LOVE IS STRONG AS DEATH

Also by Paul Kelly

How to Make Gravy

PAUL KELLY

LOVE IS STRONG AS DEATH

HAMISH HAMILTON
an imprint of
PENGUIN BOOKS

HAMISH HAMILTON
UK | USA | Canada | Ireland | Australia
India | New Zealand | South Africa | China

Hamish Hamilton is part of the Penguin Random House group of companies whose addresses can be found at global.penguinrandomhouse.com.

Penguin Random House Australia

First published by Hamish Hamilton in 2019

Cover image from *The Creation of Adam*, Michelangelo, fresco painting in the Sistine Chapel, c. 1508–12.
Cover design by Alex Ross © Penguin Random House Australia Pty Ltd
Internal design by Post Prepress, Australia
Typeset in 11.5/17 pt Bembo by Post Prepress

Printed and bound in Australia by Griffin Press, part of Ovato, an accredited ISO AS/NZS 14001 Environmental Management Systems printer

NATIONAL LIBRARY OF AUSTRALIA
A catalogue record for this book is available from the National Library of Australia

ISBN 978 1 76089 268 5
penguin.com.au

FSC www.fsc.org
MIX
Paper from responsible sources
FSC® C009448

Contents

INTRODUCTION 1

An Absolutely Ordinary Rainbow Les Murray 7
Act of Union Seamus Heaney 9
Advice for Good Love Yehuda Amichai 10
After Love Maxine Kumin 11
Afterwards Thomas Hardy 12
'All the world's a stage' William Shakespeare 13
And death shall have no dominion Dylan Thomas 14
'And so their spirits soared' Homer 15
The Armenian Language Is the Home of the Armenian
Moushegh Ishkhan 15
Asking the Way Ko Un 16
At Grass Philip Larkin 16
Aubade with Burning City Ocean Vuong 18
Aunt Julia Norman MacCaig 20
Auto Mirror Adam Zagajewski 22
Autobiography of Eve Ansel Elkins 22
Backwards Warsan Shire 23
The Ball Poem John Berryman 24
The Ballad of the Lonely Masturbator Anne Sexton 25
'The barge she sat in, like a burnish'd throne'
William Shakespeare 27
Barn Owl Gwen Harwood 28
A Barred Owl Richard Wilbur 30
Basking Shark Norman MacCaig 31
'Be absolute for death' William Shakespeare 31
La Belle Dame sans Merci John Keats 33

beneviolence Alison Whittaker 35
Binsey Poplars Gerard Manley Hopkins 35
A Birthday Christina Rossetti 36
Black Cockatoos Judith Wright 37
Bride and Groom Lie Hidden for Three Days Ted Hughes 38
'Bright star, would I were stedfast as thou art' John Keats 39
Broadcast Philip Larkin 40
Brown Maxine Beneba Clarke 41
'But I do think it is their husbands' faults' William Shakespeare 42
Canoe Ali Cobby Eckermann 43
Celibate's Ode to Balls Sharon Olds 44
Child Burial Paula Meehan 45
Clancy of the Overflow Banjo Paterson 47
Closed Path Rabindranath Tagore 48
'Come, you spirits' William Shakespeare 49
Coming to It Sam Hunt 49
Composed upon Westminster Bridge, September 3, 1802
William Wordsworth 50
The Composer W. H. Auden 51
Conjecture Number One Thousand Caroline Finkelstein 52
Corinna Ovid 53
Country Football Philip Hodgins 54
The Cows on Killing Day Les Murray 55
Cute Michel Faber 57
Danny Boy Frederic E. Weatherly 58
The Darkling Thrush Thomas Hardy 59
Days of 1903 C. P. Cavafy 60
'Death, be not proud' John Donne 61
The Death of the Bird A. D. Hope 61
Departure Arthur Rimbaud 63
The Diameter of the Bomb Yehuda Amichai 63
Digging Seamus Heaney 64

Diptych Robert Gray 65
Dirge on the Death of Art O'Leary Eibhlín Dubh Ní Chonaill (Dark Eileen) 70
Do not go gentle into that good night Dylan Thomas 78
Donal Og Anonymous 79
Dover Beach Matthew Arnold 81
A Dream of Mountaineering Po Chü-I 82
Drifters Bruce Dawe 83
Driving Alone on a Snowy Evening (After Frost) Sinéad Morrissey 84
Drowning in Wheat John Kinsella 85
Dublinesque Philip Larkin 86
Dulce et Decorum Est Wilfred Owen 87
Earth Presses Against Us Mahmoud Darwish 88
Elegy from Balmoral Beach Robert Adamson 89
The Elwood Organic Fruit and Vegetable Shop Alison Croggon 90
Eurydice and the Tawny Frogmouth Robert Adamson 91
Everything Is Plundered Anna Akhmatova 92
The Excrement Poem Maxine Kumin 92
'Th' expense of spirit in a waste of shame' William Shakespeare 93
Father and Son F. R. Higgins 94
Finding a Box of Family Letters Dana Gioia 95
First Sight Philip Larkin 97
First Time (I Met My Grandmother) Ali Cobby Eckermann 98
Five Bells Kenneth Slessor 99
The fly Miroslav Holub 103
Folklore Les Murray 105
Follower Seamus Heaney 106
The force that through the green fuse drives the flower Dylan Thomas 107
Four A.M. Wislawa Szymborska 108
'Friends, Romans, countrymen' William Shakespeare 109

From far, from eve and morning A. E. Housman 110
Funeral Blues W. H. Auden 111
The Garden of Love William Blake 111
Gift Czeslaw Milosz 112
Gifts Oodgeroo Noonuccal 112
The God Abandons Antony C. P. Cavafy 113
God's Grandeur Gerard Manley Hopkins 114
God's World Edna St.Vincent Millay 115
The Great Secret Hafiz 115
The Hag of Beare Anonymous 116
Hardcastle Crags Sylvia Plath 121
Hatred Wislawa Szymborska 123
'He is more than a hero' Sappho 125
Her Kind Anne Sexton 126
Heredity Thomas Hardy 127
Home Warsan Shire 128
'Hope' is the thing with feathers Emily Dickinson 130
House Tusiata Avia 131
The Hungry Grass Donagh MacDonagh 132
I Ask My Mother to Sing Li-Young Lee 133
I Belong There Mahmoud Darwish 133
i carry your heart with me E. E. Cummings 134
'I celebrate myself' Walt Whitman 135
'I dream'd there was an Emperor Antony' William Shakespeare 142
'I go, but first will tell thee why I came' Sophocles 143
I Never Loved You More Bertolt Brecht 143
'I think I could turn and live with animals' Walt Whitman 144
'I think of thee!' Elizabeth Barrett Browning 145
I Want to Go with the One I Love Bertolt Brecht 145
If Rudyard Kipling 146
'If thou must love me' Elizabeth Barrett Browning 147
'If we are mark'd to die, we are enow' William Shakespeare 148

I'm Explaining a Few Things Pablo Neruda 149
I'm nobody! Who are you? Emily Dickinson 152
I've Been Moved Kev Carmody 153
Immigrant Blues Li-Young Lee 154
In Dream Anna Akhmatova 156
In Paris with You James Fenton 156
In Praise of Darkness Jorge Luis Borges 157
In Praise of Doubt Bertolt Brecht 159
In the Middle of This Century Yehuda Amichai 161
In the Park Gwen Harwood 162
'In this world' Izumi Shikibu 163
Incantation Czeslaw Milosz 163
Inevitable Mahogany L. Browne 164
An Irish Airman Foresees His Death W. B. Yeats 165
Ithaka C. P. Cavafy 165
Japanese Maple Clive James 167
The Journey of the Magi T. S. Eliot 168
Katie Cruel Anonymous 170
Keats Is Dead So Fuck Me From Behind Hera Lindsay Bird 171
The Lake Isle of Innisfree W. B. Yeats 172
Last Dawn Octavio Paz 172
The Last Hellos Les Murray 173
'Lead, kindly Light, amid th'encircling gloom'
John Henry Newman 176
Leda and the Swan W. B. Yeats 177
A Letter of Recommendation Yehuda Amichai 178
The Letters of the Dead Wislawa Szymborska 179
Life-cycle Bruce Dawe 179
Life Is Fine Langston Hughes 181
'Like as the waves make towards the pebbled shore'
William Shakespeare 183
Little Bit Long Time Ali Cobby Eckermann 183

'The Lord is my shepherd' King James Bible 184
Loss and Gain Henry Wadsworth Longfellow 185
Love Czeslaw Milosz 185
'Love, never conquered in battle' Sophocles 186
Lucky Dorothy Porter 187
Lullaby W. H. Auden 188
Lyric Alison Croggon 189
The Magpies Denis Glover 190
Man for Whom I Endured . . . Máire Mhac an tSaoi 191
The Man from Ironbark Banjo Paterson 192
Man Splitting Wood in the Daybreak Galway Kinnell 194
A Man's a Man for A' That Robert Burns 195
A Man's Household Wislawa Szymborska 197
'Many in aftertimes will say of you' Christina Rossetti 198
Mary Hogan's Quatrains Máire Mhac an tSaoi 198
May John Shaw Neilson 202
The Members of the Orchestra Kevin Hart 203
Men Maya Angelou 204
'Methought I heard a voice cry' William Shakespeare 206
Milk Cream Butter Philip Hodgins 206
Mirror Sylvia Plath 208
The Mistake James Fenton 209
The Mitchells Les Murray 210
Morning Birdsong Ko Un 210
Morning Song Sylvia Plath 211
Mother Zbigniew Herbert 212
The Mother Pádraig Pearse 212
Musée des Beaux Arts W. H. Auden 213
Museum Wislawa Szymborska 214
Mushrooms Sylvia Plath 215
My At-Last Lover Dorothy Porter 216
'My love is as a fever, longing still' William Shakespeare 217

My True Love Hath My Heart Sir Philip Sidney 218
Nativity John Donne 218
Never Give All the Heart W. B. Yeats 219
The New Colossus Emma Lazarus 219
'Night deepens' Ono No Komachi 220
Night Mail W. H. Auden 220
The Night of the Dance Thomas Hardy 223
The Night-Ride Kenneth Slessor 224
'No different, really' Izumi Shikibu 224
No End of Fun Wislawa Szymborska 225
No, Thank You, John Christina Rossetti 226
'Now from his breast into the eyes the ache' Homer 228
'O Lord, thou hast searched me, and known me'
King James Bible 228
'O mistress mine' William Shakespeare 230
'O, pardon me, thou bleeding piece of earth'
William Shakespeare 230
Ode on Melancholy John Keats 231
Ode to a Nightingale John Keats 232
Ode to the Clitoris Sharon Olds 235
Ode to the Hymen Sharon Olds 237
'Of comfort no man speak' William Shakespeare 238
Old Love and New Sara Teasdale 240
On His Blindness John Milton 240
On Seeing the First Flasher Vicki Raymond 241
'Once I pass'd through a populous city' Walt Whitman 242
Once in a Lifetime, Snow Les Murray 242
One need not be a chamber to be haunted Emily Dickinson 244
1:30 AM Ko Un 245
'Or I shall live your epitaph to make' William Shakespeare 246
Ordinance on Arrival Naomi Lazard 246
Ordinary People's Lithograph Yannis Ritsos 247

The Oxen Thomas Hardy 248
Ozymandias Percy Bysshe Shelley 248
The Panther Rainer Maria Rilke 249
The Past Kevin Hart 250
Pied Beauty Gerard Manley Hopkins 251
Pillow Talk Paula Meehan 251
A Pity, We Were Such a Good Invention Yehuda Amichai 253
The Planter's Daughter Austin Clarke 254
Pleasures Bertolt Brecht 254
A Poem on the Assassination of Robert F. Kennedy
Nikki Giovanni 255
A Poison Tree William Blake 256
Postscript Seamus Heaney 256
Prayer Before Birth Louis MacNeice 257
Proud Songsters Thomas Hardy 259
'The quality of mercy is not strained' William Shakespeare 259
Quarantine Eavan Boland 260
The Railroad Station Wislawa Szymborska 261
Recalling the Past at T'ung Pass Chang Yang-Hao 263
Resumé Dorothy Parker 263
Riddle 25 from the Anglo-Saxon Riddle Hoard Anonymous 264
Rider's Song Federico García Lorca 264
'Ring out, wild bells' Alfred, Lord Tennyson 265
The Rubáiyát of Omar Khayyám Omar Khayyám 267
Said Hanrahan P. J. Hartigan 268
Sailing to Byzantium W. B. Yeats 272
The Second Coming W. B. Yeats 273
Seduction Poem Alison Croggon 274
Sermon on the Mount King James Bible 274
Sex Without Love Sharon Olds 276
'Shall I compare thee to a summer's day?' William Shakespeare 277
She Hears the Storm Thomas Hardy 277

She Walks in Beauty George Gordon, Lord Byron 278
Shooting the Dogs Philip Hodgins 279
The Sick Rose William Blake 281
Sign of Love Catullus 281
A Simple Story Gwen Harwood 281
'Since brass, nor stone, nor earth, nor boundless sea'
William Shakespeare 283
'Sing a song of sixpence' Anonymous 284
Sir from Biology Zbigniew Herbert 285
Song of Solomon 1–5 King James Bible 287
Songs for a Woman Yehuda Amichai 293
Songs of Grass Alison Croggon 294
Sonnets 44 and 45 William Shakespeare 295
Sorcery Sandra Simonds 296
Spleen Charles Baudelaire 296
'The spotted hawk swoops by and accuses me' Walt Whitman 297
Spring and Fall Gerard Manley Hopkins 298
The Statue of the Virgin at Granard Speaks Paula Meehan 299
Stopping by Woods on a Snowy Evening Robert Frost 301
The Streets of Laredo Anonymous 302
The Summer Day Mary Oliver 304
Summer Night Antonio Machado 304
The Sun Rising John Donne 305
Sunset Tu Fu 306
Surely God Was a Lover John Shaw Neilson 307
'Sweet is the breath of Morn' John Milton 307
Swineherd Eiléan Ní Chuilleanáin 308
Taklamakan Desert Ko Un 309
'That time of year thou may'st in me behold'
William Shakespeare 309
Theatre Impressions Wislawa Szymborska 310
There Will Come Soft Rain Sara Teasdale 311

There's No Place Like Home Samuel Wagan Watson 312
'They say that time assuages' Emily Dickinson 313
'They told me, Heraclitus' Callimachus 313
Things I Want Decided Izumi Shikibu 314
A Thirsty Fish Rumi 315
Thornbills Judith Wright 316
'Thou, nature, art my goddess' William Shakespeare 317
'Though I speak with the tongues of men and of angels'
King James Bible 318
'Thought Is Surrounded by a Halo' Gwen Harwood 319
The Three Fates Rosemary Dobson 319
Tiresias Alison Croggon 320
to a dark moses Lucille Clifton 321
To an Athlete Dying Young A. E. Housman 321
To Be a Slave of Intensity Kabir 323
'To be or not to be' William Shakespeare 324
'To every thing there is a season' King James Bible 325
To His Mistress Going to Bed John Donne 326
To My Dear and Loving Husband Anne Bradstreet 328
To Those Born After Bertolt Brecht 328
Today we are in a hospital ward Tusiata Avia 330
'Tomorrow, and tomorrow, and tomorrow' William Shakespeare 331
Took the Children Away Archie Roach 332
Torture Ko Un 334
The Trees Philip Larkin 334
Triads Vincent Buckley 335
Try to Remember Some Details Yehuda Amichai 336
'Twenty-eight young men' Walt Whitman 337
The Tyger William Blake 338
Uluru Statement from the Heart 250 Aboriginal and
Torres Strait Islander delegates from all around Australia 340
Us Anne Sexton 342

La Vie C'est La Vie Jessie Redmon Fauset 343
Waiting for the Barbarians C. P. Cavafy 344
Watching six seasons of the Nanny while my long-term relationship slowly fell apart Hera Lindsay Bird 346
We Did It Yehuda Amichai 347
We grow accustomed to the Dark Emily Dickinson 348
'Well, say there is no kingdom then for Richard' William Shakespeare 349
Western Arrernte rain poem Anonymous 351
What Kind of a Person Yehuda Amichai 352
'When all the others were away at Mass' Seamus Heaney 354
When I Am With You Rumi 354
'When my love swears that she is made of truth' William Shakespeare 355
'When to the sessions of sweet silent thought' William Shakespeare 356
When You Are Old W. B. Yeats 356
Where Does Such Tenderness Come From? Marina Tsvetaeva 357
White Sunday/Lotu Tamaiti Tusiata Avia 358
'Who killed Cock Robin?' Anonymous 359
Why I Love Your Body Dorothy Porter 362
Wild Swans Edna St. Vincent Millay 363
The Windhover Gerard Manley Hopkins 363
Windy Mick and the Falcon Neil Murray 364
Wine Raymond Carver 368
Woman to Child Judith Wright 369
Woman to Man Judith Wright 370
'Women of Corinth' Euripides 371
'Your children are not your children' Kahlil Gibran 372
Your Feet Pablo Neruda 373
Your Kiss Kevin Hart 374
Youth Czeslaw Milosz 375

INDEX OF POETS AND THEIR WORKS 379
INDEX OF FIRST LINES 388
INDEX OF PAUL KELLY'S MUSICAL ARRANGEMENTS 397
ACKNOWLEDGEMENTS 399
PERMISSIONS 401

Introduction

Many people I know say they feel poetry is difficult. That it seems 'worthwhile' but that 'worthiness' puts them off. Fair enough. But poetry is friendlier than they think. It hovers close by us. It's in pop songs everywhere we shop, work and play. We often reach for it on ritual occasions. Poems are read or quoted at funerals, at weddings, at ceremonies. And good speechmakers – Barack Obama, Noel Pearson, the mother of the bride at my friend's wedding earlier this year – all consciously and subconsciously adopt poetry's techniques of rhythm, repetition, rhetoric, assonance and cadence.

It lives in our everyday speech, though we may be unaware of it. The common phrases, 'without rhyme or reason', 'vanished into thin air', 'played fast and loose', 'tongue-tied', 'tower of strength', 'short shrift', 'cold comfort', 'good riddance', 'high time', 'foul play', 'the long and short of it', 'it's neither here nor there', and a host of others, all sprang from the plays of Shakespeare which, for the most part, were written in ten-syllable lines of verse.

Shakespeare was where it started for me. We did *Macbeth* at high school and I was hooked. When Lady Macbeth said, 'Come, you spirits that tend on mortal thoughts, unsex me here,' the hairs rose all over my skin. His language always gives me a jolt. I still have a physical reaction to Shakespeare even when it's done badly.

At school we also studied Keats' 'Ode to a Nightingale' and it gave me the same kind of thrill. It's the first poem I consciously memorised and it's stayed with me ever since.

The language of Keats and Shakespeare, highly charged and deeply playful, can sound over-rich to modern ears. Many contemporary poets work in an elevated register, too. But not all. Ko Un's 'Morning Birdsong', the shortest poem in this anthology, has only one line:

I didn't die – waking up I hear that.

As plain as can be. And poetry to me.

So where to start with poetry if you want to read it but are overwhelmed by the myriad paths before you? If you were put off by the way you were taught at school? My own experience may be encouraging. I discovered W. H. Auden and E. E. Cummings (he of the lower case) through movies. John Hannah reciting 'Stop all the clocks' ('Funeral Blues') in *Four Weddings and a Funeral*; Cameron Diaz saying 'I carry your heart with me' in *In Her Shoes*. But when I went and followed these poets up I found that most of their poems were opaque. I didn't get them. Only a small fraction knocked my socks off. That small fraction, though, can add up to quite a lot. This happens with most of the poets and poems I read. The strike rate per poet is low. Yet, when I'm asked now who my favourite poets are, Auden – most of whose work is unintelligible to me – is one of the first names on my list.

So let yourself off the hook when you're reading a poet someone's recommended, or following a lead gleaned from an article, book, movie, song or any other source. Many poems are obscure, full of insider information and private symbolism. Finding a poem you love requires patience, luck and a willingness to cover a wide range.

Anthologies can be helpful. I looked at many of them while hunting poems for this one, which I hope, in turn, will send you hunting. Three in particular led me down rich byways: *The Rattle*

Bag, edited by Seamus Heaney and Ted Hughes; *60 Classic Australian Poems*, with commentaries by Geoff Page; and *A Book of Luminous Things*, compiled by Czeslaw Milosz.

Like Ted and Seamus did in *The Rattle Bag*, I have arranged the poems here in alphabetical order by title or first line. Undeniably, I have a thing for the alphabet. Within its unshiftable structure, randomness is given full rein. Grouping the poems alphabetically by author would make the book too blocky. By theme, too textbooky. The best poems straddle multiple themes, anyway. And ordering the poems chronologically would seem too much like an incomplete history lesson. Listing the poems alphabetically by title allows them to jostle one another in a democratic manner – the transcendent with the earthy, the loquacious with the sparse, the hymnic with the polemic. In one sequence under H, for example, Sappho, Anne Sexton, Thomas Hardy, Warsan Shire, Emily Dickinson and Tusiata Avia all get to hang out together and have sparky conversations.

As that short list shows, I have felt free, fortified by the sturdy alphabet, to roam far and wide across centuries and countries to gather my poems. Homer and the Greek tragedians speak to us from thousands of years ago. The three-thousand-year-old or more Song of Solomon, first written in Hebrew, translated into Greek, then Latin, then into English via the King James Bible, rubs shoulders with Walt Whitman and Yehuda Amichai, giants of the nineteenth and twentieth centuries, both of whom, as it happens, drew heavily on the Bible for their own work.

There are many very well-known poems here. Some are so popular that their inclusion may seem banal. But my simple rule was if I love a poem, it goes in, no matter how worn out others may think it to be. You can't wear out a good poem, anyway. Sometimes at our big family Christmases or get-togethers we have a kind of talent night where everyone chooses to perform an item – a song, a poem, a trick, a joke or a dance. Rudyard Kipling's 'If', one of the most popular English poems ever, was memorably recited by my English nephew one Christmas, and Banjo Paterson's 'The Man From Ironbark' is my brother John's go-to performance each year, complete with acted dialogue and throat-cutting gestures.

My Aunt Pat lived to ninety-seven and could still quote poems she'd learnt and loved at school. My visits to her over her last ten years were mostly spent reading Wordsworth, Shelley, Tennyson, Keats and co. to each other, popular poems that ring down the generations.

I did have another rule. Not to include song lyrics. I know many could be claimed as a form of poetry. The Kinks' 'Waterloo Sunset', The Triffids' 'Wide Open Road', Sam Cooke's 'A Change Is Gonna Come' and Joni Mitchell's 'River' jump straight to mind. A lot of rap and hip-hop, too. For most of human history poetry has been sung. Homer was. And much of the Greek tragedies. Many songs were poems before they were songs; 'Danny Boy' is a famous example. But including songs here would have opened up a huge other well, one I wasn't prepared to dive down.

However, when you make the rules you're allowed a few exceptions, so I've included 'Took the Children Away' by Archie Roach, one of the most important Australian songs of the twentieth century. And Kev Carmody's 'I've Been Moved', a song which, like many of his, was written as a poem first. 'Danny Boy' gets a pass, too. And I've thrown in the old folk song 'Katie Cruel', for these lines which describe more succinctly than any other words I know the hunger of being human, the longing for love, earthly or divine:

If I was where I would be
Then I'd be where I am not

Here I am where I must be
Where I would be, I can not

Another notable exception is a piece of prose – the Uluru Statement from the Heart. It has the heart, hurt and urgency of great poetry.

I believe poems are best heard. Even poems read in private can generate new pleasures spoken aloud. Over the last seven years I have been in the habit of putting poems I like to music. So, along with the usual Contents list and indexes – titles, authors, first lines – I have included an index of those poems as well.

The work on this anthology hasn't been done on my own. My partner, Siân, has the uncanny knack of sending me poems that apply to a situation we've just been in, something we've been talking about or work I'm involved with. Over and over again.

I've been fortunate, too, over the years, to have had friends and family send me poems in letters and emails or books in the mail. Fifteen years ago my cousin Fiona gave me for my birthday a book of poems by a Polish poet with a name I couldn't pronounce. Wislawa Szymborska. It languished in my pile of books by the bed for almost a year. Then one day I opened it again and fell in love. The stunning 'The Statue of the Virgin at Granard Speaks' by Paula Meehan landed in my inbox like a bomb from my friend Martin and soon led me down dark and beautiful paths of Irish women's poetry. My friend Grant, now hid in death's dateless night, once sent me a postcard from America with a few scribbled lines from John Berryman's 'The Ball Poem'. Those lines gave me a song. And forty years ago in a Paddington bookshop the poet Robert Gray, whom I barely knew, a friend of my cousin (another cousin), gave me a book of Thomas Hardy poems. Until then I'd only known Thomas Hardy as a novelist. When I opened it I saw Robert's favourites lightly marked with pencil. I started with those poems, some of them included here, and so began my long march with Tom. I still have the book. Thank you, Robert.

Poems are to be passed on. They're pocketable, transferable. Little mind bombs. Wherever you are, on the tram or stuck in a queue or waiting on a friend, they're fun to commit to memory. That's what poetry has been ever since Homer. Something to memorise. The great poets have the knack of writing unforgettable lines:

I put your body
    between me
        and the history of horrors

Lay your sleeping head, my love,
Human on my faithless arm

'Hope' is the thing with feathers –
That perches in the soul

When you do nice things to me
all heavy industry shuts down

Poetry is deep play. It's comfort. It's challenge. Just like a friend. May this book be a friend. To be approached any time, any way. Day or night. In a light mood or dark.

I've never formally studied poetry. I'm an amateur following my nose, with huge gaps in my knowledge and a wide streak of bias in my choices. By the time this book is published I'll be kicking myself for the poems I've left out. The poems I've missed. Please pick them up for me. Pick them up and pass them on.

And let poetry be your friend. It can take you to the end.

PK, October, 2019

An Absolutely Ordinary Rainbow

The word goes round Repins,
the murmur goes round Lorenzinis,
at Tattersalls, men look up from sheets of numbers,
the Stock Exchange scribblers forget the chalk in their hands
and men with bread in their pockets leave the Greek Club:
There's a fellow crying in Martin Place. They can't stop him.

The traffic in George Street is banked up for half a mile
and drained of motion. The crowds are edgy with talk
and more crowds come hurrying. Many run in the back streets
which minutes ago were busy main streets, pointing:
There's a fellow weeping down there. No one can stop him.

The man we surround, the man no one approaches
simply weeps, and does not cover it, weeps
not like a child, not like the wind, like a man
and does not declaim it, nor beat his breast, nor even
sob very loudly – yet the dignity of his weeping

holds us back from his space, the hollow he makes about him
in the midday light, in his pentagram of sorrow,
and uniforms back in the crowd who tried to seize him
stare out at him, and feel, with amazement, their minds
longing for tears as children for a rainbow.

Some will say, in the years to come, a halo
or force stood around him. There is no such thing.
Some will say they were shocked and would have stopped him

but they will not have been there. The fiercest manhood,
the toughest reserve, the slickest wit amongst us

trembles with silence, and burns with unexpected
judgements of peace. Some in the concourse scream
who thought themselves happy. Only the smallest children
and such as look out of Paradise come near him
and sit at his feet, with dogs and dusty pigeons.

Ridiculous, says a man near me, and stops
his mouth with his hands, as if it uttered vomit –
and I see a woman, shining, stretch her hand
and shake as she receives the gift of weeping;
as many as follow her also receive it

and many weep for sheer acceptance, and more
refuse to weep for fear of all acceptance,
but the weeping man, like the earth, requires nothing,
the man who weeps ignores us, and cries out
of his writhen face and ordinary body

not words, but grief, not messages, but sorrow,
hard as the earth, sheer, present as the sea –
and when he stops, he simply walks between us
mopping his face with the dignity of one
man who has wept, and now has finished weeping.

Evading believers, he hurries off down Pitt Street.

Les Murray

Act of Union

I

Tonight, a first movement, a pulse,
As if the rain in bogland gathered head
To slip and flood: a bog-burst,
A gash breaking open the ferny bed.
Your back is a firm line of eastern coast
And arms and legs are thrown
Beyond your gradual hills. I caress
The heaving province where our past has grown.
I am the tall kingdom over your shoulder
That you would neither cajole nor ignore.
Conquest is a lie. I grow older
Conceding your half-independent shore
Within whose borders now my legacy
Culminates inexorably.

II

And I am still imperially
Male, leaving you with pain,
The rending process in the colony,
The battering ram, the boom burst from within.
The act sprouted an obstinate fifth column
Whose stance is growing unilateral.
His heart beneath your heart is a wardrum
Mustering force. His parasitical
And ignorant little fists already
Beat at your borders and I know they're cocked
At me across the water. No treaty

I foresee will salve completely your tracked
And stretchmarked body, the big pain
That leaves you raw, like opened ground, again

Seamus Heaney

Advice for Good Love

Advice for good love: Don't love
those from far away. Take yourself one
from nearby.
The way a sensible house will take
local stones for its building,
stones which have suffered in the same cold
and were scorched by the same sun.
Take the one with the golden wreath
around her dark eye's pupil, she
who has a certain knowledge
about your death. Love also inside
a ruin, like taking honey out of
the lion's carcass that Samson killed.

And advice for bad love: With
the love left over
from the previous one
make a new woman for yourself,
then with what is left of that woman
make again a new love,
and go on like that
until nothing remains.

Yehuda Amichai, translated by the author and Ted Hughes

After Love

Afterward, the compromise.
Bodies resume their boundaries.

These legs, for instance, mine.
Your arms take you back in.

Spoons of our fingers, lips
admit their ownership.

The bedding yawns, a door
blows aimlessly ajar

and overhead, a plane
singsongs coming down.

Nothing is changed, except
there was a moment when

the wolf, the mongering wolf
who stands outside the self

lay lightly down, and slept.

Maxine Kumin

Afterwards

When the Present has latched its postern behind my tremulous stay,
And the May month flaps its glad green leaves like wings,
Delicate-filmed as new-spun silk, will the neighbours say,
'He was a man who used to notice such things'?

If it be in the dusk when, like an eyelid's soundless blink,
The dewfall-hawk comes crossing the shades to alight
Upon the wind-warped upland thorn, a gazer may think,
'To him this must have been a familiar sight.'

If I pass during some nocturnal blackness, mothy and warm,
When the hedgehog travels furtively over the lawn,
One may say, 'He strove that such innocent creatures should come to
no harm,
But he could do little for them; and now he is gone.'

If, when hearing that I have been stilled at last, they stand at the door,
Watching the full-starred heavens that winter sees,
Will this thought rise on those who will meet my face no more,
'He was one who had an eye for such mysteries'?

And will any say when my bell of quittance is heard in the gloom,
And a crossing breeze cuts a pause in its outrollings,
Till they rise again, as they were a new bell's boom,
'He hears it not now, but used to notice such things'?

Thomas Hardy

'All the world's a stage'

All the world's a stage,
And all the men and women merely players;
They have their exits and their entrances;
And one man in his time plays many parts,
His acts being seven ages. At first the infant,
Mewling and puking in the nurse's arms;
And then the whining school-boy, with his satchel
And shining morning face, creeping like snail
Unwillingly to school. And then the lover,
Sighing like furnace, with a woeful ballad
Made to his mistress' eyebrow. Then a soldier,
Full of strange oaths, and bearded like the pard,
Jealous in honour, sudden and quick in quarrel,
Seeking the bubble reputation
Even in the cannon's mouth. And then the justice,
In fair round belly with good capon lin'd,
With eyes severe and beard of formal cut,
Full of wise saws and modern instances;
And so he plays his part. The sixth age shifts
Into the lean and slipper'd pantaloon,
With spectacles on nose and pouch on side;
His youthful hose, well sav'd, a world too wide
For his shrunk shank; and his big manly voice,
Turning again toward childish treble, pipes
And whistles in his sound. Last scene of all,
That ends this strange eventful history,
Is second childishness and mere oblivion;
Sans teeth, sans eyes, sans taste, sans everything.

Jacques in As You Like It, *William Shakespeare*

And death shall have no dominion

And death shall have no dominion.
Dead men naked they shall be one
With the man in the wind and the west moon;
When their bones are picked clean and the clean bones gone,
They shall have stars at elbow and foot;
Though they go mad they shall be sane,
Though they sink through the sea they shall rise again;
Though lovers be lost love shall not;
And death shall have no dominion.

And death shall have no dominion.
Under the windings of the sea
They lying long shall not die windily;
Twisting on racks when sinews give way,
Strapped to a wheel, yet they shall not break;
Faith in their hands shall snap in two,
And the unicorn evils run them through;
Split all ends up they shan't crack;
And death shall have no dominion.

And death shall have no dominion.
No more may gulls cry at their ears
Or waves break loud on the seashores;
Where blew a flower may a flower no more
Lift its head to the blows of the rain;
Though they be mad and dead as nails,
Heads of the characters hammer through daisies;
Break in the sun till the sun breaks down,
And death shall have no dominion.

Dylan Thomas

'And so their spirits soared'

And so their spirits soared
as they took their positions down the passageways of battle
all night long, and the watchfires blazed among them.
Hundreds strong, as stars in the night sky glittering
round the moon's brilliance blaze in all their glory
when the air falls to a sudden, windless calm . . .
all the lookout peaks stand out and the jutting cliffs
and the steep ravines and down from the high heavens bursts
the boundless bright air and all the stars shine clear
and the shepherd's heart exults – so many fires burned
between the ships and Xanthus' whirling rapids
set by the men of Troy, bright against their walls.
A thousand fires were burning there on the plain
and beside each fire sat fifty fighting men
poised in the leaping blaze, and champing oats
and glistening barley, stationed by their chariots,
stallions waited for Dawn to mount her glowing throne.

Homer, The Iliad, *from Book 8, translated by Robert Fagles*

The Armenian Language Is the Home of the Armenian

The Armenian language is the home
and haven where the wanderer can own
roof and wall and nourishment.
He can enter to find love and pride,
locking the hyena and the storm outside.
For centuries its architects have toiled
to give its ceilings height.

How many peasants working
day and night have kept
its cupboards full, lamps lit, ovens hot.
Always rejuvenated, always old, it lasts
century to century on the path
where every Armenian can find it when he's lost
in the wilderness of his future, or his past.

Moushegh Ishkhan, translated by Diana Der Hovanessian

Asking the Way

You fools who ask what god is
should ask what life is instead.
Find a port where lemon trees bloom.
Ask about places to drink in the port.
Ask about the drinkers.
Ask about the lemon trees.
Ask and ask until nothing's left to ask.

Ko Un, translated by Suji Kwock Kim and Sunja Kim Kwock

At Grass

The eye can hardly pick them out
From the cold shade they shelter in,
Till wind distresses tail and main;
Then one crops grass, and moves about
– The other seeming to look on –
And stands anonymous again.

Yet fifteen years ago, perhaps
Two dozen distances sufficed
To fable them: faint afternoons
Of Cups and Stakes and Handicaps,
Whereby their names were artificed
To inlay faded, classic Junes –

Silks at the start: against the sky
Numbers and parasols: outside,
Squadrons of empty cars, and heat,
And littered grass: then the long cry
Hanging unhushed till it subside
To stop-press columns on the street.

Do memories plague their ears like flies?
They shake their heads. Dusk brims the shadows.
Summer by summer all stole away,
The starting-gates, the crowd and cries –
All but the unmolesting meadows.
Almanacked, their names live; they

Have slipped their names, and stand at ease,
Or gallop for what must be joy,
And not a fieldglass sees them home,
Or curious stop-watch prophesies:
Only the groom, and the groom's boy,
With bridles in the evening come.

Philip Larkin

Aubade with Burning City

South Vietnam, April 29, 1975: Armed Forces Radio played Irving Berlin's 'White Christmas' as a code to begin Operation Frequent Wind, the ultimate evacuation of American civilians and Vietnamese refugees by helicopter during the fall of Saigon.

Milkflower petals on the street
like pieces of a girl's dress.

May your days be merry and bright . . .

He fills a teacup with champagne, brings it to her lips.
Open, he says.
She opens.
Outside, a soldier spits out
his cigarette as footsteps fill the square like stones
fallen from the sky. *May*
all your Christmases be white
as the traffic guard unstraps his holster.

His fingers running the hem
of her white dress. A single candle.
Their shadows: two wicks.

A military truck speeds through the intersection, children
shrieking inside. A bicycle hurled
through a store window. When the dust rises, a black dog
lies panting in the road. Its hind legs
crushed into the shine
of a white Christmas.

On the bed stand, a sprig of magnolia expands like a secret heard
for the first time.

The treetops glisten and children listen, the chief of police
facedown in a pool of Coca-Cola.
A palm-sized photo of his father soaking
beside his left ear.

The song moving through the city like a widow.
A white . . . A white . . . I'm dreaming of a curtain of snow

falling from her shoulders.

Snow scraping against the window. Snow shredded
with gunfire. Red sky.
Snow on the tanks rolling over the city walls.
A helicopter lifting the living just
out of reach.

The city so white it is ready for ink.

The radio saying run run run.
Milkflower petals on a black dog
like pieces of a girl's dress.

May your days be merry and bright. She is saying
something neither of them can hear. The hotel rocks
beneath them. The bed a field of ice.

Don't worry, he says, as the first shell flashes
their faces, *my brothers have won the war*

and tomorrow . . .
The lights go out.

I'm dreaming. I'm dreaming . . .
to hear sleigh bells in the snow . . .
In the square below: a nun, on fire,
runs silently toward her god –

Open, he says.
She opens.

Ocean Vuong

Aunt Julia

Aunt Julia spoke Gaelic
very loud and very fast.
I could not answer her –
I could not understand her.

She wore men's boots
when she wore any.
– I can see her strong foot,
stained with peat,
paddling with the treadle of the spinningwheel
while her right hand drew yarn
marvellously out of the air.

Hers was the only house
where I've lain at night
in the absolute darkness
of a box bed, listening to
crickets being friendly.

She was buckets
and water flouncing into them.
She was winds pouring wetly
round house-ends.
She was brown eggs, black skirts
and a keeper of threepennybits
in a teapot.

Aunt Julia spoke Gaelic
very loud and very fast.
By the time I had learned
a little, she lay
silenced in the absolute black
of a sandy grave
at Luskentyre. But I hear her still, welcoming me
with a seagull's voice
across a hundred yards
of peatscrapes and lazybeds
and getting angry, getting angry
with so many questions
unanswered.

Norman MacCaig

Auto Mirror

In the rear-view mirror suddenly
I saw the bulk of the Beauvais Cathedral;
great things dwell in small ones
for a moment.

Adam Zagajewski, translated by Czeslaw Milosz and Robert Hass

Autobiography of Eve

Wearing nothing but snakeskin
boots, I blazed a footpath, the first
radical road out of that old kingdom
toward a new unknown.
When I came to those great flaming gates
of burning gold,
I stood alone in terror at the threshold
between Paradise and Earth.
There I heard a mysterious echo:
my own voice
singing to me from across the forbidden
side. I shook awake –
at once alive in a blaze of green fire.

Let it be known: I did not fall from grace.

I leapt
to freedom.

Ansel Elkins

Backwards

for Saaid Shire

The poem can start with him walking backwards into a room.
He takes off his jacket and sits down for the rest of his life;
that's how we bring Dad back.
I can make the blood run back up my nose, ants rushing into a hole.
We grow into smaller bodies, my breasts disappear,
your cheeks soften, teeth sink back into gums.
I can make us loved, just say the word.
Give them stumps for hands if even once they touched us
without consent,
I can write the poem and make it disappear.
Step-Dad spits liquor back into glass,
Mum's body rolls back up the stairs, the bone pops back into place,
maybe she keeps the baby.
Maybe we're okay kid?
I'll rewrite this whole life and this time there'll be so much love,
you won't be able to see beyond it.

You won't be able to see beyond it,
I'll rewrite this whole life and this time there'll be so much love.
Maybe we're okay kid,
maybe she keeps the baby.
Mum's body rolls back up the stairs, the bone pops back into place,
Step-Dad spits liquor back into glass.
I can write the poem and make it disappear,
Give them stumps for hands if even once they touched us
without consent,
I can make us loved, just say the word.
Your cheeks soften, teeth sink back into gums

we grow into smaller bodies, my breasts disappear.
I can make the blood run back up my nose, ants rushing into a hole,
that's how we bring Dad back.
He takes off his jacket and sits down for the rest of his life.
The poem can start with him walking backwards into a room.

Warsan Shire

The Ball Poem

What is the boy now, who has lost his ball.
What, what is he to do? I saw it go
Merrily bouncing, down the street, and then
Merrily over – there it is in the water!
No use to say 'O there are other balls':
An ultimate shaking grief fixes the boy
As he stands rigid, trembling, staring down
All his young days into the harbour where
His ball went. I would not intrude on him,
A dime, another ball, is worthless. Now
He senses first responsibility
In a world of possessions. People will take balls,
Balls will be lost always, little boy,
And no one buys a ball back. Money is external.
He is learning, well behind his desperate eyes,
The epistemology of loss, how to stand up
Knowing what every man must one day know
And most know many days, how to stand up
And gradually light returns to the street,
A whistle blows, the ball is out of sight.
Soon part of me will explore the deep and dark

Floor of the harbour . . . I am everywhere,
I suffer and move, my mind and my heart move
With all that move me, under the water
Or whistling, I am not a little boy.

John Berryman

The Ballad of the Lonely Masturbator

The end of the affair is always death.
She's my workshop. Slippery eye,
out of the tribe of myself my breath
finds you gone. I horrify
those who stand by. I am fed.
At night, alone, I marry the bed.

Finger to finger, now she's mine.
She's not too far. She's my encounter.
I beat her like a bell. I recline
in the bower where you used to mount her.
You borrowed me on the flowered spread.
At night, alone, I marry the bed.

Take for instance this night, my love,
that every single couple puts together
with a joint overturning, beneath, above,
the abundant two on sponge and feather,
kneeling and pushing, head to head.
At night alone, I marry the bed.

I break out of my body this way,
an annoying miracle. Could I
put the dream market on display?
I am spread out. I crucify.
My little plum is what you said.
At night, alone, I marry the bed.

Then my black-eyed rival came.
The lady of water, rising on the beach,
a piano at her fingertips, shame
on her lips and a flute's speech.
And I was the knock-kneed broom instead.
At night, alone, I marry the bed.

She took you the way a woman takes
a bargain dress off the rack
and I broke the way a stone breaks.
I give back your books and fishing tack.
Today's paper says that you are wed.
At night, alone, I marry the bed.

The boys and girls are one tonight.
They unbutton blouses. They unzip flies.
They take off shoes. They turn off the light.
The glimmering creatures are full of lies.
They are eating each other. They are overfed.
At night, alone, I marry the bed.

Anne Sexton

'The barge she sat in, like a burnish'd throne'

The barge she sat in, like a burnish'd throne,
Burn'd on the water: the poop was beaten gold,
Purple the sails, and so perfumed that
The winds were love-sick with them; the oars were silver,
Which to the tune of flutes kept stroke, and made
The water which they beat to follow faster,
As amorous of their strokes. For her own person,
It beggar'd all description: she did lie
In her pavilion – cloth-of-gold of tissue –
O'er-picturing that Venus where we see
The fancy outwork nature: on each side her
Stood pretty dimpled boys, like smiling Cupids,
With divers-colour'd fans, whose wind did seem
To glow the delicate cheeks which they did cool,
And what they undid did.

Her gentlewomen, like the Nereides,
So many mermaids, tended her i' the eyes,
And made their bends adornings: at the helm
A seeming mermaid steers: the silken tackle
Swell with the touches of those flower-soft hands,
That yarely frame the office. From the barge
A strange invisible perfume hits the sense
Of the adjacent wharfs. The city cast
Her people out upon her; and Antony,
Enthron'd i' the market-place, did sit alone,
Whistling to the air; which, but for vacancy,
Had gone to gaze on Cleopatra too,
And made a gap in nature.

Upon her landing, Antony sent to her,
Invited her to supper: she replied,
It should be better he became her guest;
Which she entreated: our courteous Antony,
Whom ne'er the word of 'No' woman heard speak,
Being barber'd ten times o'er, goes to the feast,
And for his ordinary pays his heart
For what his eyes eat only.

I saw her once
Hop forty paces through the public street;
And having lost her breath, she spoke, and panted,
That she did make defect perfection,
And, breathless, power breathe forth.

Age cannot wither her, nor custom stale
Her infinite variety: other women cloy
The appetites they feed: but she makes hungry
Where most she satisfies; for vilest things
Become themselves in her: that the holy priests
Bless her when she is riggish.

Enobarbus in **Antony and Cleopatra**, *William Shakespeare*

Barn Owl

Daybreak: the household slept.
I rose, blessed by the sun.
A horny fiend, I crept
out with my father's gun.
Let him dream of a child
obedient, angel-mind –

old No-Sayer, robbed of power
by sleep. I knew my prize
who swooped home at this hour
with daylight-riddled eyes
to his place on a high beam
in our old stables, to dream

light's useless time away.
I stood, holding my breath,
in urine-scented hay,
master of life and death,
a wisp-haired judge whose law
would punish beak and claw.

My first shot struck. He swayed,
ruined, beating his only
wing, as I watched, afraid
by the fallen gun, a lonely
child who believed death clean
and final, not this obscene

bundle of stuff that dropped,
and dribbled through the loose straw
tangling in bowels, and hopped
blindly closer. I saw
those eyes that did not see
mirror my cruelty

while the wrecked thing that could
not bear the light nor hide
hobbled in its own blood.

My father reached my side,
gave me the fallen gun.
'End what you have begun.'

I fired. The blank eyes shone
once into mine, and slept.
I leaned my head upon
my father's arm, and wept,
owl-blind in early sun
for what I had begun

Gwen Harwood

A Barred Owl

The warping night air having brought the boom
Of an owl's voice into her darkened room,
We tell the wakened child that all she heard
Was an odd question from a forest bird,
Asking of us, if rightly listened to,
'Who cooks for you?' and then 'Who cooks for you?'

Words, which can make our terrors bravely clear,
Can also thus domesticate a fear,
And send a small child back to sleep at night
Not listening for the sound of stealthy flight
Or dreaming of some small thing in a claw
Borne up to some dark branch and eaten raw.

Richard Wilbur

Basking Shark

To stub an oar on a rock where none should be,
To have it rise with a slounge out of the sea
Is a thing that happened once (too often) to me.

But not too often – though enough. I count as gain
That once I met, on a sea tin-tacked with rain,
That roomsized monster with a matchbox brain.

He displaced more than water. He shoggled me
Centuries back – this decadent townee
Shook on a wrong branch of his family tree.

Swish up the dirt and, when it settles, a spring
Is all the clearer. I saw me, in one fling,
Emerging from the slime of everything.

So who's the monster? The thought made me grow pale
For twenty seconds while, sail after sail,
The tail fin slid away, and then the tail.

Norman MacCaig

'Be absolute for death'

Be absolute for death; either death or life
Shall thereby be the sweeter. Reason thus with life:
If I do lose thee, I do lose a thing
That none but fools would keep: a breath thou art,
Servile to all the skyey influences,

That dost this habitation, where thou keep'st,
Hourly afflict. Merely, thou art death's fool;
For him thou labour'st by thy flight to shun,
And yet run'st toward him still. Thou art not noble:
For all th' accommodations that thou bear'st
Are nurs'd by baseness. Thou art by no means valiant;
For thou dost fear the soft and tender fork
Of a poor worm. Thy best of rest is sleep,
And that thou oft provok'st; yet grossly fear'st
Thy death, which is no more. Thou art not thyself;
For thou exist'st on many a thousand grains
That issue out of dust. Happy thou art not;
For what thou hast not, still thou striv'st to get,
And what thou hast, forget'st. Thou art not certain;
For thy complexion shifts to strange effects,
After the moon. If thou art rich, thou'rt poor;
For, like an ass whose back with ingots bows,
Thou bear'st thy heavy riches but a journey,
And death unloads thee. Friend hast thou none;
For thine own bowels, which do call thee sire,
The mere effusion of thy proper loins,
Do curse the gout, serpigo, and the rheum,
For ending thee no sooner. Thou hast nor youth nor age;
But, as it were, an after-dinner's sleep,
Dreaming on both; for all thy blessed youth
Becomes as aged, and doth beg the alms
Of palsied eld; and when thou art old and rich,
Thou hast neither heat, affection, limb, nor beauty,
To make thy riches pleasant. What's yet in this
That bears the name of life? Yet in this life

Lie hid moe thousand deaths: yet death we fear,
That makes these odds all even.

The Duke in Measure for Measure, *William Shakespeare*

La Belle Dame sans Merci

O what can ail thee, knight-at-arms,
  Alone and palely loitering?
The sedge has wither'd from the lake,
  And no birds sing.

O what can ail thee, knight-at-arms,
  So haggard and so woe-begone?
The squirrel's granary is full,
  And the harvest's done.

I see a lily on thy brow,
  With anguish moist and fever-dew,
And on thy cheeks a fading rose
  Fast withereth too.

I met a lady in the meads,
  Full beautiful – a faery's child,
Her hair was long, her foot was light,
  And her eyes were wild.

I made a garland for her head,
  And bracelets too, and fragrant zone;
She look'd at me as she did love,
  And made sweet moan.

I set her on my pacing steed,
    And nothing else saw all day long,
For sidelong would she bend, and sing
    A faery's song.

She found me roots of relish sweet,
    And honey wild, and manna-dew,
And sure in language strange she said –
    'I love thee true'.

She took me to her elfin grot,
    And there she wept and sigh'd full sore,
And there I shut her wild wild eyes
    With kisses four.

And there she lulled me asleep,
    And there I dream'd – Ah! woe betide! –
The latest dream I ever dream'd
    On the cold hill side.

I saw pale kings and princes too,
    Pale warriors, death-pale were they all;
They cried – 'La Belle Dame sans Merci
    Hath thee in thrall!'

I saw their starved lips in the gloam,
    With horrid warning gaped wide,
And I awoke and found me here,
    On the cold hill's side.

And this is why I sojourn here,
  Alone and palely loitering,
Though the sedge is wither'd from the lake,
  And no birds sing.

John Keats

beneviolence

THIS IS *GOOD* FOR YOU!
THIS IS FOR *YOUR* GOOD. YOUR OWN
GOOD. THIS IS FOR *YOU*.

FOR THIS GOOD, IS YOU. IS *YOU* GOOD? GOOD.
IS THIS GOOD? IS GOOD?
YOU IS GOOD FOR *THIS*. *OWN* THIS!

FOR *YOU*, THIS IS GOOD.
FOR GOOD. FOR *YOU* IS GOOD. FOR
YOUR OWN, YOU OWN THIS GOOD.

THIS GOOD IS FOR YOU.

Alison Whittaker

Binsey Poplars

Felled 1879

My aspens dear, whose airy cages quelled,
 Quelled or quenched in leaves the leaping sun,
 All felled, felled, are all felled;
  Of a fresh and following folded rank

Not spared, not one
That dandled a sandalled
Shadow that swam or sank
On meadow and river and wind-wandering weed-winding bank.

O if we but knew what we do
When we delve or hew –
Hack and rack the growing green!
Since country is so tender
To touch, her being so slender,
That, like this sleek and seeing ball
But a prick will make no eye at all,
Where we, even where we mean
To mend her we end her,
When we hew or delve:
After-comers cannot guess the beauty been.
Ten or twelve, only ten or twelve
Strokes of havoc unselve
The sweet especial scene,
Rural scene, a rural scene,
Sweet especial rural scene.

Gerard Manley Hopkins

A Birthday

My heart is like a singing bird
Whose nest is in a water'd shoot;
My heart is like an apple-tree
Whose boughs are bent with thickset fruit;
My heart is like a rainbow shell

That paddles in a halcyon sea;
My heart is gladder than all these
Because my love is come to me.

Raise me a dais of silk and down;
Hang it with vair and purple dyes;
Carve it in doves and pomegranates,
And peacocks with a hundred eyes;
Work it in gold and silver grapes,
In leaves and silver fleurs-de-lys;
Because the birthday of my life
Is come, my love is come to me.

Christina Rossetti

Black Cockatoos

Each certain kind of weather or of light
has its own creatures. Somewhere else they wait
as though they but inhabited heat or cold,
twilight or dawn, and knew no other state.
Then at their time they come, timid or bold.

So when the long drought-winds sandpaper-harsh,
were still, and the air changed, and the clouds came,
and other birds were quiet in prayer or fear,
these knew their hour. Before the first far flash
lit up, or the first thunder spoke its name,
in heavy flight they came, till I could hear
the wild black cockatoos, tossed on the crest
of their high trees, crying the world's unrest.

Judith Wright

Bride and Groom Lie Hidden for Three Days

She gives him his eyes, she found them
Among some rubble, among some beetles

He gives her her skin
He just seemed to pull it down out of the air and lay it over her
She weeps with fearfulness and astonishment

She has found his hands for him, and fitted them freshly at the wrists
They are amazed at themselves, they go feeling all over her

He has assembled her spine, he cleaned each piece carefully
And sets them in perfect order
A superhuman puzzle but he is inspired
She leans back twisting this way and that, using it and
    laughing, incredulous

Now she has brought his feet, she is connecting them
So that his whole body lights up

And he has fashioned her new hips
With all fittings complete and with newly wound coils,
    all shiningly oiled
He is polishing every part, he himself can hardly believe it

They keep taking each other to the sun, they find they can easily
To test each new thing at each new step

And now she smooths over him the plates of his skull
So that the joints are invisible

And now he connects her throat, her breasts and the pit
    of her stomach
With a single wire

She gives him his teeth, tying the roots to the centrepin of his body

He sets the little circlets on her fingertips

She stitches his body here and there with steely purple silk

He oils the delicate cogs of her mouth

She inlays with deep-cut scrolls the nape of his neck

He sinks into place the inside of her thighs

So, gasping with joy, with cries of wonderment
Like two gods of mud
Sprawling in the dirt, but with infinite care

They bring each other to perfection.

Ted Hughes

'Bright star, would I were stedfast as thou art'

Bright star, would I were stedfast as thou art –
    Not in lone splendour hung aloft the night
And watching, with eternal lids apart,
    Like nature's patient, sleepless Eremite,
The moving waters at their priestlike task

Of pure ablution round earth's human shores,
Or gazing on the new soft-fallen mask
Of snow upon the mountains and the moors –
No – yet still stedfast, still unchangeable,
Pillow'd upon my fair love's ripening breast,
To feel for ever its soft fall and swell,
Awake for ever in a sweet unrest,
Still, still to hear her tender-taken breath,
And so live ever – or else swoon to death.

John Keats

Broadcast

Giant whispering and coughing from
Vast Sunday-full and organ-frowned-on spaces
Precede a sudden scuttle on the drum,
'The Queen', and huge resettling. Then begins
A snivel of the violins:
I think of your face among all those faces,

Beautiful and devout before
Cascades of monumental slithering,
One of your gloves unnoticed on the floor
Beside those new, slightly-outmoded shoes.
Here it goes quickly dark. I lose
All but the outline of the still and withering

Leaves on half-emptied trees. Behind
The glowing wavebands, rabid storms of chording
By being distant overpower my mind

All the more shamelessly, their cut-off shout
Leaving me desperate to pick out
Your hands, tiny in all that air, applauding.

Philip Larkin

Brown

sometimes
bronzed terracotta mahogany
i wake
burnished hazelnut beige
with rope
scarlet brown cedar
tanned sandstone
oaked earth
and red-rusted caramel gold
round my neck
chocolate
raw umber
scorched hazel
dripping
burnt macadamian cream
sweat
walnut sienna
and mapled sahara
ripe olive on dark aubergine
out of
earth clayed treacle
breath

dog at my
honeyed tree sap
heels

bleeding but
carmine coffee bean
free

afraid to
stained pine sunset
dream

Maxine Beneba Clarke

'But I do think it is their husbands' faults'

But I do think it is their husbands' faults
If wives do fall. Say that they slack their duties,
And pour our treasures into foreign laps,
Or else break out in peevish jealousies,
Throwing restraint upon us. Or say they strike us,
Or scant our former having in despite.
Why, we have galls, and though we have some grace,
Yet have we some revenge. Let husbands know
Their wives have sense like them. They see, and smell,
And have their palates both for sweet and sour,
As husbands have. What is it that they do
When they change us for others? Is it sport?
I think it is. And doth affection breed it?
I think it doth. Is't frailty that thus errs?

It is so too. And have not we affections,
Desires for sport, and frailty, as men have?
Then let them use us well. Else let them know,
The ills we do, their ills instruct us so.

Emilia in Othello, *William Shakespeare*

Canoe

a girl watches a bead of sweat roll
tracing the muscles on his arms
as he lowers the freshly cut bark
moist grass provides a cushion

he turns to stare at her stillness
her eyes remain above his head
the soft flesh of the tree expires
the scar bleeds on the trunk

outside the smoky fire she stands
he dries and shapes the fresh canoe
the structure forms to nature's laws
a new dais of voyage prepared

at midnight they sail the river
she turns without causing a ripple
looking back along the darkness
to the neon of the scar tree

it shines like a bended doorway
a light within beckons as if a

sacred star has fallen and a
yearning will soon be done

Ali Cobby Eckermann

Celibate's Ode to Balls

When I first saw a naked man,
there they were, visible,
in air, in light, hidden in
their carrying case, inside them the miniscule
people, teeming seeds of them,
the world populations, the crowds
rushing across enormous capital-
city squares, as if a man
could feel his known world tilt
and the oceans lift up out of their beds.
And when I was no longer married,
once I was a spinster again,
every day I missed living with them
– with him, but the longer I went without him,
the more the longing was general, cate-
gorical, and imperative.
I missed the two who are with the one
which enters, while they do not enter,
they loll intense,
I missed how they are two in one –
once, in a dream, I wandered in one,
my oldest home, my hobo-sack home,
I underwater-breaststroked through
the dessert of it, like the inside

of a tongue, and light came through into the pink
male sewing reticule,
basket of tangles of brilliant polished
thread – and then the skin would shift
like my scalp when the hairs stood straight on end.
All those years, when I was celibate again,
I'd cry out to balls, 'O purses of X's
and Y's, O inside-out pocket with its dear
seam, O dear,' I knew that some
would laugh when I said it, 'I love balls,'
and others would groan with me a moment, missing them.

Sharon Olds

Child Burial

Your coffin looked unreal,
fancy as a wedding cake.

I chose your grave clothes with care,
your favourite stripey shirt,

your blue cotton trousers.
They smelt of woodsmoke, of October,

your own smell there too.
I chose a gansy of handspun wool,

warm and fleecy for you. It is
so cold down in the dark.

No light can reach you and teach you
the paths of wild birds,

the names of the flowers,
the fishes, the creatures.

Ignorant you must remain
of the sun and its work,

my lamb, my calf, my eaglet,
my cub, my kid, my nestling,

my suckling, my colt. I would spin
time back, take you again

within my womb, your amniotic lair,
and further spin you back

through nine waxing months
to the split seeding moment

you chose to be made flesh,
word within me.

I'd cancel the love feast
the hot night of your making.

I would travel alone
to a quiet mossy place,

you would spill from me into the earth
drop by bright red drop.

Paula Meehan

Clancy of the Overflow

I had written him a letter which I had, for want of better
  Knowledge, sent to where I met him down the Lachlan, years ago,
He was shearing when I knew him, so I sent the letter to him,
  Just 'on spec', addressed as follows, 'Clancy, of The Overflow'.

And an answer came directed in a writing unexpected,
  (And I think the same was written with a thumb-nail dipped in tar)
'Twas his shearing mate who wrote it, and *verbatim* I will quote it:
  'Clancy's gone to Queensland droving, and we don't know where he are.'

In my wild erratic fancy visions come to me of Clancy
  Gone a-droving 'down the Cooper' where the Western drovers go;
As the stock are slowly stringing, Clancy rides behind them singing,
  For the drover's life has pleasures that the townsfolk never know.

And the bush hath friends to meet him, and their kindly voices greet him
  In the murmur of the breezes and the river on its bars,
And he sees the vision splendid of the sunlit plains extended,
  And at night the wond'rous glory of the everlasting stars.

I am sitting in my dingy little office, where a stingy
  Ray of sunlight struggles feebly down between the houses tall,
And the foetid air and gritty of the dusty, dirty city
  Through the open window floating, spreads its foulness over all.

And in place of lowing cattle, I can hear the fiendish rattle
  Of the tramways and the 'buses making hurry down the street,
And the language uninviting of the gutter children fighting,
  Comes fitfully and faintly through the ceaseless tramp of feet.

And the hurrying people daunt me, and their pallid faces haunt me
  As they shoulder one another in their rush and nervous haste,
With their eager eyes and greedy, and their stunted forms and weedy,
  For townsfolk have no time to grow, they have no time to waste.

And I somehow rather fancy that I'd like to change with Clancy,
  Like to take a turn at droving where the seasons come and go,
While he faced the round eternal of the cash-book and the journal –
  But I doubt he'd suit the office, Clancy, of 'The Overflow'.

Banjo Paterson

Closed Path

I thought that my voyage had come to its end
at the last limit of my power, – that the path before me was closed,
that provisions were exhausted
and the time come to take shelter in a silent obscurity.

But I find that thy will knows no end in me.
And when old words die out on the tongue,
new melodies break forth from the heart;
and where the old tracks are lost,
new country is revealed with its wonders.

Rabindranath Tagore, from Gitanjali, *translated by the author*

'Come, you spirits'

Come, you spirits
That tend on mortal thoughts, unsex me here,
And fill me from the crown to the toe top-full
Of direst cruelty. Make thick my blood,
Stop up th'access and passage to remorse,
That no compunctious visitings of nature
Shake my fell purpose, nor keep peace between
Th'effect and it. Come to my woman's breasts,
And take my milk for gall, you murd'ring ministers,
Wherever in your sightless substances
You wait on nature's mischief. Come, thick night,
And pall thee in the dunnest smoke of hell,
That my keen knife see not the wound it makes,
Nor heaven peep through the blanket of the dark,
To cry 'Hold, hold!'

Lady Macbeth in Macbeth, *William Shakespeare*

Coming to It

Three kids down at the front gate
wait the school bus;
fog hung low down the valley,
the house in sore need of paint,
the bright washing on the line,
a Van Morrison morning.

A man without a dog is not a man.
You don't have to believe it,

you really don't.
But it's all to do with the farm gate,
the three kids waiting the bus,
the man singing, the man we're listening to.
He knows where buses go
and why they never painted the house;
and if it's songs about fog you want,
Van Morrison's your boy.

So come over here,
take a look:
the fog is lifting – or is it just drifting? –
the bus has taken the kids to school.
And there's a man singing.
Wait for it –
the bright-washing-on-the-line bit –
we're all just
coming to it.

Sam Hunt

Composed upon Westminster Bridge, September 3, 1802

Earth has not any thing to show more fair:
Dull would he be of soul who could pass by
A sight so touching in its majesty:
This City now doth, like a garment, wear
The beauty of the morning; silent, bare,
Ships, towers, domes, theatres, and temples lie
Open unto the fields, and to the sky;
All bright and glittering in the smokeless air.

Never did sun more beautifully steep
In his first splendour, valley, rock, or hill;
Ne'er saw I, never felt, a calm so deep!
The river glideth at his own sweet will:
Dear God! the very houses seem asleep;
And all that mighty heart is lying still!

William Wordsworth

The Composer

All the others translate: the painter sketches
A visible world to love or reject;
Rummaging into his living, the poet fetches
The images out that hurt and connect.

From Life to Art by painstaking adaption,
Relying on us to cover the rift;
Only your notes are pure contraption,
Only your song is an absolute gift.

Pour out your presence, a delight cascading
The falls of the knee and the weirs of the spine,
Our climate of silence and doubt invading;

You alone, alone, imaginary song,
Are unable to say an existence is wrong,
And pour out your forgiveness like a wine.

W. H. Auden

Conjecture Number One Thousand

If I loved him – I loved him –
I cannot remember the whole middle part
where the gods never go, they'd be bored.

Of the beginning – how many poems
to describe his buoyancy,
and gaze, and hands –

how many times can the act of whispering together
be a remonstrance to the underworld?

And the end is completely remembered –
flinging his clothes in the driveway,
like a movie – domestic comedy they call it.

Okay, finito.

But no, I want to know, still, what it was
there in the everyday
that turned the connection into threat.

If I could I would blame the blameless
spoons, or the air where springtime bluebirds
– all rufous breasts – returned.

They had been to the Amazon.

Maybe we went wrong – we lacked
a winter vacation – never gambling in Miami,
never asking some beautiful Cuban

to deflect the ordinary.

This cold light – New Hampshire fall –
illuminates a trembling,
probably the wind. Or something with a purpose.

Caroline Finkelstein

Corinna

It was hot – the day already more than half gone.
  I lay where I'd dropped on the bed.
It happened a window was half open. Light filtered in
  like light falling in a forest;
like the afterglow of twilight or when it's dawn
  but the night hasn't quite faded.
That's the kind of dim light shy girls like – it gives
  their modesty some cover.
The door opens. In comes Corinna, her dress half buttoned,
  her hair fixed to show off that lovely neck.
She looked as lovely as Semiramis on her wedding night
  or Lais in anyone's bed.
I tore off the dress. To make it more fun she fought
  to keep the flimsy thing half on.
We struggled; I won! Her protests betrayed
  the truth: she had wanted to lose.
Clothes littered the room. There stood Corinna nude.
  God, what a masterpiece she was!
Looking was not enough; I had to touch those shoulders, those arms;
  mold my hands round each round breast.
Her belly's subtle curves coaxed my fingers on. Soon I felt
  the supple swell of hips and thighs.

But why catalogue the store of pleasure her body held?
    I held her naked in my arms.
You can fantasize the rest. We were exhausted and slept.
    May many afternoons be so well spent.

Ovid, Amores*: 1.5, translated by John Svarlien*

Country Football

The ellipse, Hindu symbol of fertility,
is flanked by crowded cars
nosing up to the rails.
It suckles like a sow.

Inside the cars voices report
from significant, never been there places –
Kardinia, Moorabbin, Windy Hill.

Reflecting each other from the cusps
rise two-dimensional white cathedrals.
Today they will be temples to apostasy twice.
Their entrances are guarded by clones
whose torches blaze pure white.

From corrugated iron purgatory
many men feed out in lines like parachutists
limbs varnished with an intoxicating wake
of eucalyptus oil.

Landing near afflatus
they disperse into pairs
of cryptic numerical combinations.

But one without a number,
as resolutely white as the cue ball,
omnipotent in a classical pose,
holds aloft a red ellipse

and whistles up
a terrible trumpeting of car horns
for this afternoon's do or die.

Philip Hodgins

The Cows on Killing Day

All me are standing on feed. The sky is shining.

All me have just been milked. Teats all tingling still
from that dry toothless sucking by the chilly mouths
that gasp loudly in in in, and never breathe out.

All me standing on feed, move the feed inside me.
One me smells of needing the bull, that heavy urgent me,
the back-climber, who leaves me humped, straining, but light
and peaceful again, with crystalline moving inside me.

Standing on wet rock, being milked, assuages the calf-sorrow in me.
Now the me who needs mounts on me, hopping, to signal the bull.

The tractor comes trotting in its grumble; the heifer human
bounces on top of it, and cud comes with the tractor,
big rolls of tight dry feed: lucerne, clovers, buttercup, grass,
that's been bitten but never swallowed, yet is cud.

She walks up over the tractor and down it comes, roll on roll
and all me following, eating it, and dropping the good pats.

The heifer human smells of needing the bull human
and is angry. All me look nervously at her
as she chases the dog me dream of horning dead: our enemy
of the light loose tongue. Me'd jam him in his squeals.

Me, facing every way, spreading out over feed.

One me is still in the yard, the place skinned of feed.
Me, old and sore-boned, little milk in that me now,
licks at the wood. The oldest bull human is coming.

Me in the peed yard. A stick goes out from the human
and cracks, like the whip. Me shivers and falls down
with the terrible, the blood of me, coming out behind an ear.
Me, that other me, down and dreaming in the bare yard.

All me come running. It's like the Hot Part of the sky
that's hard to look at, this that now happens behind wood
in the raw yard. A shining leaf, like off the bitter gum tree
is with the human. It works in the neck of me
and the terrible floods out, swamped and frothy. All me make the Roar,
some leaping stiff-kneed, trying to horn that worst horror.
The wolf-at-the-calves is the bull human. Horn the bull human!

But the dog and the heifer human drive away all me.

Looking back, the glistening leaf is still moving.
All of dry old me is crumpled, like the hills of feed,
and a slick me like a huge calf is coming out of me.

The carrion-stinking dog, who is calf of human and wolf,
is chasing and eating little blood things the humans scatter,
and all me run away, over smells, toward the sky.

Les Murray

Cute

You cannot feel your toes, and so
you walk like a child,
that hint of a toddle,
that newness to bipedal poise.
You would have walked like this, I guess,
in 1960, hand-in-hand with mummy,
fearless in your infancy.
Now your illness has taken fifty years
of confidence off your gait
and made you quite
adorable again.

Beside you, casual and sly,
I keep an eye on your most fetching lack
of balance; the winsome lollop
that might cause a fall.
Half a century back, you'd scrape your knees,
need kisses for your momentary distress,
perhaps get mud stains on your dress.
Today, you might break bones.
Today, your flesh might rend.
Today, something might happen which, in hindsight,
was the omen of your end.

I reach out for your hand.
You walk ahead, oblivious, intent
on the rhythm of your steps,
refreshing your memory
of how this walking trick is done.
One foot in front
of the other one.
Oh, my little girl, how unbearably
cute you have become.

Michel Faber

Danny Boy

Oh, Danny boy, the pipes, the pipes are calling
From glen to glen, and down the mountain side.
The summer's gone, and all the roses falling,
It's you, it's you must go and I must bide.

But come ye back when summer's in the meadow,
Or when the valley's hushed and white with snow,
I'll be here in sunshine or in shadow,
Oh, Danny boy, oh Danny boy, I love you so!

But when ye come, and all the flowers are dying,
If I am dead, as dead I well may be,
You'll come and find the place where I am lying,
And kneel and say an Ave there for me.

And I shall hear, though soft you tread above me,
And all my grave will warmer, sweeter be,

For you will bend and tell me that you love me,
And I shall sleep in peace until you come to me!

Frederic E. Weatherly

The Darkling Thrush

I leant upon a coppice gate
    When Frost was spectre-grey,
And Winter's dregs made desolate
    The weakening eye of day.
The tangled bine-stems scored the sky
    Like strings of broken lyres,
And all mankind that haunted nigh
    Had sought their household fires.

The land's sharp features seemed to be
    The Century's corpse outleant,
His crypt the cloudy canopy,
    The wind his death-lament.
The ancient pulse of germ and birth
    Was shrunken hard and dry,
And every spirit upon earth
    Seemed fervourless as I.

At once a voice arose among
    The bleak twigs overhead
In a full-hearted evensong
    Of joy illimited;
An aged thrush, frail, gaunt and small,
    In blast-beruffled plume,

Had chosen thus to fling his soul
    Upon the growing gloom.

So little cause for carolings
    Of such ecstatic sound
Was written on terrestrial things
    Afar or nigh around,
That I could think there trembled through
    His happy good-night air
Some blessed Hope, whereof he knew
    And I was unaware.

Thomas Hardy

Days of 1903

I never found them again – all lost so quickly . . .
the poetic eyes, the pale face . . .
in the darkening street . . .

I never found them again – mine entirely by chance,
and so easily given up,
then longed for so painfully.
The poetic eyes, the pale face,
those lips – I never found them again.

C. P. Cavafy, translated by Edmund Keeley and Philip Sherrard

'Death, be not proud'

Death, be not proud, though some have called thee
Mighty and dreadful, for thou art not so;
For those whom thou think'st thou dost overthrow
Die not, poor Death, nor yet canst thou kill me.
From rest and sleep, which but thy pictures be,
Much pleasure; then from thee much more must flow,
And soonest our best men with thee do go,
Rest of their bones, and soul's delivery.
Thou art slave to fate, chance, kings, and desperate men,
And dost with poison, war, and sickness dwell,
And poppy or charms can make us sleep as well
And better than thy stroke; why swell'st thou then?
One short sleep past, we wake eternally
And death shall be no more; Death, thou shalt die.

Holy Sonnet 10, John Donne

The Death of the Bird

For every bird there is this last migration:
Once more the cooling year kindles her heart;
With a warm passage to the summer station
Love pricks the course in lights across the chart.

Year after year a speck on the map, divided
By a whole hemisphere, summons her to come;
Season after season, sure and safely guided,
Going away she is also coming home.

And being home, memory becomes a passion
With which she feeds her brood and straws her nest,
Aware of ghosts that haunt the heart's possession
And exiled love mourning within the breast.

The sands are green with a mirage of valleys;
The palm-tree casts a shadow not its own;
Down the long architrave of temple or palace
Blows a cool air from moorland scarps of stone.

And day by day the whisper of love grows stronger;
That delicate voice, more urgent with despair,
Custom and fear constraining her no longer,
Drives her at last on the waste leagues of air.

A vanishing speck in those inane dominions,
Single and frail, uncertain of her place,
Alone in the bright host of her companions,
Lost in the blue unfriendliness of space,

She feels it close now, the appointed season:
The invisible thread is broken as she flies;
Suddenly, without warning, without reason,
The guiding spark of instinct winks and dies.

Try as she will, the trackless world delivers
No way, the wilderness of light no sign,
The immense and complex map of hills and rivers
Mocks her small wisdom with its vast design.

And darkness rises from the eastern valleys,
And the winds buffet her with their hungry breath,
And the great earth, with neither grief nor malice,
Receives the tiny burden of her death.

A. D. Hope

Departure

Enough seen. The vision has been encountered in all skies.
Enough had. Sounds of cities, in the evening, and in sunlight,
    and always.
Enough known. The stations of life. – O Sounds and Visions!
Departure amid new noise and affection!

Arthur Rimbaud, translated by John Ashbery

The Diameter of the Bomb

The diameter of the bomb was thirty centimeters
and the diameter of its effective range about seven meters,
with four dead and eleven wounded.
And around these, in a larger circle
of pain and time, two hospitals are scattered
and one graveyard. But the young woman
who was buried in the city she came from,
at a distance of more than a hundred kilometers,
enlarges the circle considerably,
and the solitary man mourning her death
at the distant shores of a country far across the sea
includes the entire world in the circle.

And I won't even mention the howl of orphans
that reaches up to the throne of God and
beyond, making
a circle with no end and no God.

Yehuda Amichai, translated by Chana Bloch

Digging

Between my finger and my thumb
The squat pen rests; snug as a gun.

Under my window, a clean rasping sound
When the spade sinks into gravelly ground:
My father, digging. I look down

Till his straining rump among the flowerbeds
Bends low, comes up twenty years away
Stooping in rhythm through potato drills
Where he was digging.

The coarse boot nestled on the lug, the shaft
Against the inside knee was levered firmly.
He rooted out tall tops, buried the bright edge deep
To scatter new potatoes that we picked,
Loving their cool hardness in our hands.

By God, the old man could handle a spade.
Just like his old man.

My grandfather cut more turf in a day
Than any other man on Toner's bog.
Once I carried him milk in a bottle
Corked sloppily with paper. He straightened up
To drink it, then fell to right away
Nicking and slicing neatly, heaving sods
Over his shoulder, going down and down
For the good turf. Digging.

The cold smell of potato mould, the squelch and slap
Of soggy peat, the curt cuts of an edge
Through living roots awaken in my head.
But I've no spade to follow men like them.

Between my finger and my thumb
The squat pen rests.
I'll dig with it.

Seamus Heaney

Diptych

1

My mother told me that she'd often stayed awake
in those years, and of a certain night
at a rented farm,
on the end of the dark leaf-mulch of the drive,
where she sat in a doorway with mosquito-smoke,
listening for my father, after the pubs had closed, knowing he would
    have to walk

'miles, in his state', or sleep in weeds by the road,
if no one dropped him at our gate
(since long before this he had driven his own car off a mountain-side
and becoming legend had ridden
on the easily-felled banana palms
of a steep plantation, right to the foot and a kitchen door,
the car reared high, and slipping fast, on a vast
raft of sap-oozing fibre,
from which he'd climbed down, unharmed, his most soberly polite,
had doffed his hat
to a terrified
young woman with her child in arms
and never driven again).
This other night, my mother was reluctant to go out, poking with a stick
under the lantana, down every slope,
and leave us kids in the house asleep, a cough
trundled among us,
and fell asleep herself, clothed, on the unopened bed,
but leapt upright, sometime later, with the foulest taste – glimpsed
  at once
he was still not home – and rushed out, gagging,
to find that, asleep, she'd bitten off the tail
of a small lizard, dragged through her lips. That bitterness, I used
  to imagine;
she running onto the verandah to spit,
and standing there, spat dry, seeing across the silent, frosty bush
the distant lights of town had died.

And yet my mother never ceased from what philosophers invoke,
from extending 'care',

though she only read the *Women's Weekly*,
and although she could be 'damned impossible' through a few
meal-times, of course.
That care for things, I see, was her one real companion in those years.
It was as if there were two of her,
a harassed person, and a calm, who saw what needed to be done, and
stepped through her, again.
Her care you could watch reappear like the edge of tidal water
in salt flats, about everything.
It was this made her drive out the neighbour's bull from our garden
with a broom,
when she saw it trample her seedlings –
back, step by step, she forced it, through the broken fence,
it bellowing and hooking either side sharply at her all the way, and I
six years old on the back steps calling
'Let it have a few old bloody flowers, Mum.'
No. She locked the broom handle straight-armed across its nose
and was pushed right back herself
quickly across the yard. She
ducked behind some tomato stakes,
and beat with the handle, all over that deep hollowness of the muzzle,
poked with the straw at its eyes,
and had her way, drove it out bellowing;
and me, slapping into the steps, the rail, with an ironing cord,
or rushing down there, quelled also,
repelled to the bottom step, barracking. And all,
I saw, for those little flimsy leaves
she fell to at once, small as mouse prints, among the
chopped-up loam.

2

Whereas, my father only seemed to care that he would never
    appear a drunkard
while ever his shoes were clean.
A drunkard he defined as someone who had forgotten the mannerisms
of a gentleman. The gentleman, after all, is only known,
only exists, through manner. He himself had the most perfect manners,
of a kind. I can imagine no one
with a style more easily and coolly precise. With him,
manner had subsumed all of feeling. To brush and dent the hat
which one would re-settle, or to look about over each of us
and then unfold a napkin
to allow the meal, in that town where probably all of the men
sat to eat of a hot evening without a shirt,
was his dry passion. After all, he was a university man
(although ungraduated), something more rare then.
My father, I see, was hopelessly melancholic –
the position of those wary
small eyes, and thin lips, on the long-boned face
proclaimed the bitterness of every pleasure, except those of form.
He often drank alone
at the RSL club, and had been known to wear a
    carefully-considered tie
to get drunk in the sandhills, watching the sea.
When he was ill and was at home at night, I would look into
    his bedroom,
on the end of a gauzed verandah,
from around the door and a little behind him,
and see his frighteningly high-domed skull under the lamp-light,
    as he read

in a curdle of cigarette smoke.
Light shone through wire mesh onto the packed hydrangea heads,
and on the great ragged mass of insects, like bees over a comb,
that crawled tethered
and ignored right beside him. He seemed content, at these times,
as though he'd done all he need
to make a case against himself, and had been forced, objectively, to
    give up.
He appeared to like his bland ulcer-patient food
and the heap of library books I brought. (My instructions always were:
'Nothing by Faulkner;
    nothing by New York Jews; nothing by 'proletarian' writers;
    nothing by women, except for those who are shelved under Crime;
    nothing 'spiritual', or translated from the Russian.')
And yet, the only time I heard him say that he'd enjoyed anything
was when he spoke of the bush, once. 'Up in those hills,'
he advised me, pointing around, 'when the sun is coming out of the sea,
    standing among
that lifting timber, you can feel at peace.'
I was impressed. He asked me, another time, that when he died
I should take his ashes somewhere, and not put him with the locals,
    in the cemetery.
I went up to one of the places he had named
years earlier, at the time of day he had spoken of, when the half-risen sun
was as strongly-spiked as the one
on his Infantry badge,
and I scattered him there, utterly reduced at last, among the wet,
    breeze-woven grass.
For all his callousness to my mother, I had long accepted him,
who had shown me the best advice
and left me to myself. And I'd come by then to see that all

are pathetic.
Opening his plastic, brick-sized box, that morning,
my pocket-knife slid
sideways and pierced my hand – and so I dug with that one
into his ashes, which I found were like a mauvish-grey marble dust,
and felt I needn't think of anything else to say.

Robert Gray

Dirge on the Death of Art O'Leary

I

My closest and dearest!
From the first day I saw you
From the top of the market-house,
My eyes gave heed to you,
My heart gave affection to you,
I fled from my friends with you,
Far from my home with you,
No lasting sorrow this to me.

II

Thou didst bring me to fair chambers,
Rooms you had adorned for me;
Ovens were reddened for me,
Fresh trout were caught for me,
Roast flesh was carved for me
From beef that was felled for me;
On beds of down I lay

Till the coming of the milking-time,
Or so long as was pleasing to me.

III

Rider of the white palm!
With the silver-hilted sword!
Well your beaver hat became you
With its band of graceful gold;
Your suit of solid homespun yarn
Wrapped close around your form;
Slender shoes of foreign fashion,
And a pin of brightest silver
Fastened in your shirt.
As you rode in stately wise
On your slender steed, white-faced,
After coming over seas,
Even the Saxons bowed before you
Bowed down to the very ground;
Not because they loved you well
But from deadly hate;
For it was by them you fell,
Darling of my soul.

IV

My friend and my little calf!
Offsprings of the Lords of Antrim,
And the chiefs of Immokely!
Never had I thought you dead,
Until there came to me your mare

Her bridle dragged beside her to the ground;
Upon her brow your heart-blood splashed,
Even to the carven saddle flowing down
Where you were wont to sit or stand.
I did not stay to cleanse it –
I gave a quick leap with my hands
Upon the wooden stretcher of the bed:
A second leap was to the gate,
And the third leap upon thy mare.

V

In haste I clapped my hands together,
I followed on your tracks
As well as I could,
Till I found you laid before me dead
At the foot of a lowly bush of furze;
Without pope, without bishop,
Without cleric or priest
To read a psalm for thee;
But only an old bent wasted crone
Who flung over thee the corner of her cloak.

VI

My dear and beloved one!
When it will come to me to reach our home,
Little Conor, of our love,
And Fiac, his toddling baby-brother,
Will be asking of me quickly
Where I left their dearest father?

I shall answer them with sorrow
That I left him in Kill Martyr;
They will call upon their father;
He will not be there to answer.

VII

My love and my chosen one!
When you were going forward from the gate,
You turned quickly back again!
You kissed your two children,
You threw a kiss to me.
You said, 'Eileen, arise now, be stirring,
And set your house in order,
Be swiftly moving.
I am leaving our home,
It is likely that I may not come again.'
I took it only for a jest
You used often to be jesting thus before.

VIII

My friend and my heart's love!
Arise up, my Art,
Leap on thy steed,
Arise out to Macroom
And to Inchegeela after that;
A bottle of wine in thy grasp,
As was ever in the time of thy ancestors.
Arise up, my Art,
Rider of the shining sword;

Put on your garments,
Your fair noble clothes;
Don your black beaver,
Draw on your gloves;
See, here hangs your whip,
Your good mare waits without;
Strike eastward on the narrow road,
For the bushes will bare themselves before you,
For the streams will narrow on your path,
For men and women will bow themselves before you
If their own good manners are upon them yet,
But I am much a-feared they are not now.

IX

Destruction to you and woe,
O Morris, hideous the treachery
That took from me the man of the house,
The father of my babes;
Two of them running about the house,
The third beneath my breast,
It is likely that I shall not give it birth.

X

My long wound, my bitter sorrow,
That I was not beside thee
When the shot was fired;
That I might have got it in my soft body
Or in the skirt of my gown;
Till I would give you freedom to escape,

O Rider of the grey eye,
Because it is you would best have followed after them.

XI

My dear and my heart's love!
Terrible to me the way I see thee,
To be putting our hero,
Our rider so true of heart,
In a little cap in a coffin!
Thou who used to be fishing along the streams,
Thou who didst drink within wide halls
Among the gentle women white of breast;
It is my thousand afflictions
That I have lost your companionship!
My love and my darling,
Could my shouts but reach thee
West in mighty Derrynane,
And in Carhen of the yellow apples after that;
Many a light-hearted young horseman,
And woman with white, spotless kerchief
Would swiftly be with us here,
To wail above thy head
Art O'Leary of the joyous laugh!
O women of the soft, wet eyes,
Stay now your weeping,
Till Art O'Leary drinks his drink
Before his going back to school;
Not to learn reading or music does he go there now,
But to carry clay and stones.

XII

My love and my secret thou.
Thy corn-stacks are piled,
And thy golden kine are milking,
But it is upon my own heart is the grief!
There is no healing in the Province of Munster,
Nor in the Island smithy of the Fians,
Till Art O'Leary will come back to me;
But all as if it were a lock upon a trunk
And the key of it gone straying;
Or till rust will come upon the screw.

XIII

My friend and my best one!
Art O'Leary, son of Conor,
Son of Cadach, son of Lewis,
Eastward from wet wooded glens,
Westward from the slender hill
Where the rowan-berries grow,
And the yellow nuts are ripe upon the branches;
Apples trailing, as it was in my day.
Little wonder to myself
If fires were lighted in O'Leary's country,
And at the mouth of Ballingeary,
Or at holy Gougane Barra of the cells,
After the rider of the smooth grip,
After the huntsman unwearied
When, heavy breathing with the chase,
Even thy lithe deerhounds lagged behind.

O horseman of the enticing eyes,
What happened thee last night?
For I myself thought
That the whole world could not kill you
When I bought for you that shirt of mail.

XIV

My friend and my darling!
A cloudy vision through the darkness
Came to me last night,
At Cork lately
And I alone upon my bed!
I saw the wooded glen withered,
I saw our lime-washed court fallen;
No sound of speech came from thy hunting-dogs
No sound of singing from the birds
When you were found in the clay,
On the side of the hill without;
When you were found fallen
Art O'Leary;
With your drop of blood oozing out
Through the breast of your shirt.

XV

It is known to Jesus Christ,
I will put no cap upon thy head,
Nor body-linen on my side,
Nor shoes upon my feet,
Nor gear throughout the house:

Even on the brown mare will be no bridle,
But I shall spend all in taking the law.
I will go across the seas
To seek the villain of the black blood
But if they will give no heed to me,
It is I that will come back again
To speak with the King;
Who cut off my treasure from me.
O Morris, who killed my hero,
Was there not one man in Erin
Would put a bullet through you?
The affection of this heart to you,
O white women of the mill,
For the edged poetry that you have shed
Over the horseman of the brown mare.
It is I who am the lonely one
In Inse Carriganane.

Eibhlín Dubh Ní Chonaill (Dark Eileen), translated by Eleanor Hull

Do not go gentle into that good night

Do not go gentle into that good night,
Old age should burn and rave at close of day;
Rage, rage against the dying of the light.

Though wise men at their end know dark is right,
Because their words had forked no lightning they
Do not go gentle into that good night.

Good men, the last wave by, crying how bright
Their frail deeds might have danced in a green bay,
Rage, rage against the dying of the light.

Wild men who caught and sang the sun in flight,
And learn, too late, they grieved it on its way,
Do not go gentle into that good night.

Grave men, near death, who see with blinding sight
Blind eyes could blaze like meteors and be gay,
Rage, rage against the dying of the light.

And you, my father, there on the sad height,
Curse, bless, me now with your fierce tears, I pray.
Do not go gentle into that good night.
Rage, rage against the dying of the light.

Dylan Thomas

Donal Og

It is late last night the dog was speaking of you;
the snipe was speaking of you in her deep marsh.
It is you are the lonely bird through the woods;
and that you may be without a mate until you find me.

You promised me, and you said a lie to me,
that you would be before me where the sheep are flocked;
I gave a whistle and three hundred cries to you,
and I found nothing there but a bleating lamb.

You promised me a thing that was hard for you,
a ship of gold under a silver mast;
twelve towns with a market in all of them,
and a fine white court by the side of the sea.

You promised me a thing that is not possible,
that you would give me gloves of the skin of a fish;
that you would give me shoes of the skin of a bird;
and a suit of the dearest silk in Ireland.

When I go by myself to the Well of Loneliness,
I sit down and I go through my trouble;
when I see the world and do not see my boy,
he that has an amber shade in his hair.

It was on that Sunday I gave my love to you;
the Sunday that is last before Easter Sunday
and myself on my knees reading the Passion;
and my two eyes giving love to you for ever.

My mother has said to me not to be talking with you today,
or tomorrow, or on the Sunday;
it was a bad time she took for telling me that;
it was shutting the door after the house was robbed.

My heart is as black as the blackness of the sloe,
or as the black coal that is on the smith's forge;
or as the sole of a shoe left in white halls;
it was you put that darkness over my life.

You have taken the east from me, you have taken the west from me;
you have taken what is before me and what is behind me;
you have taken the moon, you have taken the sun from me;
and my fear is great that you have taken God from me!

Anonymous, translated by Lady Gregory

Dover Beach

The sea is calm tonight.
The tide is full, the moon lies fair
Upon the straits; on the French coast the light
Gleams and is gone; the cliffs of England stand,
Glimmering and vast, out in the tranquil bay.
Come to the window, sweet is the night-air!
Only, from the long line of spray
Where the sea meets the moon-blanched land,
Listen! you hear the grating roar
Of pebbles which the waves draw back, and fling,
At their return, up the high strand,
Begin, and cease, and then again begin,
With tremulous cadence slow, and bring
The eternal note of sadness in.

Sophocles long ago
Heard it on the Aegean, and it brought
Into his mind the turbid ebb and flow
Of human misery; we
Find also in the sound a thought,
Hearing it by this distant northern sea.

The Sea of Faith
Was once, too, at the full, and round earth's shore
Lay like the folds of a bright girdle furled.
But now I only hear
Its melancholy, long, withdrawing roar,
Retreating, to the breath
Of the night-wind, down the vast edges drear
And naked shingles of the world.

Ah, love, let us be true
To one another! for the world, which seems
To lie before us like a land of dreams,
So various, so beautiful, so new,
Hath really neither joy, nor love, nor light,
Nor certitude, nor peace, nor help for pain;
And we are here as on a darkling plain
Swept with confused alarms of struggle and flight,
Where ignorant armies clash by night.

Matthew Arnold

A Dream of Mountaineering

At night, in my dream, I stoutly climbed a mountain,
Going out alone with my staff of holly-wood.
A thousand crags, a hundred hundred valleys –
In my dream-journey none were unexplored
And all the while my feet never grew tired
And my step was as strong as in my young days.
Can it be that when the mind travels backward

The body also returns to its old state?
And can it be, as between body and soul,
That the body may languish, while the soul is still strong?
Soul and body – both are vanities;
Dreaming and waking – both alike unreal.
In the days my feet are palsied and tottering;
In the night my steps go striding over the hills.
As day and night are divided in equal parts –
Between the two I *get* as much as I *lose*.

Po Chü-I, translated by Arthur Waley

Drifters

One day soon he'll tell her it's time to start packing,
and the kids will yell 'Truly?' and get wildly excited for no reason,
and the brown kelpie pup will start dashing about,
    tripping everyone up,
and she'll go out to the vegetable-patch and pick all the green
    tomatoes from the vines,
and notice how the oldest girl is close to tears because
    she was happy here,
and how the youngest girl is beaming because she wasn't.
And the first thing she'll put on the trailer will be the bottling-set she
    never unpacked from Grovedale,
and when the loaded ute bumps down the drive past the blackberry-
    canes with their last shrivelled fruit,
she won't even ask why they're leaving this time, or where
    they're headed for
– she'll only remember how, when they came here,

she held out her hands bright with berries,
the first of the season, and said:
'Make a wish, Tom, make a wish.'

Bruce Dawe

Driving Alone on a Snowy Evening (After Frost)

There is no reason that I know
To go on waking, eating, so
I turn the urgent wipers off
And watch the screen sift up with snow.

They'll conjure emptiness, despair,
Disease in the wings, a failed career.
Those inward, ticking moments when
The seduction of stopping obliterates fear.

The car purrs on. I do not brake.
The choice of crash I leave to fate.
A tree, a bridge, a railway line.
Behind the brightness dark shapes wait.

The snow and ceiling kiss, then meet.
The view's as white as a winding sheet.
The heart still beats repeat repeat.
The heart still beats repeat repeat.

Sinéad Morrissey

Drowning in Wheat

They'd been warned
on every farm
that playing
in the silos
would lead to death.
You sink in wheat.
Slowly. And the more
you struggle the worse it gets.
'You'll see a rat sail past
your face, nimble on its turf,
and then you'll disappear.'
In there, hard work
has no reward.
So it became a kind of test
to see how far they could sink
without needing a rope
to help them out.
But in the midst of play
rituals miss a beat – like both
leaping in to resolve
an argument
as to who'd go first
and forgetting
to attach the rope.
Up to the waist
and afraid to move.
That even a call for help
would see the wheat
trickle down.

The painful consolidation
of time. The grains
in the hourglass
grotesquely swollen.
And that acrid
chemical smell
of treated wheat
coaxing them into
a near-dead sleep.

John Kinsella

Dublinesque

Down stucco sidestreets,
Where light is pewter
And afternoon mist
Brings lights on in shops
Above race-guides and rosaries,
A funeral passes.

The hearse is ahead,
But after there follows
A troop of streetwalkers
In wide flowered hats,
Leg-of-mutton sleeves,
And ankle-length dresses.

There is an air of great friendliness,
As if they were honouring
One they were fond of;

Some caper a few steps,
Skirts held skilfully
(Someone claps time),

And of great sadness also.
As they wend away
A voice is heard singing
Of Kitty, or Katy,
As if the name meant once
All love, all beauty.

Philip Larkin

Dulce et Decorum Est

Bent double, like old beggars under sacks,
Knock-kneed, coughing like hags, we cursed through sludge,
Till on the haunting flares we turned our backs,
And towards our distant rest began to trudge.
Men marched asleep. Many had lost their boots,
But limped on, blood-shod. All went lame; all blind;
Drunk with fatigue; deaf even to the hoots
Of gas-shells dropping softly behind.

Gas! GAS! Quick, boys! – An ecstasy of fumbling,
Fitting the clumsy helmets just in time,
But someone still was yelling out and stumbling,
And flound'ring like a man in fire or lime. –
Dim, through the misty panes and thick green light,
As under a green sea, I saw him drowning.

In all my dreams, before my helpless sight,
He plunges at me, guttering, choking, drowning.

If in some smothering dreams you too could pace
Behind the wagon that we flung him in,
And watch the white eyes writhing in his face,
His hanging face, like a devil's sick of sin;
If you could hear, at every jolt, the blood
Come gargling from the froth-corrupted lungs,
Obscene as cancer, bitter as the cud
Of vile, incurable sores on innocent tongues, –
My friend, you would not tell with such high zest
To children ardent for some desperate glory,
The old Lie; *Dulce et Decorum est*
Pro patria mori.

Wilfred Owen

Earth Presses Against Us

Earth is pressing against us, trapping us in the final passage.
To pass through, we pull off our limbs.
Earth is squeezing us. If only we were its wheat, we might die and yet live.
If only it were our mother so that she might temper us with mercy.
If only we were pictures of rocks held in our dreams like mirrors.
We glimpse faces in their final battle for the soul, of those who will be killed
by the last living among us. We mourn their children's feast.
We saw the faces of those who would throw our children out of the windows
of this last space. A star to burnish our mirrors.

Where should we go after the last border? Where should birds fly
after the last sky?
Where should plants sleep after the last breath of air?
We write our names with crimson mist!
We end the hymn with our flesh.
Here we will die. Here, in the final passage.
Here or there, our blood will plant olive trees.

Mahmoud Darwish, translated by Munir Akash and Carolyn Forché

Elegy from Balmoral Beach

For Arkie Deya Whiteley

A beach. Small waves and a shark net.
Moonlight on a fig tree, the bay a black mirror.

Music coming from a house, an exquisite guitar.
Tonight, there's nothing more bitter.

Resonating chords float above the school yard,
night birds beat the humid air. The ebb tide

exposes the moon's haul: squabbling seagulls
slicing open the body of a drowned rat.

A light flickers, a newspaper floats. Doc Watson's
playing sounds like a waterfall, almost gentle.

Tonight the harbour's incandescent.
You arrive in an empty boat.

Robert Adamson

The Elwood Organic Fruit and Vegetable Shop

I will go walking in Elwood with my mind as smooth as a marrow
winking at the unruffled sky throwing its light down for free
letting the gardens exude their well-groomed scents and thinking
    everything good
to the Elwood Organic Fruit and Vegetable Shop:
for the counter is democratically in the centre and everyone smiles
for people go on with the civil business of buying and selling under
    the handwritten notices
for bawling children are solaced with grapes and handled to leave
    no bruises
for the mangoes are soft yellow thighs and the strawberries are
    klaxons of sweetness
for the mignonette purses its frilly lips and snowpeas pout their
    discreet bellies
and the melons hug their quirky shapes under their marvellous rinds
for onions ringing their coppery globes and o the silver shallots and
    the hairy trumpets of leeks
for the cabbages folding crisp linens and the broccolis blooming in
    purple tulles and the dense green skirts of lettuces
for peaches like breasts of angels and passionfruits hard and dark and
    bursting with seed in your palm
for the dull gold flesh of pontiacs and knotty umbers of yams and
    new potatoes like the heels of babies
for the tubs of sweet william and heart-lifting freesias and orchids
    damp and beautiful as clitoral kisses
for poignant basil and maiden-haired fennel and prim blue-lipped
    rosemary and o! irrepressible mint!

how they nestle up the vegetables, promising them the fragrance of
    their ardour!
the marriages which await them! the lips that moisten to meet them!
    glorious speech of the earth!

Alison Croggon

Eurydice and the Tawny Frogmouth

On the low arch
above our gate,
he looks out
through a fringe
of feathers,
hunting,
then places one
foot on black
cast iron and ruffles
his head. His other
foot is clenched
in the night air,
held out
in an atmosphere
of waiting – then
unclenched.
Those nights
flying with you
weighed no more
or less than
this.

Robert Adamson

Everything Is Plundered

Everything is plundered, betrayed, sold,
Death's great black wing scrapes the air,
Misery gnaws to the bone.
Why then do we not despair?

By day, from the surrounding woods,
Cherries blow summer into town;
At night the deep transparent skies
Glitter with new galaxies.

And the miraculous comes so close
To the ruined, dirty houses –
Something not known to anyone at all,
But wild in our breast for centuries.

Anna Akhmatova, translated by Stanley Kunitz with Max Hayward

The Excrement Poem

It is done by us all, as God disposes, from
the least cast of worm to what must have been
in the case of the brontosaur, say, spoor
of considerable heft, something awesome.

We eat, we evacuate, survivors that we are.
I think these things each morning with shovel
and rake, drawing the risen brown buns
toward me, fresh from the horse oven, as it were,

or culling the alfalfa-green ones, expelled
in a state of ooze, through the sawdust bed
to take a serviceable form, as putty does,
so as to lift out entire from the stall.

And wheeling to it, storming up the slope,
I think of the angle of repose the manure
pile assumes, how sparrows come to pick
the redelivered grain, how inky-cap

coprinous mushrooms spring up in a downpour.
I think of what drops from us and must then
be moved to make way for the next and next.
However much we stain the world, spatter

it with our leavings, make stenches, defile
the great formal oceans with what leaks down,
trundling off today's last barrowful,
I honor shit for saying: We go on.

Maxine Kumin

'Th' expense of spirit in a waste of shame'

Th' expense of spirit in a waste of shame
Is lust in action; and till action, lust
Is perjured, murd'rous, bloody, full of blame,
Savage, extreme, rude, cruel, not to trust,
Enjoyed no sooner but despisèd straight,
Past reason hunted; and, no sooner had
Past reason hated as a swallowed bait

On purpose laid to make the taker mad;
Mad in pursuit and in possession so,
Had, having, and in quest to have, extreme;
A bliss in proof and proved, a very woe;
Before, a joy proposed; behind, a dream.
    All this the world well knows; yet none knows well
    To shun the heaven that leads men to this hell.

Sonnet 129, William Shakespeare

Father and Son

Only last week, walking the hushed fields
Of our most lovely Meath, now thinned by November,
I came to where the road from Laracor leads
To the Boyne river – that seems more lake than river,
Stretched in uneasy light and stript of reeds.

And walking longside an old weir
Of my people's, where nothing stirs – only the shadowed
Leaden flight of a heron up the lean air –
I went unmanly with grief, knowing how my father,
Happy though captive in years, walked last with me there.

Yes, happy in Meath with me for a day
He walked, taking stock of herds hid in their own breathing;
And naming colts, gusty as wind, once steered by his hand,
Lightnings winked in the eyes that were half shy in greeting
Old friends – the wild blades, when he gallivanted the land.

For that proud, wayward man now my heart breaks –
Breaks for that man whose mind was a secret eyrie,
Whose kind hand was sole signet of his race,
Who curbed me, scorned my green ways, yet increasingly loved me
Till Death drew its grey blind down his face.

And yet I am pleased that even my reckless ways
Are living shades of his rich calms and passions –
Witnesses for him and for those faint namesakes
With whom now he is one, under yew branches,
Yes, one in a graven silence no bird breaks.

F. R. Higgins

Finding a Box of Family Letters

The dead say little in their letters
they haven't said before.
We find no secrets, and yet
how different every sentence sounds
heard across the years.

My father breaks my heart
simply by being so young and handsome.
He's half my age, with jet-black hair.
Look at him in his navy uniform
grinning beside his dive-bomber.

Come back, Dad! I want to shout.
He says he misses all of us
(though I haven't yet been born).

He writes from places I never knew he saw,
and everyone he mentions now is dead.

There is a large, long photograph
curled like a diploma – a banquet sixty years ago.
My parents sit uncomfortably
among tables of dark-suited strangers.
The mildewed paper reeks of regret.

I wonder what song the band was playing,
just out of frame, as the photographer
arranged your smiles. A waltz? A foxtrot?
Get out there on the floor and dance!
You don't have forever.

What does it cost to send a postcard
to the underworld? I'll buy
a penny stamp from World War II
and mail it downtown at the old post office
just as the courthouse clock strikes twelve.

Surely the ghost of some postal worker
still makes his nightly rounds, his routine
too tedious for him to notice when it ended.
He works so slowly he moves back in time
carrying our dead letters to their lost addresses.

It's silly to get sentimental.
The dead have moved on. So should we.
But isn't it equally simple-minded to miss

the special expertise of the departed
in clarifying our long-term plans?

They never let us forget that the line
between them and us is only temporary.
Get out there and dance! the letters shout
adding, *Love always. Can't wait to get home!*
And soon we will be. *See you there.*

Dana Gioia

First Sight

Lambs that learn to walk in snow
When their bleating clouds the air
Meet a vast unwelcome, know
Nothing but a sunless glare.
Newly stumbling to and fro
All they find, outside the fold,
Is a wretched width of cold.

As they wait beside the ewe,
Her fleeces wetly caked, there lies
Hidden round them, waiting too,
Earth's immeasurable surprise.
They could not grasp it if they knew,
What so soon will wake and grow
Utterly unlike the snow.

Philip Larkin

First Time (I Met My Grandmother)

For Rosina

Sit down in the dirt and brush away the flies
Sit down in the dirt and avoid the many eyes

I never done no wrong to you, so why you look at me?
But if you gotta check me out, well go ahead – feel free!

I feel that magic thing you do, you crawl beneath my skin
To read the story of my Soul, to find out where I been

And now yous' mob you make me wait, so I just sit and sit
English words seem useless, I know Language just a bit

I sit quiet way, not lonely, 'cos this country sings loud Songs
I never been out here before, but I feel like I belong

It's three days now, the mob comes back, big smiles are on their face
'This your Grandmother's Country here, this is your homeland place'

'We got a shock when we seen you, you got your Nana's face
We was real sad when she went missing in that cold Port Pirie place'

I understand the feelings now, tears push behind my eyes
I'll sit on this soil anytime, and brush away the flies

I'll dance with mob on this red Land, munda wiru place
I'll dance away them half caste lies 'cos I got my Nana's face!

Ali Cobby Eckermann

Five Bells

Time that is moved by little fidget wheels
Is not my Time, the flood that does not flow.
Between the double and the single bell
Of a ship's hour, between a round of bells
From the dark warship riding there below,
I have lived many lives, and this one life
Of Joe, long dead, who lives between five bells.

Deep and dissolving verticals of light
Ferry the falls of moonshine down. Five bells
Coldly rung out in a machine's voice. Night and water
Pour to one rip of darkness, the Harbour floats
In the air, the Cross hangs upside-down in water.

Why do I think of you, dead man, why thieve
These profitless lodgings from the flukes of thought
Anchored in Time? You have gone from earth,
Gone even from the meaning of a name;
Yet something's there, yet something forms its lips
And hits and cries against the ports of space,
Beating their sides to make its fury heard.

Are you shouting at me, dead man, squeezing your face
In agonies of speech on speechless panes?
Cry louder, beat the windows, bawl your name!

But I hear nothing, nothing . . . only bells,
Five bells, the bumpkin calculus of Time.
Your echoes die, your voice is dowsed by Life,

There's not a mouth can fly the pygmy strait –
Nothing except the memory of some bones
Long shoved away, and sucked away, in mud;
And unimportant things you might have done,
Or once I thought you did; but you forgot,
And all have now forgotten – looks and words
And slops of beer; your coat with buttons off,
Your gaunt chin and pricked eye, and raging tales
Of Irish kings and English perfidy,
And dirtier perfidy of publicans
Groaning to God from Darlinghurst.

Five bells.

Then I saw the road, I heard the thunder
Tumble, and felt the talons of the rain
The night we came to Moorebank in slab-dark,
So dark you bore no body, had no face,
But a sheer voice that rattled out of air
(As now you'd cry if I could break the glass),
A voice that spoke beside me in the bush,
Loud for a breath or bitten off by wind,
Of Milton, melons, and the Rights of Man,
And blowing flutes, and how Tahitian girls
Are brown and angry-tongued, and Sydney girls
Are white and angry-tongued, or so you'd found.
But all I heard was words that didn't join
So Milton became melons, melons girls,
And fifty mouths, it seemed, were out that night,
And in each tree an Ear was bending down,
Or something that had just run, gone behind the grass,

When blank and bone-white, like a maniac's thought,
The naphtha-flash of lightning slit the sky,
Knifing the dark with deathly photographs.
There's not so many with so poor a purse
Or fierce a need, must fare by night like that,
Five miles in darkness on a country track,
But when you do, that's what you think.

In Melbourne, your appetite had gone,
Your angers too; they had been leeched away
By the soft archery of summer rains
And the sponge-paws of wetness, the slow damp
That stuck the leaves of living, snailed the mind,
And showed your bones, that had been sharp with rage,
The sodden ectasies of rectitude.
I thought of what you'd written in faint ink,
Your journal with the sawn-off lock, that stayed behind
With other things you left, all without use,
All without meaning now, except a sign
That someone had been living who now was dead:
'At Labassa. Room 6 x 8
On top of the tower; because of this, very dark
And cold in winter. Everything has been stowed
Into this room – 500 books all shapes
And colours, dealt across the floor
And over sills and on the laps of chairs;
Guns, photoes of many differant things
And differant curioes that I obtained . . .'

In Sydney, by the spent aquarium-flare
Of penny gaslight on pink wallpaper,

We argued about blowing up the world,
But you were living backward, so each night
You crept a moment closer to the breast,
And they were living, all of them, those frames
And shapes of flesh that had perplexed your youth,
And most your father, the old man gone blind,
With fingers always round a fiddle's neck,
That graveyard mason whose fair monuments
And tablets cut with dreams of piety
Rest on the bosoms of a thousand men
Staked bone by bone, in quiet astonishment
At cargoes they had never thought to bear,
These funeral-cakes of sweet and sculptured stone.

Where have you gone? The tide is over you,
The turn of midnight water's over you,
As Time is over you, and mystery,
And memory, the flood that does not flow.
You have no suburb, like those easier dead
In private berths of dissolution laid –
The tide goes over, the waves ride over you
And let their shadows down like shining hair,
But they are Water; and the sea-pinks bend
Like lilies in your teeth, but they are Weed;
And you are only part of an Idea.
I felt the wet push its black thumb-balls in,
The night you died, I felt your eardrums crack,
And the short agony, the longer dream,
The Nothing that was neither long nor short;
But I was bound, and could not go that way,
But I was blind, and could not feel your hand.

If I could find an answer, could only find
Your meaning, or could say why you were here
Who now are gone, what purpose gave you breath
Or seized it back, might I not hear your voice?

I looked out my window in the dark
At waves with diamond quills and combs of light
That arched their mackerel-backs and smacked the sand
In the moon's drench, that straight enormous glaze,
And ships far off asleep, and Harbour-buoys
Tossing their fireballs wearily each to each,
And tried to hear your voice, but all I heard
Was a boat's whistle, and the scraping squeal
Of seabirds' voices far away, and bells,
Five bells. Five bells coldly ringing out.

Five bells.

Kenneth Slessor

The fly

She sat on a willow-trunk
watching
part of the battle of Crécy,
the shouts,
the gasps,
the groans,
the trampling and the tumbling.

During the fourteenth charge
of the French cavalry
she mated
with a brown-eyed male fly
from Vadincourt.

She rubbed her legs together
as she sat on a disembowelled horse
meditating
on the immortality of flies.

With relief she alighted
on the blue tongue
of the Duke of Clervaux.

When silence settled
and only the whisper of decay
softly circled the bodies

and only
a few arms and legs
still twitched jerkily under the trees,

she began to lay her eggs
on the single eye
of Johann Uhr,
the Royal Armourer.

And thus it was
that she was eaten by a swift

fleeing
from the fires of Estrées.

Miroslav Holub, translated by George Theiner

Folklore

What are the sights of our town?

Well, there is that skeleton they hang
some nights in the bar of the Rest
and everyone laughing in whispers
the barmaid broke down one time, laughing.
The cord goes up through the ceiling
to the undersprings of the big
white bed in the Honeymoon Suite
and when those bones even jiggle
there's cheers (and a donnybrook once)
and when they joggle, there's whooping
and folk stalking out in emotions
and when they dance – hoo, when they dance!
he knows every tune on the honeymoon
flute, does the hollow-hipped fellow.
There are a few, mind, who drink on
straight through it all. Steady drinkers.
Up over the pub there's the sky
full of stars, as I have reflected
outside, while guiding the course of my
thoughts. Some say there's a larger
cord goes on up there, but I doubt it

I mean
but then I'm no dancer.

Besides that, there's meatworks and mines.

Les Murray

Follower

My father worked with a horse-plough,
His shoulders globed like a full sail strung
Between the shafts and the furrow.
The horse strained at his clicking tongue.

An expert. He would set the wing
And fit the bright steel-pointed sock.
The sod rolled over without breaking.
At the headrig, with a single pluck

Of reins, the sweating team turned round
And back into the land. His eye
Narrowed and angled at the ground,
Mapping the furrow exactly.

I stumbled in his hob-nailed wake,
Fell sometimes on the polished sod;
Sometimes he rode me on his back
Dipping and rising to his plod.

I wanted to grow up and plough,
To close one eye, stiffen my arm.

All I ever did was follow
In his broad shadow round the farm.

I was a nuisance, tripping, falling,
Yapping always. But today
It is my father who keeps stumbling
Behind me, and will not go away.

Seamus Heaney

The force that through the green fuse drives the flower

The force that through the green fuse drives the flower
Drives my green age; that blasts the roots of trees
Is my destroyer.
And I am dumb to tell the crooked rose
My youth is bent by the same wintry fever.

The force that drives the water through the rocks
Drives my red blood; that dries the mouthing streams
Turns mine to wax.
And I am dumb to mouth unto my veins
How at the mountain spring the same mouth sucks.

The hand that whirls the water in the pool
Stirs the quicksand; that ropes the blowing wind
Hauls my shroud sail.
And I am dumb to tell the hanging man
How of my clay is made the hangman's lime.

The lips of time leech to the fountain head;
Love drips and gathers, but the fallen blood
Shall calm her sores.
And I am dumb to tell a weather's wind
How time has ticked a heaven round the stars.

And I am dumb to tell the lover's tomb
How at my sheet goes the same crooked worm.

Dylan Thomas

Four A.M.

The hour between night and day.
The hour between toss and turn.
The hour of thirty-year-olds.

The hour swept clean for roosters' crowing.
The hour when the earth takes back its warm embrace.
The hour of cool drafts from extinguished stars.
The hour of do-we-vanish-too-without-a-trace.

Empty hour.
Hollow. Vain.
Rock bottom of all the other hours.

No one feels fine at four a.m.
If ants feel fine at four a.m.,
we're happy for the ants. And let five a.m. come
if we've got to go on living.

Wislawa Szymborska, translated by Stanislaw Baranczak and Clare Cavanagh

'Friends, Romans, countrymen'

Friends, Romans, countrymen, lend me your ears;
I come to bury Caesar, not to praise him.
The evil that men do lives after them;
The good is oft interred with their bones;
So let it be with Caesar. The noble Brutus
Hath told you Caesar was ambitious:
If it were so, it was a grievous fault,
And grievously hath Caesar answer'd it.
Here, under leave of Brutus and the rest –
For Brutus is an honourable man;
So are they all, all honourable men –
Come I to speak in Caesar's funeral.
He was my friend, faithful and just to me:
But Brutus says he was ambitious;
And Brutus is an honourable man.
He hath brought many captives home to Rome
Whose ransoms did the general coffers fill:
Did this in Caesar seem ambitious?
When that the poor have cried, Caesar hath wept:
Ambition should be made of sterner stuff:
Yet Brutus says he was ambitious;
And Brutus is an honourable man.
You all did see that on the Lupercal
I thrice presented him a kingly crown,
Which he did thrice refuse: was this ambition?
Yet Brutus says he was ambitious;
And, sure, he is an honourable man.
I speak not to disprove what Brutus spoke,
But here I am to speak what I do know.

You all did love him once, not without cause:
What cause withholds you then, to mourn for him?
O judgment! thou art fled to brutish beasts,
And men have lost their reason. Bear with me;
My heart is in the coffin there with Caesar,
And I must pause till it come back to me.

Antony in Julius Caesar, *William Shakespeare*

'From far, from eve and morning'

From far, from eve and morning
        And yon twelve-winded sky,
The stuff of life to knit me
        Blew hither: here am I.

Now – for a breath I tarry
        Nor yet disperse apart –
Take my hand quick and tell me,
        What have you in your heart.

Speak now, and I will answer;
        How shall I help you, say;
Ere to the wind's twelve quarters
        I take my endless way.

A. E. Housman

Funeral Blues

Stop all the clocks, cut off the telephone,
Prevent the dog from barking with a juicy bone,
Silence the pianos and with muffled drum
Bring out the coffin, let the mourners come.

Let aeroplanes circle moaning overhead
Scribbling on the sky the message He Is Dead,
Put crêpe bows round the white necks of the public doves,
Let the traffic policemen wear black cotton gloves.

He was my North, my South, my East and West,
My working week and my Sunday rest,
My noon, my midnight, my talk, my song;
I thought that love would last forever: I was wrong.

The stars are not wanted now: put out every one;
Pack up the moon and dismantle the sun;
Pour away the ocean and sweep up the wood;
For nothing now can ever come to any good.

W. H. Auden

The Garden of Love

I went to the Garden of Love,
And saw what I never had seen:
A Chapel was built in the midst,
Where I used to play on the green.

And the gates of this Chapel were shut,
And Thou shalt not, writ over the door;
So I turn'd to the Garden of Love,
That so many sweet flowers bore.

And I saw it was filled with graves,
And tomb-stones where flowers should be:
And Priests in black gowns, were walking their rounds,
And binding with briars, my joys & desires.

William Blake

Gift

A day so happy.
Fog lifted early, I worked in the garden.
Hummingbirds were stopping over honeysuckle flowers.
There was no thing on earth I wanted to possess.
I knew no one worth my envying him.
Whatever evil I had suffered, I forgot.
To think that once I was the same man did not embarrass me.
In my body I felt no pain.
When straightening up, I saw the blue sea and sails.

Czeslaw Milosz, translated by the author

Gifts

'I will bring you love,' said the young lover,
'A glad light to dance in your dark eye.
Pendants I will bring of the white bone,
And gay parrot feathers to deck your hair.'

But she only shook her head.

'I will put a child in your arms,' he said,
'Will be a great headman, great rain-maker.
I will make remembered songs about you
That all the tribes in all the wandering camps
Will sing for ever.'

But she was not impressed.

'I will bring you the still moonlight on the lagoon,
And steal for you the singing of all the birds;
I will bring down the stars of heaven to you,
And put the bright rainbow into your hand.'

'No,' she said, 'bring me tree-grubs.'

Oodgeroo Noonuccal

The God Abandons Antony

When suddenly, at midnight, you hear
an invisible procession going by
with exquisite music, voices,
don't mourn your luck that's failing now,
work gone wrong, your plans
all proving deceptive – don't mourn them uselessly.
As one long prepared, and graced with courage,
say goodbye to her, the Alexandria that is leaving.
Above all, don't fool yourself, don't say
it was a dream, your ears deceived you:

don't degrade yourself with empty hopes like these.
As one long prepared, and graced with courage,
as is right for you who proved worthy of this kind of city,
go firmly to the window
and listen with deep emotion, but not
with the whining, the pleas of a coward;
listen – your final delectation – to the voices,
to the exquisite music of that strange procession,
and say goodbye to her, to the Alexandria you are losing.

C. P. Cavafy, translated by Edmund Keeley and Philip Sherrard

God's Grandeur

The world is charged with the grandeur of God.
　It will flame out, like shining from shook foil;
　It gathers to a greatness, like the ooze of oil
Crushed. Why do men then now not reck his rod?
Generations have trod, have trod, have trod;
　And all is seared with trade; bleared, smeared with toil;
　And wears man's smudge and shares man's smell: the soil
Is bare now, nor can foot feel, being shod.

And for all this, nature is never spent;
　There lives the dearest freshness deep down things;
And though the last lights off the black West went
　Oh, morning, at the brown brink eastward, springs –
Because the Holy Ghost over the bent
　World broods with warm breast and with ah! bright wings.

Gerard Manley Hopkins

God's World

O world, I cannot hold thee close enough!
Thy winds, thy wide grey skies!
Thy mists, that roll and rise!
Thy woods, this autumn day, that ache and sag
And all but cry with colour! That gaunt crag
To crush! To lift the lean of that black bluff!
World, World, I cannot get thee close enough!

Long have I known a glory in it all,
But never knew I this;
Here such a passion is
As stretcheth me apart, – Lord, I do fear
Thou'st made the world too beautiful this year;
My soul is all but out of me, – let fall
No burning leaf; prithee, let no bird call.

Edna St. Vincent Millay

The Great Secret

God was full of Wine last night,
So full of Wine

That He let a great secret slip.

He said:

There is no man on this earth
Who needs a pardon from Me –

For there is really no such thing,
No such thing
As Sin!

The Beloved has gone completely Wild –
He has poured Himself into me!

I am Blissful and Drunk and Overflowing.

Dear world,
Draw life from my Sweet Body.

Dear wayfaring souls,
Come drink your fill of liquid rubies,
For God has made my heart
An Eternal Fountain!

Hafiz, translated by Daniel Ladinsky

The Hag of Beare

Ebb tide has come for me:
My life drifts downwards
Like a retreating sea
With no tidal turn.

I am the Hag of Beare
Fine petticoats I used to wear,
Today, gaunt with poverty,
I hunt for rags to cover me.

Girls nowadays
Dream only of money –
When we were young
We cared more for our men.

Riding over their lands
We remember how, like nobles,
They treated us well;
Courted, but didn't tell.

Today every upstart
Is a master of graft;
Skinflint, yet sure to boast
Of being a lavish host.

But I bless my King who gave –
Balanced briefly on time's wave –
Largesse of speedy chariots
And champion thoroughbreds.

These arms, so bony, thin
And useless to younger men,
Once caressed with skill
The limbs of princes!

Sadly my body seeks to join
Them soon in their dark home –
When God wishes to claim it,
He can have back his deposit.

No more gamy teasing
For me, no wedding feast:
Scant grey hair is best
Shadowed by a veil.

Why should I care?
Many's the bright scarf
Adorned my hair in the days
When I drank with the gentry.

So God be praised
That I mis-spent my days!
Whether the plunge be bold
Or timid, the blood runs cold.

After Spring and Autumn
Come age's frost and body's chill:
Even in bright sunlight
I carry my shawl.

Lovely the mantle of green
Our Lord spreads on the hillside!
Every spring the divine craftsman
Plumps its worn fleece.

But my cloak is mottled with age –
No, I'm beginning to dote –
It's only grey hair straggling
Over my skin like a lichened oak.

And my right eye has been taken away
As down payment on heaven's estate;
Likewise the ray in the left
That I may grope to heaven's gate.

No storm has overthrown
The royal standing stone.
Every year the fertile plain
Bears its crop of yellow grain.

But I, who feasted royally
By candlelight, now pray
In this darkened oratory.
Instead of heady mead

And wine, high on the bench
With kings, I sup whey
In a nest of hags:
God pity me!

Yet may this cup of whey
O! Lord, serve as my ale-feast –
Fathoming its bitterness
I'll learn that you know best.

Alas, I cannot
Again sail youth's sea;
The days of my beauty
Are departed, and desire spent.

I hear the fierce cry of the wave
Whipped by in the wintry wind.
No one will visit me today
Neither nobleman nor slave.

I hear the phantom oars
As ceaselessly they row
And row to the chill ford,
Or fall asleep by its side.

Flood tide
And the ebb dwindling on the sand!
What the flood rides ashore
The ebb snatches from your hand.

Flood tide
And the sucking ebb to follow!
Both have I come to know
Pouring down my body.

Flood tide
Has not yet rifled my pantry
But a chill has been paid
On many who in darkness visited me.

Well might the Son of Mary
Take their place under my roof-tree
For if I lack other hospitality
I never say 'No' to anybody –

Man being of all
Creatures the most miserable –
His flooding pride always seen
But never his tidal turn.

Happy the island in mid-ocean
Washed by the returning flood
But my ageing blood
Slows to final ebb.

I have hardly a dwelling
Today, upon this earth.
Where once was life's flood
All is ebb.

Anonymous, translated by John Montague

Hardcastle Crags

Flintlike, her feet struck
Such a racket of echoes from the steely street,
Tacking in moon-blued crooks from the black
Stone-built town, that she heard the quick air ignite
Its tinder and shake

A firework of echoes from wall
To wall of the dark, dwarfed cottages.
But the echoes died at her back as the walls
Gave way to fields and the incessant seethe of grasses
Riding in the full

Of the moon, manes to the wind,
Tireless, tied, as a moon-bound sea
Moves on its root. Though a mist-wraith wound
Up from the fissured valley and hung shoulder-high
Ahead, it fattened

To no family-featured ghost,
Nor did any word body with a name
The blank mood she walked in. Once past
The dream-peopled village, her eyes entertained no dream,
And the sandman's dust

Lost lustre under her footsoles.
The long wind, paring her person down
To a pinch of flame, blew its burdened whistle
In the whorl of her ear, and like a scooped-out pumpkin crown
Her head cupped the babel.

All the night gave her, in return
For the paltry gift of her bulk and the beat
Of her heart, was the humped indifferent iron
Of its hills, and its pastures bordered by black stone set
On black stone. Barns

Guarded broods and litters
Behind shut doors; the dairy herds
Knelt in the meadow mute as boulders;
Sheep drowsed stoneward in their tussocks of wool, and birds,
Twig-sleeping, wore

Granite ruffs, their shadows
The guise of leaves. The whole landscape
Loomed absolute as the antique world was
Once, in its earliest sway of lymph and sap,
Unaltered by eyes,

Enough to snuff the quick
Of her small heat out, but before the weight
Of stones and hills of stones could break
Her down to mere quartz grit in that stony light
She turned back.

Sylvia Plath

Hatred

See how efficient it still is,
how it keeps itself in shape –
our century's hatred.
How easily it vaults the tallest obstacles.
How rapidly it pounces, tracks us down.

It's not like other feelings.
At once both older and younger.
It gives birth itself to the reasons
that give it life.
When it sleeps, it's never eternal rest.
And sleeplessness won't sap its strength; it feeds it.

One religion or another –
whatever gets it ready, in position.

One fatherland or another –
whatever helps it get a running start.
Justice also works well at the outset
until hate gets its own momentum going.
Hatred. Hatred.
Its face twisted in a grimace
of erotic ecstasy.

Oh these other feelings,
listless weaklings.
Since when does brotherhood
draw crowds?
Has compassion
ever finished first?
Does doubt ever really rouse the rabble?
Only hatred has just what it takes.

Gifted, diligent, hardworking.
Need we mention all the songs it has composed?
All the pages it has added to our history books?
All the human carpets it has spread
over countless city squares and football fields?

Let's face it:
it knows how to make beauty.
The splendid fire-glow in midnight skies.
Magnificent bursting bombs in rosy dawns.
You can't deny the inspiring pathos of ruins
and a certain bawdy humor to be found
in the sturdy column jutting from their midst.

Hatred is a master of contrast –
between explosions and dead quiet,
red blood and white snow.
Above all, it never tires
of its leitmotif – the impeccable executioner
towering over its soiled victim.

It's always ready for new challenges.
If it has to wait awhile, it will.
They say it's blind. Blind?
It has a sniper's keen sight
and gazes unflinchingly at the future
as only it can.

Wislawa Szymborska, translated by Stanislaw Baranczak and Clare Cavanagh

'He is more than a hero'

He is more than a hero
he is a god in my eyes –
the man who is allowed
to sit beside you – he

who listens intimately
to the sweet murmur of
your voice, the enticing

laughter that makes my own
heart beat fast. If I meet
you suddenly, I can't

speak – my tongue is broken;
a thin flame runs under
my skin; seeing nothing,

hearing only my own ears
drumming, I drip with sweat;
trembling shakes my body

and I turn paler than
dry grass. At such times
death isn't far from me

Sappho, translated by Mary Barnard

Her Kind

I have gone out, a possessed witch,
haunting the black air, braver at night;
dreaming evil, I have done my hitch
over the plain houses, light by light:
lonely thing, twelve-fingered, out of mind.
A woman like that is not a woman, quite.
I have been her kind.

I have found the warm caves in the woods,
filled them with skillets, carvings, shelves,
closets, silks, innumerable goods;
fixed the suppers for the worms and the elves:
whining, rearranging the disaligned.
A woman like that is misunderstood.
I have been her kind.

I have ridden in your cart, driver,
waved my nude arms at villages going by,
learning the last bright routes, survivor
where your flames still bite my thigh
and my ribs crack where your wheels wind.
A woman like that is not ashamed to die.
I have been her kind.

Anne Sexton

Heredity

I am the family face;
Flesh perishes, I live on,
Projecting trait and trace
Through time to times anon,
And leaping from place to place
Over oblivion.

The years-heired feature that can
In curve and voice and eye
Despise the human span
Of durance – that is I;
The eternal thing in man,
That heeds no call to die.

Thomas Hardy

Home

No one leaves home
unless home is the mouth of a shark.

You only run for the border
when you see the whole city
running as well.

Your neighbours running faster than you,
the boy you went to school with
who kissed you dizzy behind
the old tin factory
is holding a gun bigger than his body,
you only leave home
when home won't let you stay.

No one would leave home unless home
chased you, fire under feet,
hot blood in your belly.

It's not something you ever thought about
doing, and so when you did –
you carried the anthem under your breath,
waiting until the airport toilet
to tear up the passport and swallow –
each mouthful making it clear that
you would not be going back.

You must understand,
no one puts their children in a boat
unless the water is safer than the land.

Who would choose days and nights
in the stomach of a truck,
unless the miles travelled
meant something more than the journey.

No one would choose to crawl under fences,
be beaten until your shadow leaves you
raped, then drowned, forced to the bottom of
a boat because you are darker, be sold,
starved, shot at the border like a sick animal,
be pitied, lose your name, lose your family,
make a refugee camp a home for a year or two or ten
stripped and searched, find prison everywhere
and if you survive
and you are greeted on the other side
go home blacks, refugees
dirty immigrants, asylum seekers
sucking our country dry of milk,
dark, with their hands out
smell strange, savage –
look what they've done to their own countries,
what will they do to ours?

The dirty looks in the street
feel softer than a limb torn off,
the indignity of everyday life more tender
than fourteen men who look like your father,
between your legs. Insults easier to swallow
than rubble, than your child's body

in pieces – for now, forget about pride
your survival is more important.

I want to go home,
but home is the mouth of a shark
home is the barrel of the gun
and no one would leave home
unless home chased you to the shore
unless home tells you to
leave what you could not behind,
even if it's human.

No one leaves home until home
is a damp voice in your ear saying
leave, run now, I don't know what
I've become.

Warsan Shire

'Hope' is the thing with feathers

'Hope' is the thing with feathers –
That perches in the soul –
And sings the tune without the words –
And never stops – at all –

And sweetest – in the Gale – is heard –
And sore must be the storm –
That could abash the little Bird
That kept so many warm –

I've heard it in the chillest land –
And on the strangest Sea –
Yet – never – in Extremity,
It asked a crumb – of me.

Emily Dickinson

House

Ask the god to open the house of your chest
wide enough that your enemy may enter

ask aitu: lie down with me
my heart is open as a window

ask aitu: walk with me
my heart is younger than the sun

pearl shell
whale tooth
human hair
pounamu

ask aitu: shuck off your clothes
at this edge of ocean and like a diver cut –

here is the place where I will keep you
here is the place where I will keep you.

Tusiata Avia

The Hungry Grass

Note: It is a common belief in Ireland that anyone
who steps on a famine grave will have the strength
sucked from their body by the hungry bones underneath

Crossing the shallow holdings high above sea
Where few birds nest, the luckless foot may pass
From the bright safety of experience
Into the terror of the hungry grass.

Here in a year when poison from the air
First withered in despair the growth of spring
Some skull-faced wretch whom nettle could not save
Crept on four bones to his last scattering,

Crept, and the shrivelled heart which drove his thought
Towards platters brought in hospitality
Burst as the wizened eyes measured the miles
Like dizzy walls forbidding him the city.

Little the earth reclaimed from that poor body
And yet remembering him the place has grown
Bewitched and the thin grass he nourishes
Racks with his famine, sucks marrow from the bone.

Donagh MacDonagh

I Ask My Mother to Sing

She begins, and my grandmother joins her.
Mother and daughter sing like young girls.
If my father were alive, he would play
his accordion and sway like a boat.

I've never been in Peking, or the Summer Palace,
nor stood on the great Stone Boat to watch
the rain begin on Kuen Ming Lake, the picnickers
running away in the grass.

But I love to hear it sung;
how the waterlilies fill with rain until
they overturn, spilling water into water,
then rock back, and fill with more.

Both women have begun to cry.
But neither stops her song.

Li-Young Lee

I Belong There

I belong there. I have many memories. I was born as everyone is born.
I have a mother, a house with many windows, brothers, friends, and a prison cell
with a chilly window! I have a wave snatched by seagulls, a panorama of my own.
I have a saturated meadow. In the deep horizon of my word, I have a moon,

a bird's sustenance, and an immortal olive tree.
I have lived on the land long before swords turned man into prey.
I belong there. When heaven mourns for her mother, I return heaven
to her mother.
And I cry so that a returning cloud might carry my tears.
To break the rules, I have learned all the words needed for a trial by blood.
I have learned and dismantled all the words in order to draw from
them a single word: *Home.*

Mahmoud Darwish, translated by Munir Akash and Carolyn Forché

i carry your heart with me

i carry your heart with me(i carry it in
my heart)i am never without it(anywhere
i go you go,my dear; and whatever is done
by only me is your doing,my darling)
                                                            i fear
no fate(for you are my fate, my sweet)i want
no world(for beautiful you are my world, my true)
and it's you are whatever a moon has always meant
and whatever a sun will always sing is you

here is the deepest secret nobody knows
(here is the root of the root and the bud of the bud
and the sky of the sky of a tree called life; which grows
higher than the soul can hope or mind can hide)
and this is the wonder that's keeping the stars apart

i carry your heart(i carry it in my heart)

E. E. Cummings

'I celebrate myself'

1

I celebrate myself, and sing myself,
And what I assume you shall assume,
For every atom belonging to me as good belongs to you.

I loafe and invite my soul,
I lean and loafe at my ease observing a spear of summer grass.

My tongue, every atom of my blood, form'd from this soil, this air,
Born here of parents born here from parents the same, and their
    parents the same,
I, now thirty-seven years old in perfect health begin,
Hoping to cease not till death.

Creeds and schools in abeyance,
Retiring back a while sufficed at what they are, but never forgotten,
I harbor for good or bad, I permit to speak at every hazard,
Nature without check with original energy.

2

Houses and rooms are full of perfumes, the shelves are crowded
    with perfumes,
I breathe the fragrance myself and know it and like it,
The distillation would intoxicate me also, but I shall not let it.

The atmosphere is not a perfume, it has no taste of the distillation,
    it is odorless,

It is for my mouth forever, I am in love with it,
I will go to the bank by the wood and become undisguised and naked,
I am mad for it to be in contact with me.

The smoke of my own breath,
Echoes, ripples, buzz'd whispers, love-root, silk-thread, crotch and vine
My respiration and inspiration, the beating of my heart, the passing of blood and air through my lungs,
The sniff of green leaves and dry leaves, and of the shore and dark color'd sea-rocks, and of hay in the barn,
The sound of the belch'd words of my voice loos'd to the eddies of the wind,
A few light kisses, a few embraces, a reaching around of arms,
The play of shine and shade on the trees as the supple boughs wag,
The delight alone or in the rush of the streets, or along the fields and hill-sides.
The feeling of health, the full-noon trill, the song of me rising from bed and meeting the sun.

Have you reckon'd a thousand acres much? have you reckon'd the earth much?
Have you practis'd so long to learn to read?
Have you felt so proud to get at the meaning of poems?

Stop this day and night with me and you shall possess the origin of all poems,
You shall possess the good of the earth and sun, (there are millions of suns left,)
You shall no longer take things at second or third hand, nor look
through the eyes of the dead, nor feed on the spectres in books,

You shall not look through my eyes either, nor take things from me,
You shall listen to all sides and filter them from your self.

3

I have heard what the talkers were talking, the talk of the beginning and the end
But I do not talk of the beginning or the end.

There was never any more inception than there is now,
Nor any more youth or age than there is now,
And will never be any more perfection than there is now,
Nor any more heaven or hell than there is now.

Urge and urge and urge,
Always the procreant urge of the world.

Out of the dimness opposite equals advance, always substance and increase, always sex,
Always a knit of identity, always distinction, always a breed of life.

To elaborate is no avail, learn'd and unlearn'd feel that it is so.

Sure as the most certain sure, plumb in the uprights, well entretied, braced in the beams,
Stout as a horse, affectionate, haughty, electrical,
I and this mystery here we stand.

Clear and sweet is my soul, and clear and sweet is all that is not my soul.

Lack one lacks both, and the unseen is proved by the seen,
Till that becomes unseen and receives proof in its turn.

Showing the best and dividing it from the worst age vexes age,
Knowing the perfect fitness and equanimity of things, while they
discuss I am silent, and go bathe and admire myself.

Welcome is every organ and attribute of me, and of any man hearty
and clean,
Not an inch nor a particle of an inch is vile, and none shall be less
familiar than the rest.

I am satisfied – I see, dance, laugh, sing;
As the hugging and loving bed-fellow sleeps at my side through
the night, and withdraws at the peep of the day with stealthy tread.
Leaving me baskets cover'd with white towels swelling the house
with their plenty,
Shall I postpone my acceptation and realization and scream at my eyes,
That they turn from gazing after and down the road,
And forthwith cipher and show me to a cent,
Exactly the value of one and exactly the value of two, and which
is ahead?

4

Trippers and askers surround me,
People I meet, the effect upon me of my early life or the ward and
city I live in, or the nation,
The latest dates, discoveries, inventions, societies, authors old and new,
My dinner, dress, associates, looks, compliments, dues,

The real or fancied indifference of some man or woman I love,
The sickness of one of my folks or of myself, or ill-doing or loss
or lack of money, or depressions or exaltations,
Battles, the horrors of fratricidal war, the fever of doubtful news, the
fitful events;
These come to me days and nights and go from me again,
But they are not the Me myself.

Apart from the pulling and hauling stands what I am,
Stands amused, complacent, compassionating, idle, unitary,
Looks down, is erect, or bends an arm on an impalpable certain rest,
Looking with side-curved head curious what will come next,
Both in and out of the game and watching and wondering at it.

Backward I see in my own days where I sweated through fog with
linguists and contenders,
I have no mockings or arguments, I witness and wait.

5

I believe in you my soul, the other I am must not abase itself to you,
And you must not be abased to the other.

Loafe with me on the grass, loose the stop from your throat,
Not words, not music or rhyme I want, not custom or lecture, not
even the best,
Only the lull I like, the hum of your valvèd voice.

I mind how once we lay such a transparent summer morning,
How you settled your head athwart my hips and gently turn'd over
upon me,

And parted the shirt from my bosom-bone, and plunged your tongue
to my bare-stript heart,
And reach'd till you felt my beard, and reach'd till you held my feet.

Swiftly arose and spread around me the peace and knowledge that
pass all the argument of the earth,
And I know that the hand of God is the promise of my own,
And I know that the spirit of God is the brother of my own,
And that all the men ever born are also my brothers, and the women
my sisters and lovers,
And that a kelson of the creation is love,
And limitless are leaves stiff or drooping in the fields,
And brown ants in the little wells beneath them,
And mossy scabs of the wormfence, heap'd stones, elder, mullein
and poke-weed.

6

A child said *What is the grass?* fetching it to me with full hands;
How could I answer the child? I do not know what it is any more
than he.

I guess it must be the flag of my disposition, out of hopeful green
stuff woven.

Or I guess it is the handkerchief of the Lord,
A scented gift and remembrancer designedly dropt,
Bearing the owner's name someway in the corners, that we may see
and remark, and say *Whose?*

Or I guess the grass is itself a child, the produced babe of
the vegetation.

Or I guess it is a uniform hieroglyphic,
And it means, Sprouting alike in broad zones and narrow zones,
Growing among black folks as among white,
Kanuck, Tuckahoe, Congressman, Cuff, I give them the same,
I receive them the same.

And now it seems to me the beautiful uncut hair of graves.

Tenderly will I use you curling grass,
It may be you transpire from the breasts of young men,
It may be if I had known them I would have loved them.
It may be you are from old people, or from offspring taken soon out
of their mothers' laps,
And here you are the mothers' laps.

This grass is very dark to be from the white heads of old mothers.
Darker than the colorless beards of old men,
Dark to come from under the faint red roofs of mouths.

O I perceive after all so many uttering tongues,
And I perceive they do not come from the roofs of mouths for nothing.

I wish I could translate the hints about the dead young men and women,
And the hints about old men and mothers, and the offspring taken
soon out of their laps.

What do you think has become of the young and old men?
And what do you think has become of the women and children?

They are alive and well somewhere,
The smallest sprout shows there is really no death,
And if ever there was it led forward life, and does not wait at the end
    to arrest it,
And ceas'd the moment life appear'd.

All goes onward and outward, nothing collapses,
And to die is different from what any one supposed, and luckier.

Song of Myself*: 1–6, Walt Whitman*

'I dream'd there was an Emperor Antony'

I dream'd there was an Emperor Antony:
O, such another sleep, that I might see
But such another man!
His face was as the heavens; and therein stuck
A sun and moon, which kept their course, and lighted
The little O, the earth.
His legs bestrid the ocean: his rear'd arm
Crested the world: his voice was propertied
As all the tuned spheres, and that to friends;
But when he meant to quail and shake the orb,
He was as rattling thunder. For his bounty,
There was no winter in't; an autumn 'twas
That grew the more by reaping: his delights
Were dolphin-like; they show'd his back above
The element they lived in: in his livery
Walk'd crowns and coronets; realms and islands were
As plates dropp'd from his pocket.

Cleopatra in **Antony and Cleopatra***, William Shakespeare*

'I go, but first will tell thee why I came'

I go, but first will tell thee why I came.
Thy frown I dread not, for thou canst not harm me.
Hear then: this man whom thou hast sought to arrest
With threats and warrants this long while, the wretch
Who murdered Laius – that man is here.
He passes for an alien in the land
But soon shall prove a Theban, native born.
And yet his fortune brings him little joy;
For blind of seeing, clad in beggar's weeds,
For purple robes, and leaning on his staff,
To a strange land he soon shall grope his way.
And of the children, inmates of his home,
He shall be proved the brother and the sire,
Of her who bare him son and husband both,
Co-partner, and assassin of his sire.
Go in and ponder this, and if thou find
That I have missed the mark, henceforth declare
I have no wit nor skill in prophecy.

Tiresias to Oedipus in Oedipus Rex, *Sophocles, translated by F. Storr*

I Never Loved You More

I never loved you more, ma soeur
Than as I walked away from you that evening.
The forest swallowed me, the blue forest, ma soeur
The blue forest and above it pale stars in the west.

I did not laugh, not one little bit, ma soeur
As I playfully walked towards a dark fate –
While the faces behind me
Slowly paled in the evening of the blue forest.

Everything was grand that one night, ma soeur
Never thereafter and never before –
I admit it: I was left with nothing but the big birds
And their hungry cries in the dark evening sky.

Bertolt Brecht, translated by Johannes Beilharz

'I think I could turn and live with animals'

I think I could turn and live with animals, they are so placid
    and self-contain'd,
I stand and look at them long and long.
They do not sweat and whine about their condition,
They do not lie awake in the dark and weep for their sins,
They do not make me sick discussing their duty to God,
Not one is dissatisfied, not one is demented with the mania
    of owning things,
Not one kneels to another, nor to his kind that lived thousands
    of years ago,
Not one is respectable or unhappy over the whole earth.

Song of Myself*: 32, Walt Whitman*

'I think of thee!'

I think of thee! – my thoughts do twine and bud
About thee, as wild vines, about a tree,
Put out broad leaves, and soon there's nought to see
Except the straggling green which hides the wood.
Yet, O my palm-tree, be it understood
I will not have my thoughts instead of thee
Who art dearer, better! Rather, instantly
Renew thy presence; as a strong tree should,
Rustle thy boughs and set thy trunk all bare,
And let these bands of greenery which insphere thee
Drop heavily down, – burst, shattered, everywhere!
Because, in this deep joy to see and hear thee
And breathe within thy shadow a new air,
I do not think of thee – I am too near thee.

Sonnet 29, Elizabeth Barrett Browning

I Want to Go with the One I Love

I want to go with the one I love.
I do not want to calculate the cost.
I do not want to think about whether it's good.
I do not want to know whether he loves me.
I want to go with the one I love.

Bertolt Brecht, translated by Johannes Beilharz

If

If you can keep your head when all about you
  Are losing theirs and blaming it on you,
If you can trust yourself when all men doubt you,
  But make allowance for their doubting too;
If you can wait and not be tired by waiting,
  Or being lied about, don't deal in lies,
Or being hated, don't give way to hating,
  And yet don't look too good, nor talk too wise:

If you can dream – and not make dreams your master;
  If you can think – and not make thoughts your aim;
If you can meet with Triumph and Disaster
  And treat those two impostors just the same;
If you can bear to hear the truth you've spoken
  Twisted by knaves to make a trap for fools,
Or watch the things you gave your life to, broken,
  And stoop and build 'em up with worn-out tools:

If you can make one heap of all your winnings
  And risk it on one turn of pitch-and-toss,
And lose, and start again at your beginnings
  And never breathe a word about your loss;
If you can force your heart and nerve and sinew
  To serve your turn long after they are gone,
And so hold on when there is nothing in you
  Except the Will which says to them: 'Hold on!'

If you can talk with crowds and keep your virtue,
  Or walk with Kings – nor lose the common touch,

If neither foes nor loving friends can hurt you,
    If all men count with you, but none too much;
If you can fill the unforgiving minute
    With sixty seconds' worth of distance run,
Yours is the Earth and everything that's in it,
    And – which is more – you'll be a Man, my son!

Rudyard Kipling

'If thou must love me'

If thou must love me, let it be for naught
Except for love's sake only. Do not say,
'I love her for her smile – her look – her way
Of speaking gently, – for a trick of thought
That falls in well with mine, and certes brought
A sense of pleasant ease on such a day' –
For these things in themselves, Beloved, may
Be changed, or change for thee, – and love, so wrought,
May be unwrought so. Neither love me for
Thine own dear pity's wiping my cheeks dry, –
A creature might forget to weep, who bore
Thy comfort long, and lose thy love thereby!
But love me for love's sake, that evermore
Thou mayst love on, through love's eternity.

Sonnet 14, Elizabeth Barrett Browning

'If we are mark'd to die, we are enow'

If we are mark'd to die, we are enow
To do our country loss; and if to live,
The fewer men, the greater share of honour.
God's will! I pray thee, wish not one man more.
By Jove, I am not covetous for gold,
Nor care I who doth feed upon my cost;
It yearns me not if men my garments wear;
Such outward things dwell not in my desires:
But if it be a sin to covet honour,
I am the most offending soul alive.
No, faith, my coz, wish not a man from England:
God's peace! I would not lose so great an honour
As one man more, methinks, would share from me
For the best hope I have. O, do not wish one more!
Rather proclaim it, Westmoreland, through my host,
That he which hath no stomach to this fight,
Let him depart; his passport shall be made
And crowns for convoy put into his purse:
We would not die in that man's company
That fears his fellowship to die with us.
This day is called the feast of Crispian:
He that outlives this day, and comes safe home,
Will stand a tip-toe when the day is named,
And rouse him at the name of Crispian.
He that shall live this day, and see old age,
Will yearly on the vigil feast his neighbours,
And say 'Tomorrow is Saint Crispian':
Then will he strip his sleeve and show his scars.

And say 'These wounds I had on Crispin's day.'
Old men forget: yet all shall be forgot,
But he'll remember with advantages
What feats he did that day: then shall our names,
Familiar in his mouth as household words
Harry the king, Bedford and Exeter,
Warwick and Talbot, Salisbury and Gloucester,
Be in their flowing cups freshly remember'd.
This story shall the good man teach his son;
And Crispin Crispian shall ne'er go by,
From this day to the ending of the world,
But we in it shall be remember'd;
We few, we happy few, we band of brothers;
For he today that sheds his blood with me
Shall be my brother; be he ne'er so vile,
This day shall gentle his condition:
And gentlemen in England now a-bed
Shall think themselves accursed they were not here,
And hold their manhoods cheap whiles any speaks
That fought with us upon Saint Crispin's day.

King Henry in Henry V, *William Shakespeare*

I'm Explaining a Few Things

You are going to ask: and where are the lilacs?
and the poppy-petalled metaphysics?
and the rain repeatedly spattering
its words and drilling them full
of apertures and birds?

I'll tell you all the news.

I lived in a suburb,
a suburb of Madrid, with bells,
and clocks, and trees.

From there you could look out
over Castille's dry face:
a leather ocean.
                    My house was called
the house of flowers, because in every cranny
geraniums burst: it was
a good-looking house
with its dogs and children.
                              Remember, Raúl?
Eh, Rafael?
                Federico, do you remember
from under the ground
where the light of June drowned flowers in your mouth?
                                          Brother, my brother!

Everything
loud with big voices, the salt of merchandises,
pile-ups of palpitating bread,
the stalls of my suburb of Argüelles with its statue
like a drained inkwell in a swirl of hake:
oil flowed into spoons,
a deep baying
of feet and hands swelled in the streets,
metres, litres, the sharp
measure of life,

stacked-up fish,
the texture of roofs with a cold sun in which
the weather vane falters,
the fine, frenzied ivory of potatoes,
wave on wave of tomatoes rolling down to the sea.

And one morning all that was burning,
one morning the bonfires
leapt out of the earth
devouring human beings –
and from then on fire,
gunpowder from then on,
and from then on blood.
Bandits with planes and Moors,
Bandits with finger-rings and duchesses,
Bandits with black friars spattering blessings
came through the sky to kill children
and the blood of children ran through the streets
without fuss, like children's blood.

Jackals that the jackals would despise,
stones that the dry thistle would bite on and spit out,
vipers that the vipers would abominate!

Face to face with you I have seen the blood
of Spain tower like a tide
to drown you in one wave
of pride and knives!

Treacherous
generals:

see my dead house,
look at broken Spain:

from every house burning metal flows
instead of flowers,
from every socket of Spain
Spain emerges
and from every dead child a rifle with eyes,
and from every crime bullets are born
which will one day find
the bull's eye of your hearts.

And you will ask: why doesn't his poetry
speak of dreams and leaves
and the great volcanoes of his native land?

Come and see the blood in the streets.
Come and see
the blood in the streets.
Come and see the blood
in the streets!

Pablo Neruda, translated by Nathaniel Tarn

I'm nobody! Who are you?

I'm nobody! Who are you?
Are you nobody, too?
Then there's a pair of us – don't tell!
They'd banish us, you know.

How dreary to be somebody!
How public, like a frog
To tell your name the livelong day
To an admiring bog!

Emily Dickinson

I've Been Moved

I've been moved by the wind upon the waters
And the shadows as the leaves are blown
When that old wind moans
On a weary winter Sunday
Like a friend that keeps on knocking on my home

I've been moved by the crying of the newborn
The honey sweetness of the air in spring
I've watched the moonlight flood
Across them sleepy hills and valleys
Heard the sadness in her requiem

I've been moved watching nature slowly turning
Through the seasons and the patterns that she brings
And as the morning star proceeds
The breaking of a new day
You'll find the black crow is already on the wing

I've been moved watching something that's been suffering
Be it humankind or any living thing
From the fury of the storm
That old parched ground is reborn
And the deserts blooms'd satisfy a king

I've been moved by the tireless sea a-churning
And them scarlets of an inland dusk
Or when a close friend has died
I turned away and cried
As they laid 'em down and shovelled in the dust

Kev Carmody

Immigrant Blues

People have been trying to kill me since I was born,
a man tells his son, trying to explain
the wisdom of learning a second tongue.

It's an old story from the previous century
about my father and me.

The same old story from yesterday morning
about me and my son.

It's called 'Survival Strategies
and the Melancholy of Racial Assimilation.'

It's called 'Psychological Paradigms of Displaced Persons,'

called 'The Child Who'd Rather Play than Study.'

Practice until you feel
the language inside you, says the man.

But what does he know about inside and outside,
my father who was spared nothing
in spite of the languages he used?

And me, confused about the flesh and the soul,
who asked once into a telephone,
Am I inside you?

You're always inside me, a woman answered,
at peace with the body's finitude,
at peace with the soul's disregard
of space and time.

Am I inside you? I asked once
lying between her legs, confused
about the body and the heart.

If you don't believe you're inside me, you're not,
she answered, at peace with the body's greed,
at peace with the heart's bewilderment.

It's an ancient story from yesterday evening

called 'Patterns of Love in Peoples of Diaspora,'

called 'Loss of the Homeplace
and the Defilement of the Beloved,'

called 'I Want to Sing but I Don't Know Any Songs.'

Li-Young Lee

In Dream

Black and enduring separation
I share equally with you.
Why weep? Give me your hand,
Promise me you will come again.
You and I are like high
Mountains and we can't move closer.
Just send me word
At midnight sometime through the stars.

Anna Akhmatova, translated by D. M. Thomas

In Paris with You

Don't talk to me of love. I've had an earful
And I get tearful when I've downed a drink or two.
I'm one of your talking wounded.
I'm a hostage. I'm maroonded.
But I'm in Paris with you.

Yes I'm angry at the way I've been bamboozled
And resentful at the mess that I've been through.
I admit I'm on the rebound
And I don't care where are *we* bound.
I'm in Paris with you.

 Do you mind if we do *not* go to the Louvre
 If we say sod off to sodding Notre Dame,
 If we skip the Champs Elysées
 And remain here in this sleazy

Old hotel room
Doing this and that
To what and whom
Learning who you are,
Learning what I am.

Don't talk to me of love. Let's talk of Paris,
The little bit of Paris in our view.
There's that crack across the ceiling
And the hotel walls are peeling
And I'm in Paris with you.

Don't talk to me of love. Let's talk of Paris.
I'm in Paris with the slightest thing you do.
I'm in Paris with your eyes, your mouth,
I'm in Paris with . . . all points south.
Am I embarrassing you?
I'm in Paris with you.

James Fenton

In Praise of Darkness

Old age (the name that others give it)
can be the time of our greatest bliss.
The animal has died or almost died.
The man and his spirit remain.
I live among vague, luminous shapes
that are not darkness yet.
Buenos Aires,
whose edges disintegrated

into the endless plain,
has gone back to being the Recoleta, the Retiro,
the nondescript streets of the Once,
and the rickety old houses
we still call the South.
In my life there were always too many things.
Democritus of Abdera plucked out his eyes in order to think;
Time has been my Democritus.
This penumbra is slow and does not pain me;
it flows down a gentle slope,
resembling eternity.
My friends have no faces,
women are what they were so many years ago,
these corners could be other corners,
there are no letters on the pages of books.
All this should frighten me,
but it is a sweetness, a return.
Of the generations of texts on earth
I will have read only a few –
the ones that I keep reading in my memory,
reading and transforming.
From South, East, West, and North
the paths converge that have led me
to my secret center.
Those paths were echoes and footsteps,
women, men, death-throes, resurrections,
days and nights,
dreams and half-wakeful dreams,
every inmost moment of yesterday
and all the yesterdays of the world,
the Dane's staunch sword and the Persian's moon,

the acts of the dead,
shared love, and words,
Emerson and snow, so many things.
Now I can forget them. I reach my center
my algebra and my key,
my mirror.
Soon I will know who I am.

Jorge Luis Borges, translated by Hoyt Rogers

In Praise of Doubt

Praised be doubt! I advise you to greet
Cheerfully and with respect the man
Who tests your word like a bad penny.
I'd like you to be wise and not to give
Your word with too much assurance.
Read history and see
The headlong flight of invincible armies.
Wherever you look
Impregnable strongholds collapse and
Even if the Armada was innumerable as it left port
The returning ships
Could be numbered.

Thus one day a man stood on the unattainable summit
And a ship reached the end of
The endless sea.

O Beautiful the shaking of heads
Over the indisputable truth!

O brave the doctor's cure
Of the incurable patient!

But the most beautiful of all doubts
Is when the downtrodden and despondent
Raise their heads and
Stop believing in the strength
Of their oppressors.

. . .

There are the thoughtless who never doubt
Their digestion is splendid, their judgment is infallible.
They don't believe in the facts, they believe only in themselves.
When it comes to the point
The facts must go by the board
Their patience with themselves
Is boundless. To arguments
They listen with the ear of a police spy.

The thoughtless who never doubt
Meet the thoughtful who never act.
They doubt, not in order to come to a decision but
To avoid a decision. Their heads
They use only for shaking. With anxious faces
They warn the crews of sinking ships that water is dangerous.
Beneath the murderer's axe
They ask themselves if he isn't human too.
Murmuring something
About the situation not yet being clarified, they go to bed.
Their only action is to vacillate.
Their favorite phrase is: not yet ripe for discussion.

Therefore, if you praise doubt
Do not praise
The doubt which is a form of despair.
What use is the ability to doubt to a man
Who can't make up his mind?
He who is content with too few reasons
May act wrongly
But he who needs too many
Remains inactive under danger.

Bertolt Brecht, translated by Martin Esslin

In the Middle of This Century

In the middle of this century we turned to each other
With half faces and full eyes
like an ancient Egyptian picture
And for a short while.

I stroked your hair
In the opposite direction to your journey,
We called to each other,
Like calling out the names of towns
Where nobody stops
Along the route.

Lovely is the world rising early to evil,
Lovely is the world falling asleep to sin and pity,
In the mingling of ourselves, you and I,
Lovely is the world.

The earth drinks men and their loves
Like wine,
To forget.
It can't.
And like the contours of the Judean hills,
We shall never find peace.

In the middle of this century we turned to each other,
I saw your body, throwing shade, waiting for me,
The leather straps for a long journey
Already tightening across my chest.
I spoke in praise of your mortal hips,
You spoke in praise of my passing face,
I stroked your hair in the direction of your journey,
I touched your flesh, prophet of your end,
I touched your hand which has never slept,
I touched your mouth which may yet sing.

Dust from the desert covered the table
At which we did not eat
But with my finger I wrote on it
The letters of your name.

Yehuda Amichai, translated by Assia Gutmann

In the Park

She sits in the park. Her clothes are out of date.
Two children whine and bicker, tug her skirt.
A third draws aimless patterns in the dirt.
Someone she loved once passes by – too late

to feign indifference to that casual nod.
'How nice,' *et cetera*. 'Time holds great surprises.'
From his neat head unquestionably rises
a small balloon . . . 'but for the grace of God . . .'

They stand awhile in flickering light, rehearsing
the children's names and birthdays. 'It's so sweet
to hear their chatter, watch them grow and thrive,'
she says to his departing smile. Then, nursing
the youngest child, sits staring at her feet.
To the wind she says, 'They have eaten me alive.'

Gwen Harwood

'In this world'

In this world
love has no color –
yet how deeply
my body
is stained by yours.

Izumi Shikibu, translated by Jane Hirshfield with Mariko Aratani

Incantation

Human reason is beautiful and invincible.
No bars, no barbed wire, no pulping of books,
No sentence of banishment can prevail against it.
It establishes the universal ideas in language,
And guides our hand so we write Truth and Justice

With capital letters, lie and oppression with small.
It puts what should be above things as they are,
Is an enemy of despair and a friend of hope.
It does not know Jew from Greek or slave from master,
Giving us the estate of the world to manage.
It saves austere and transparent phrases
From the filthy discord of tortured words.
It says that everything is new under the sun,
Opens the congealed fist of the past.
Beautiful and very young are Philo-Sophia
And poetry, her ally in the service of the good.
As late as yesterday Nature celebrated their birth,
The news was brought to the mountains by a unicorn and an echo.
Their friendship will be glorious, their time has no limit.
Their enemies have delivered themselves to destruction.

Czeslaw Milosz, translated by the author and Robert Pinsky

Inevitable

when I dropped my 12-year-old off at her first
homecoming dance, I tried not to look

her newly-developed breasts, all surprise and alert
in their uncertainty. I tried not to imagine her

mashed between a young man's curiousness
and the gym's sweaty wall. I tried not picture

her grinding off beat/on time to the rhythm
of a dark manchild; the one who whispered

'you are the most beautiful girl in brooklyn'
his swag so sincere, she'd easily mistaken him for a god.

Mahogany L. Browne

An Irish Airman Foresees His Death

I know that I shall meet my fate
Somewhere among the clouds above;
Those that I fight I do not hate,
Those that I guard I do not love;
My country is Kiltartan Cross,
My countrymen Kiltartan's poor,
No likely end could bring them loss
Or leave them happier than before.
Nor law, nor duty bade me fight,
Nor public men, nor cheering crowds,
A lonely impulse of delight
Drove to this tumult in the clouds;
I balanced all, brought all to mind,
The years to come seemed waste of breath,
A waste of breath the years behind
In balance with this life, this death.

W. B. Yeats

Ithaka

As you set out for Ithaka
hope your road is a long one,
full of adventure, full of discovery.

Laistrygonians and Cyclops,
angry Poseidon – don't be afraid of them:
you'll never find things like that on your way
as long as you keep your thoughts raised high,
as long as a rare excitement
stirs your spirit and your body.
Laistrygonians and Cyclops,
wild Poseidon – you won't encounter them
unless you bring them along inside your soul,
unless your soul sets them up in front of you.

Hope your road is a long one.
May there be many a summer morning when,
with what pleasure, what joy,
you enter harbors you're seeing for the first time;
may you stop at Phoenician trading stations
to buy fine things,
mother of pearl and coral, amber and ebony,
sensual perfume of every kind –
as many sensual perfumes as you can;
and may you visit many Egyptian cities
to learn and go on learning from their scholars.

Keep Ithaka always in your mind.
Arriving there is what you're destined for.
But don't hurry the journey at all.
Better if it lasts for years,
so you're old by the time you reach the island,
wealthy with all you have gained on the way,
not expecting Ithaka to make you rich.

Ithaka gave you the marvelous journey.
Without her you would not have set out.
She has nothing left to give you now.

And if you find her poor, Ithaka won't have fooled you.
Wise as you will have become, so full of experience,
you'll have understood by then what these Ithakas mean.

C. P. Cavafy, translated by Edmund Keeley

Japanese Maple

Your death, near now, is of an easy sort.
So slow a fading out brings no real pain.
Breath growing short
Is just uncomfortable. You feel the drain
Of energy, but thought and sight remain:

Enhanced, in fact. When did you ever see
So much sweet beauty as when fine rain falls
On that small tree
And saturates your brick back-garden walls,
So many Amber Rooms and mirror halls?

Ever more lavish as the dusk descends
This glistening illuminates the air.
It never ends.
Whenever the rain comes it will be there,
Beyond my time, but now I take my share.

My daughter's choice, the maple tree is new.
Come autumn and its leaves will turn to flame.
What I must do
Is live to see that. That will end the game
For me, though life continues all the same:

Filling the double doors to bathe my eyes,
A final flood of colours will live on
As my mind dies,
Burned by my vision of a world that shone
So brightly at the last, and then was gone.

Clive James

The Journey of the Magi

'A cold coming we had of it,
Just the worst time of the year
For a journey, and such a long journey:
The ways deep and the weather sharp,
The very dead of winter.'
And the camels galled, sore-footed, refractory,
Lying down in the melting snow.
There were times we regretted
The summer palaces on slopes, the terraces,
And the silken girls bringing sherbet.
Then the camel men cursing and grumbling
And running away, and wanting their liquor and women,
And the night-fires going out, and the lack of shelters,
And the cities hostile and the towns unfriendly
And the villages dirty and charging high prices:

A hard time we had of it.
At the end we preferred to travel all night,
Sleeping in snatches,
With the voices singing in our ears, saying
That this was all folly.

Then at dawn we came down to a temperate valley,
Wet, below the snow line, smelling of vegetation;
With a running stream and a water-mill beating the darkness,
And three trees on the low sky,
And an old white horse galloped away in the meadow.
Then we came to a tavern with vine-leaves over the lintel,
Six hands at an open door dicing for pieces of silver,
And feet kicking the empty wine-skins.
But there was no information, and so we continued
And arriving at evening, not a moment too soon
Finding the place; it was (you might say) satisfactory.

All this was a long time ago, I remember,
And I would do it again, but set down
This set down
This: were we led all that way for
Birth or Death? There was a Birth, certainly
We had evidence and no doubt. I had seen birth and death,
But had thought they were different; this Birth was
Hard and bitter agony for us, like Death, our death.
We returned to our places, these Kingdoms,
But no longer at ease here, in the old dispensation,
With an alien people clutching their gods.
I should be glad of another death.

T. S. Eliot

Katie Cruel

When I first came to town
They called me the roving jewel
Now they've changed their tune
Call me Katie Cruel

Through the woods I'm going
And through the boggy mire
Straight way down the road
'Til I come to my heart's desire

If I was where I would be
Then I'd be where I am not
Here I am where I must be
Where I would be, I can not

When I first came to town
They bought me drinks plenty
Now they've changed their tune
And hand me the bottles empty

If I was where I would be
Then I'd be where I am not
Here I am where I must be
Where I would be, I can not

Anonymous

Keats Is Dead So Fuck Me From Behind

Keats is dead so fuck me from behind
Slowly and with carnal purpose
Some black midwinter afternoon
While all the children are walking home from school
Peel my stockings down with your teeth
Coleridge is dead and Auden too
Of laughing in an overcoat
Shelley died at sea and his heart wouldn't burn
& Wordsworth . . .
They never found his body
His widow mad with grief, hammering nails into an empty meadow
Byron, Whitman, our dog crushed by the garage door
Finger me slowly
In the snowscape of your childhood
Our dead floating just below the surface of the earth
Bend me over like a substitute teacher
& pump me full of shivering arrows
O emotional vulnerability
Bosnian folk-song, birds in the chimney
Tell me what you love when you think I'm not listening
Wallace Stevens's mother is calling him in for dinner
But he's not coming, he's dead too, he died sixty years ago
And nobody cared at his funeral
Life is real
And the days burn off like leopard print
Nobody, not even the dead, can tell me what to do
Eat my pussy from behind
Bill Manhire's not getting any younger

Hera Lindsay Bird

The Lake Isle of Innisfree

I will arise and go now, and go to Innisfree,
And a small cabin build there, of clay and wattles made;
Nine bean rows will I have there, a hive for the honeybee,
And live alone in the bee-loud glade.

And I shall have some peace there, for peace comes dropping slow,
Dropping from the veils of the morning to where the cricket sings;
There midnight's all a-glimmer, and noon a purple glow,
And evening full of the linnet's wings.

I will arise and go now, for always night and day
I hear lake water lapping with low sounds by the shore;
While I stand on the roadway, or on the pavements grey,
I hear it in the deep heart's core.

W. B. Yeats

Last Dawn

Your hair is lost in the forest,
your feet touching mine.
Asleep you are bigger than the night,
but your dream fits within this room.
How much we are who are so little!
Outside a taxi passes
with its load of ghosts.
The river that runs by
is always

running back.
Will tomorrow be another day?

Octavio Paz, translated by Eliot Weinberger

The Last Hellos

Don't die, Dad –
but they die.

This last year he was wandery:
took off a new chainsaw blade
and cobbled a spare from bits.
Perhaps if I lay down
my head'll come better again.
His left shoulder kept rising
higher in his cardigan.

He could see death in a face.
Family used to call him in
to look at sick ones and say.
At his own time, he was told.

The knob found in his head
was duck-egg size. Never hurt.
Two to six months, Cecil.

I'll be right, he boomed
to his poor sister on the phone
I'll do that when I finish dyin.

o

Don't die, Cecil.
But they do.

Going for last drives
in the bush, odd massive
board-slotted stumps bony white
in whipstick second growth.
I could chop all day.

I could always cash
a cheque, in Sydney or anywhere.
Any of the shops.

Eating, still at the head
of the table, he now missed
food on his knife side.

Sorry, Dad, but like
have you forgiven your enemies?
Your father and all them?
All his lifetime of hurt.

I must have,(grin). *I don't*
think about that now.

o

People can't say goodbye
any more. They say last hellos.

Going fast, over Christmas,
he'd still stumble out
of his room, where his photos
hang over the other furniture,
and play host to his mourners.

The courage of his bluster,
firm big voice of his confusion.

Two last days in the hospital:
his long forearms were still
red mahogany. His hands
gripped steel frame. *I'm dyin.*

On the second day:
You're bustin to talk
but I'm too busy dyin.

o

Grief ended when he died,
the widower like soldiers who
won't live life their mates had missed.

Good boy Cecil! No more Bluey dog.
No more cowtime. No more stories.
We're still using your imagination,
it was stronger than all ours.

Your grave's got littler
somehow in the three months.

More pointy as the clay's shrivelled,
like a stuck zip in a coat.

Your cricket boots are in
the State museum! Odd letters
still come. Two more's died since you:
Annie and Stewart. Old Stewart.

On your day there was a good crowd,
family, and people from away.
But of course a lot had gone
to their own funerals first.

Snobs mind us off religion
nowadays, if they can.
Fuck thém. I wish you God.

Les Murray

'Lead, kindly Light, amid th'encircling gloom'

Lead, kindly Light, amid th'encircling gloom,
Lead thou me on!
The night is dark, and I am far from home;
Lead thou me on!
Keep thou my feet; I do not ask to see
The distant scene; one step enough for me.

I was not ever thus, nor prayed that thou
Shouldst lead me on;

I loved to choose and see my path; but now,
Lead thou me on!
I loved the garish day, and, spite of fears,
Pride ruled my will: remember not past years!

So long thy power hath blessed me, sure it still
Will lead me on.
O'er moor and fen, o'er crag and torrent, till
The night is gone,
And with the morn those angel faces smile,
Which I have loved long since, and lost awhile!

John Henry Newman

Leda and the Swan

A sudden blow: the great wings beating still
Above the staggering girl, her thighs caressed
By the dark webs, her nape caught in his bill,
He holds her helpless breast upon his breast.

How can those terrified vague fingers push
The feathered glory from her loosening thighs?
And how can body, laid in that white rush,
But feel the strange heart beating where it lies?

A shudder in the loins engenders there
The broken wall, the burning roof and tower
And Agamemnon dead.
                Being so caught up,
So mastered by the brute blood of the air,

Did she put on his knowledge with his power
Before the indifferent beak could let her drop?

W. B. Yeats

A Letter of Recommendation

On summer nights I sleep naked
in Jerusalem. My bed
stands on the brink of a deep valley
without rolling down into it.

In the daytime I walk around with the Ten
Commandments on my lips
like an old tune someone hums to himself.

Oh touch me, touch me, good woman!
That's not a scar you feel under my shirt, that's
a letter of recommendation, folded up tight,
from my father:
'All the same, he's a good boy, and full of love.'

I remember my father waking me for early prayers.
He would do it by gently stroking my forehead, not
by tearing away the blanket.

Since then I love him even more.
And as his reward, may he be wakened
gently and with love
on the Day of the Resurrection.

Yehuda Amichai, translated by Chana Bloch

The Letters of the Dead

We read the letters of the dead like helpless gods,
but gods, nonetheless, since we know the dates that follow.
We know which debts will never be repaid.
Which widows will remarry with the corpse still warm.
Poor dead, blindfolded dead,
gullible, fallible, pathetically prudent.
We see the faces people make behind their backs.
We catch the sound of wills being ripped to shreds.
The dead sit before us comically, as if on buttered bread,
or frantically pursue the hats blown from their heads.
Their bad taste, Napoleon, steam, electricity,
their fatal remedies for curable diseases,
their foolish apocalypse according to St. John,
their counterfeit heaven on earth according to Jean-Jacques . . .
We watch the pawns on their chessboards in silence,
even though we see them three squares later.
Everything the dead predicted has turned out completely different.
Or a little bit different – which is to say, completely different.
The most fervent of them gaze confidingly into our eyes:
their calculations tell them that they'll find perfection there.

Wislawa Szymborska, translated by Stanislaw Baranczak and Clare Cavanagh

Life-cycle

For Big Jim Phelan

When children are born in Victoria
they are wrapped in club-colours, laid in beribboned cots,
having already begun a lifetime's barracking.

Carn, they cry, Carn . . . feebly at first
while parents playfully tussle with them
for possession of a rusk: Ah, he's a little Tiger! (And they are . . .)

Hoisted shoulder-high at their first League game
they are like innocent monsters who have been years swimming
towards the daylight's roaring empyrean

Until, now, hearts shrapnelled with rapture,
they break surface and are forever lost,
their minds rippling out like streamers

In the pure flood of sound, they are scarfed with light, a voice
like the voice of God booms from the stands
Ooohh you bludger! and the covenant is sealed.

Hot pies and potato-crisps they will eat,
they will forswear the Demons, cling to the Saints
and behold their team going up the ladder into Heaven,

And the tides of life will be the tides of the home-team's fortunes
– the reckless proposal after the one-point win,
the wedding and honeymoon after the grand final . . .

They will not grow old as those from the more northern states
    grow old,
for them it will always be three-quarter time
with the scores level and the wind advantage in the final term,

That passion persisting, like a race-memory, through the welter
    of seasons,

enabling old-timers by boundary fences to dream of resurgent lions
and centaur-figures from the past to replenish continually the present,

So that mythology may be perpetually renewed
and Chicken Smallhorn return like the maize-god
in a thousand shapes, the dancers changing

But the dance forever the same – the elderly still
loyally crying Carn . . . Carn . . . (if feebly) unto the very end,
having seen in the six-foot recruit from Eaglehawk their hope
    of salvation

Bruce Dawe

Life Is Fine

I went down to the river,
I set down on the bank.
I tried to think but couldn't,
So I jumped in and sank.

I came up once and hollered!
I came up twice and cried!
If that water hadn't a-been so cold
I might've sunk and died.

But it was
Cold in that water!
It was cold!

I took the elevator
Sixteen floors above the ground.
I thought about my baby
And thought I would jump down.

I stood there and I hollered!
I stood there and I cried!
If it hadn't a-been so high
I might've jumped and died.

But it was
High up there!
It was high!

So since I'm still here livin',
I guess I will live on.
I could've died for love –
But for livin' I was born.

Though you may hear me holler,
And you may see me cry –
I'll be dogged, sweet baby,
If you gonna see me die.

Life is fine!
Fine as wine!
Life is fine!

Langston Hughes

'Like as the waves make towards the pebbled shore'

Like as the waves make towards the pebbled shore,
So do our minutes hasten to their end;
Each changing place with that which goes before,
In sequent toil all forwards do contend.
Nativity, once in the main of light,
Crawls to maturity, wherewith being crown'd,
Crooked eclipses 'gainst his glory fight,
And Time, that gave, doth now his gift confound.
Time doth transfix the flourish set on youth,
And delves the parallels in beauty's brow,
Feeds on the rarities of nature's truth,
And nothing stands but for his scythe to mow.
    And yet to times in hope my verse shall stand,
    Praising thy worth, despite his cruel hand.

Sonnet 60, William Shakespeare

Little Bit Long Time

stay here
he whispers gruffly   holds her roughly
hugs her   then hides her
little bit long time

big eyes young face   stare from hiding place
watch her Dad pause   check nature's laws
sniffing the air   eyes filled with despair
little bit long time

he just wants some water to give to his daughter
he steps from the trees   crawls on his knees
squats on the sand   drinks with his hands
little bit long time

her eyes do not waver   good lessons he gave her
sees Dad fall over strange   there is a hole in his brains
gun noise fills her ears   her eyes lose their tears
little bit long time

rough white hands snatch her   cruel voices scratch her
she is too scared to run   she's learnt respect for the gun
two different eyes clash   and she knows in a flash
this killer had watched them

little bit long time

Ali Cobby Eckermann

'The Lord is my shepherd'

The Lord is my shepherd; I shall not want.
He maketh me to lie down in green pastures: he leadeth me beside
    the still waters.
He restoreth my soul: he leadeth me in the paths of righteousness for
    his name's sake.
Yea, though I walk through the valley of the shadow of death,
    I will fear no evil: for thou art with me; thy rod and thy staff they
    comfort me.
Thou preparest a table before me in the presence of mine enemies:
    thou anointest my head with oil; my cup runneth over.

Surely goodness and mercy shall follow me all the days of my life:
  and I will dwell in the house of the Lord for ever.

Psalm 23, King James Bible

Loss and Gain

When I compare
What I have lost with what I have gained,
What I have missed with what attained,
Little room do I find for pride.

I am aware
How many days have been idly spent;
How like an arrow the good intent
Has fallen short or been turned aside.

But who shall dare
To measure loss and gain in this wise?
Defeat may be victory in disguise;
The lowest ebb is the turn of the tide.

Henry Wadsworth Longfellow

Love

Love means to learn to look at yourself
The way one looks at distant things
For you are only one thing among many.
And whoever sees that way heals his heart,

Without knowing it, from various ills –
A bird and a tree say to him: Friend

Then he wants to use himself and things
So they stand in the glow of ripeness.
It doesn't matter whether he knows what he serves:
Who serves best doesn't always understand.

Czeslaw Milosz, translated by the author

'Love, never conquered in battle'

Love, never conquered in battle
Love, the plunderer laying waste the rich!
Love standing the night-watch guarding a girl's soft cheek,
you range the seas, the shepherds' steadings off in the wilds –
not even the deathless gods can flee your onset,
nothing human born for a day –
whoever feels your grip is driven mad. Love! –
you wrench the minds of the righteous into outrage,
swerve them to their ruin – you have ignited this,
this kindred strife, father and son at war and Love alone the victor –
warm glance of the bride triumphant, burning with desire!
Throned in power, side-by-side with the mighty laws!
Irresistible Aphrodite, never conquered –
Love, you mock us for your sport.

Chorus in Antigone, *Sophocles, translated by Robert Fagles*

Lucky

For Andy

There's a damp melancholy
in T'ang poetry
that smudges
the lovely jade
precision.

I love Walt Whitman's
spunky company
but under his bardic
whistling
I can hear his lonely heart
howling
at the turned back
of some deaf rough trade.

So many poets
starve
in the cold faery spaces
between their frost-bitten ears.

How lucky I am
to hear you, darling,
coming up the stairs
to smell the coffee
floating ahead of you
like my favourite incense.

Dorothy Porter

Lullaby

Lay your sleeping head, my love,
Human on my faithless arm;
Time and fevers burn away
Individual beauty from
Thoughtful children, and the grave
Proves the child ephemeral:
But in my arms till break of day
Let the living creature lie,
Mortal, guilty, but to me
The entirely beautiful.

Soul and body have no bounds:
To lovers as they lie upon
Her tolerant enchanted slope
In their ordinary swoon,
Grave the vision Venus sends
Of supernatural sympathy,
Universal love and hope;
While an abstract insight wakes
Among the glaciers and the rocks
The hermit's carnal ecstasy.

Certainty, fidelity
On the stroke of midnight pass
Like vibrations of a bell,
And fashionable madmen raise
Their pedantic boring cry:
Every farthing of the cost,
All the dreaded cards foretell,

Shall be paid, but from this night
Not a whisper, not a thought,
Not a kiss nor look be lost.

Beauty, midnight, vision dies:
Let the winds of dawn that blow
Softly round your dreaming head
Such a day of welcome show
Eye and knocking heart may bless.
Find our mortal world enough;
Noons of dryness see you fed
By the involuntary powers,
Nights of insult let you pass
Watched by every human love.

W. H. Auden

Lyric

As brazen as the naked day
he came and stole my heart away
though I was wanton, sly and fey:
merry meet and merry part
my heart.

No modest ban, no practised play
could keep his gentle hands at bay
for all my armours fell away:
merry meet and merry part
my heart.

And all my blood grows on his bone
and in his ribs my heart is sewn
when one and one make only one:
merry meet and merry part
my heart.

And if one day the ruthless sun
wakes us to show our love has gone
then of us two there will be none:
merry meet and merry part
my heart.

Alison Croggon

The Magpies

When Tom and Elizabeth took the farm
The bracken made their bed,
And *Quardle oodle ardle wardle doodle*
The magpies said.

Tom's hand was strong to the plough
Elizabeth's lips were red,
And *Quardle oodle ardle wardle doodle*
The magpies said.

Year in year out they worked
While the pines grew overhead,
And *Quardle oodle ardle wardle doodle*
The magpies said.

But all the beautiful crops soon went
To the mortgage-man instead,
And *Quardle oodle ardle wardle doodle*
The magpies said.

Elizabeth is dead now (it's years ago)
Old Tom went light in the head;
And *Quardle oodle ardle wardle doodle*
The magpies said.

The farm's still there. Mortgage corporations
Couldn't give it away.
And *Quardle oodle ardle wardle doodle*
The magpies say.

Denis Glover

Man for Whom I Endured . . .

Man, for whom I suffered love
In secret, I now call a halt.
I'll no longer dance in step.
Far too long I've been enthralled.

Know that I desire surcease,
Reckon up what love has cost
In racking sighs, in blighted nights
When every hope of sleep is lost.

Harrowed heart, strangled laughter;
Though you're dead to shame, I charge you

With my luckless graceless plight
And pain that plagues me sorely.

Yet, can I blame you that the sun
Darkens when you are in sight?
Until I'm free each day is dark –
False freedom to swap day for night!

Cruel my fate, if by your side.
Crueller still, if set apart.
A bad bargain either way
To love you or to love you not.

Máire Mhac an tSaoi, translated by Biddy Jenkinson

The Man from Ironbark

It was the man from Ironbark who struck the Sydney town,
He wandered over street and park, he wandered up and down.
He loitered here, he loitered there, till he was like to drop,
Until at last in sheer despair he sought a barber's shop.
''Ere! shave my beard and whiskers off, I'll be a man of mark,
I'll go and do the Sydney toff up home in Ironbark.'

The barber man was small and flash, as barbers mostly are,
He wore a strike-your-fancy sash, he smoked a huge cigar;
He was a humorist of note and keen at repartee,
He laid the odds and kept a 'tote', whatever that may be,
And when he saw our friend arrive, he whispered, 'Here's a lark!
Just watch me catch him all alive, this man from Ironbark.'

There were some gilded youths that sat along the barber's wall.
Their eyes were dull, their heads were flat, they had no brains at all;
To them the barber passed the wink, his dexter eyelid shut,
'I'll make this bloomin' yokel think his bloomin' throat is cut.'
And as he soaped and rubbed it in he made a rude remark:
'I s'pose the flats is pretty green up there in Ironbark.'

A grunt was all reply he got; he shaved the bushman's chin,
Then made the water boiling hot and dipped the razor in.
He raised his hand, his brow grew black, he paused awhile to gloat,
Then slashed the red-hot razor-back across his victim's throat;
Upon the newly-shaven skin it made a livid mark –
No doubt it fairly took him in – the man from Ironbark.

He fetched a wild up-country yell might wake the dead to hear,
And though his throat, he knew full well, was cut from ear to ear,
He struggled gamely to his feet, and faced the murd'rous foe:
'You've done for me! you dog, I'm beat! one hit before I go!
'I only wish I had a knife, you blessed murdering shark!
'But you'll remember all your life the man from Ironbark.'

He lifted up his hairy paw, with one tremendous clout
He landed on the barber's jaw, and knocked the barber out.
He set to work with nail and tooth, he made the place a wreck;
He grabbed the nearest gilded youth, and tried to break his neck.
And all the while his throat he held to save his vital spark,
And 'Murder! Bloody Murder!' yelled the man from Ironbark.

A peeler who had heard the din came in to see the show;
He tried to run the bushman in, but he refused to go.
And when at last the barber spoke, and said 'Twas all in fun –

'Twas just a little harmless joke, a trifle overdone.'
'A joke!' he cried, 'By George, that's fine; a lively sort of lark;
'I'd like to catch that murdering swine some night in Ironbark.'

And now while round the shearing floor the list'ning shearers gape,
He tells the story o'er and o'er, and brags of his escape.
'Them barber chaps what keeps a tote, By George, I've had enough,
'One tried to cut my bloomin' throat, but thank the Lord it's tough.'
And whether he's believed or no, there's one thing to remark,
That flowing beards are all the go way up in Ironbark.

Banjo Paterson

Man Splitting Wood in the Daybreak

The man splitting wood in the daybreak
looks strong, as though, if one weakened,
one could turn to him and he would help.
Gus Newland was strong. When he split wood
he struck hard, flashing the bright steel
through the air so hard the hard maple
leapt apart, as it's feared marriages will do
in countries reluctant to permit divorce,
and even willow, which, though stacked
to dry a full year, on being split
actually weeps – totem wood, therefore,
to the married-until-death – sunders
with many little lip-wetting gasp-noises.
But Gus is dead. We could turn to our fathers,
but they help us only by the unperplexed
looking-back of the numerals cut into headstones.

Or to our mothers, whose love, so devastated,
can't, even in spring, break through the hard earth.
Our spouses weaken at the same rate we do.
We have to hold our children up to lean on them.
Everyone who could help goes or hasn't arrived.
What about the man splitting wood in the daybreak,
who looked strong? That was years ago. That was me.

Galway Kinnell

A Man's a Man for A' That

Is there for honest Poverty
That hangs his head, an' a' that;
The coward slave, we pass him by,
We dare be poor for a' that!
For a' that, an' a' that.
Our toils obscure an' a' that,
The rank is but the guinea's stamp,
The Man's the gowd for a' that.

What though on hamely fare we dine,
Wear hoddin grey, an' a that;
Gie fools their silks, and knaves their wine;
A Man's a Man for a' that:
For a' that, and a' that,
Their tinsel show, an' a' that;
The honest man, tho' e'er sae poor,
Is king o' men for a' that.

Ye see yon birkie, ca'd a lord,
Wha struts, an' stares, an' a' that;
Tho' hundreds worship at his word,
He's but a coof for a' that:
For a' that, an' a' that,
His ribband, star, an' a' that:
The man o' independent mind
He looks an' laughs at a' that.

A prince can mak a belted knight,
A marquis, duke, an' a' that;
But an honest man's aboon his might,
Gude faith, he mauna fa' that!
For a' that, an' a' that,
Their dignities an' a' that;
The pith o' sense, an' pride o' worth,
Are higher rank than a' that.

Then let us pray that come it may,
(As come it will for a' that,)
That Sense and Worth, o'er a' the earth,
Shall bear the gree, an' a' that.
For a' that, an' a' that,
It's coming yet for a' that,
That Man to Man, the world o'er,
Shall brothers be for a' that.

Robert Burns

A Man's Household

He's one of those men who want to do everything by themselves.
You need to love him along with drawers, cabinets, and shelves,
with what's on top of cupboards, or inside or sticking out.
Everything is going to come in handy without a doubt.
Drills, hammers, files, chisels, melting pots and pliers.
bundles of string, springs and umbrella wires,
squeezed-out tubes, dried-out glue,
jars big and small where something already grew,
an assortment of pebbles, a little anvil, a vise,
an alarm clock that's already been broken twice,
a dead beetle in a soap dish, beside an empty vial,
on which a skull and crossbones have been painted in grand style,
a batten, short and long plugs, buckles and a gasket,
a Lake Mamry water hen's three feathers in a basket,
a few champagne corks stuck in cement,
two glass slides scorched in the course of an experiment,
a pile of bars, some cardboard boxes, tiles, a gutter spout,
and fitting uses for them all might soon be figured out,
some handles to something, scraps of leather, a blanket torn to shreds,
a boyish slingshot, scads of keys and screws of varied threads . . .
May I throw out a thing or two? – I put this to him dearly,
but in response the man I love just looked at me severely.

Wislawa Szymborska, translated by Joanna Trzeciak

'Many in aftertimes will say of you'

Vien dietro a me e lascia dir le genti – Dante
Contando i casi della vita nostra – Petrarch

Many in aftertimes will say of you
'He loved her' – while of me what will they say?
Not that I loved you more than just in play,
For fashion's sake as idle women do.
Even let them prate; who know not what we knew
Of love and parting in exceeding pain.
Of parting hopeless here to meet again,
Hopeless on earth, and heaven is out of view.
But by my heart of love laid bare to you,
My love that you can make not void nor vain,
Love that foregoes you but to claim anew
Beyond this passage of the gate of death,
I charge you at the Judgment make it plain
My love of you was life and not a breath.

Christina Rossetti

Mary Hogan's Quatrains

I

O to be disentangled from this net –
And may God not let that be long –
Perhaps the memory will help
Of all the ease I had in your arms.

When I shall have the ability to pray,
Take communion and hear Mass,
Who will say then that it is not seemly
To intercede on yours and on my behalf?

But meanwhile my advice to you,
Don't get too firmly enmeshed,
For I am determined to let loose
Whatever bond between us is tied.

II

I care little for people's suspicions,
I care little for priests' prohibitions,
For anything save to lie stretched
Between you and the wall –

I am indifferent to the night's cold,
I am indifferent to the squall or rain,
When in this warm narrow secret world
Which does not go beyond the edge of the bed –

We shall not contemplate what lies before us,
What has already been done,
Time is on our side, my dearest,
And it will last til morning.

III

For the space of a year I have been
Lying with you in your embrace,

Hard to say now
What I was hoping for!

You trampled on love,
That was freely given at first,
Unaware of the suffering
Of the flesh you crushed under foot.

And yet the flesh is willing
For the sake of an old familiar pledge,
But since the heart's singing has ceased
The joy of pleasure ebbs.

IV

The child of jealousy is sucking my breast,
While I nurse it day and night;
The ugly brat is cutting teeth,
My veins throb with the venom of its bite.

My love, may the little wretch not remain between us,
Seeing how healthy and full was our knowledge of each other;
It was a skin warranty that kept us together,
And a seal of hand that knew no bounds.

See how I am not determined to deny love,
Though doubt has plunged its roots deep;
Do not force a willing mare,
And she will recompense you in her own season.

V

Pain is a powerful thing,
How it consumes the breast,
It gives no respite day or night,
It gives no peace or rest –

Anyone who feels pain like me,
Has never been lonely or alone,
But is ever bearing company
Like a pregnant woman, in her womb.

VI

'I do not sleep at night' –
Of no account, but will we ever know
With open eyes
The burden of the night?

VII

Tonight seems never-ending!
There was once such a night
Which with you was not long –
Dare I call to mind.

That would not be hard, for sure,
The road on which I would return –
If it were permitted
After repentance.

Lying down for joy
And rising to pleasure
That is what we practised –
If only I could return to it.

Máire Mhac an tSaoi, translated by James Gleasure

May

Shyly the silver-hatted mushrooms make
  Soft entrance through,
And undelivered lovers, half awake,
  Hear noises in the dew

Yellow in all the earth and in the skies,
  The world would seem
Faint as a widow mourning with soft eyes
  And falling into dream.

Up the long hill I see the slow plough leave
  Furrows of brown;
Dim is the day and beautiful: I grieve
  To see the sun go down.

But there are suns a many for mine eyes
  Day after day:
Delightsome in grave greenery they rise,
  Red oranges in May.

John Shaw Neilson

The Members of the Orchestra

Walk onto the dark stage dressed for a funeral
Or a wedding and we, the anxious ones, quieten
As we wait to discover which it will be tonight:

They sit or stand before thin books written
In a foreign script, more alien than Chinese,
But its secret contents will be revealed now

As at the reading of a dead relation's will,
For the last member has entered, slightly late
As befits his honour, like a famous lecturer

With a new theory and a pointer to make it clear.
Alas, he too cannot talk except in the language
Of the deaf and dumb, but as he waves his hands

The members of the orchestra commence their act
Of complicated ventriloquism, each making
His instrument speak our long-forgotten native tongue.

Now one violin speaks above the rest, rehearsing
The articulate sorrow of things in this world
Where we have suddenly woken to find a music

As curious as the relation between an object
And its name. We are taken by the hand and led
Through the old darkness that separates us

From things in themselves, through the soft fold
Of evening that keeps two days apart. And now
Each instrument tells its story in details

That become the whole, the entire forest contained
Within a leaf: the orchestra is quickly building
A city of living air about us where we can live

And know ourselves at last, for we have given up
Our selves, as at our wedding or our funeral,
To take on something new, something that was always there.

Kevin Hart

Men

When I was young, I used to
Watch behind the curtains
As men walked up and down
The street. Wino men, old men.
Young men sharp as mustard.
See them. Men are always
Going somewhere.
They knew I was there. Fifteen
Years old and starving for them.
Under my window, they would pause,
Their shoulders high like the
Breasts of a young girl,
Jacket tails slapping over
Those behinds,
Men.

One day they hold you in the
Palms of their hands, gentle, as if you
Were the last raw egg in the world. Then
They tighten up. Just a little. The
First squeeze is nice. A quick hug.
Soft into your defenselessness. A little
More. The hurt begins. Wrench out a
Smile that slides around the fear. When the
Air disappears,
Your mind pops, exploding fiercely, briefly,
Like the head of a kitchen match. Shattered.
It is your juice
That runs down their legs. Staining their shoes.
When the earth rights itself again,
And taste tries to return to the tongue,
Your body has slammed shut. Forever.
No keys exist.

Then the window draws full upon
Your mind. There, just beyond
The sway of curtains, men walk.
Knowing something.
Going someplace.
But this time, you will simply
Stand and watch.

Maybe.

Maya Angelou

'Methought I heard a voice cry'

Methought I heard a voice cry, 'Sleep no more!
Macbeth does murder sleep' – the innocent sleep,
Sleep that knits up the ravelled sleave of care,
The death of each day's life, sore labour's bath,
Balm of hurt minds, great nature's second course,
Chief nourisher in life's feast.

Macbeth in Macbeth, *William Shakespeare*

Milk Cream Butter

He'd get up every morning before the sun
had cleared the treeline on his neighbour's creek,
and while the sound of magpies trickled in
the slightly opened window of his room
he'd take whatever clothes he'd worn all week,
a tattered pile that mostly smelled of him,
and shake them out and put them on again.
That time of day the paddock by the house
was brittle with a covering of frost
so when he went to get his seven cows
it left a zig-zag trail of darker prints
where the silver grass got crushed beneath his boots.
The cows would wander down along a fence
that led them through a set of open gates
and when they'd turn into the narrow lane
he'd notice now their cautious feet would mince
the gravel-filling with the mud again.
Arriving at the milking shed the queue

of weighted cows would always be the same.
They'd practised twice a day and now they knew
the sequence and the distance off by heart.
They knew the routine of the single bail
and after that how far to keep apart.
So there was nothing much he had to do
except to chain them in and wet the teats
then draw the lines of milk into the pail
between his legs, a tight metallic gasp
that changed into exquisite frothy breaths.
In less than half an hour he'd have them done
and while they sauntered back the way they'd come
he'd go out to the separating room
and tip the previous morning's creamless milk
into two pig troughs that used to be a drum
and then he'd pour each bucketful of warm
fresh milk into a metal cooling dish.
Beside them was a wooden butter-churn
that looked like some sideshow magician's prop.
He'd fill it up with sour cream and turn
the handle steadily until the fat
began to float in globules on the top.
A final rapid stirring firmed them up,
he'd slide a bucket underneath, then pull
the plug and let the buttermilk escape
before he'd fill the small vat nearly full
of water, rinse the butter clean, then add
some salt and take the soapy mixture out
in handfuls, which he'd torture like a rag,
removing with a twist the final drops.
The rest was just a kind of copyright.

He'd press the butter into one-pound pats
with an emu imprinted on the tops
denoting him, and when the job was done
he'd notice that those blocks of golden light
were glowing deeper than the early sun.

Philip Hodgins

Mirror

I am silver and exact. I have no preconceptions.
Whatever I see I swallow immediately
Just as it is, unmisted by love or dislike.
I am not cruel, only truthful –
The eye of a little god, four-cornered.
Most of the time I meditate on the opposite wall.
It is pink, with speckles. I have looked at it so long
I think it is a part of my heart. But it flickers.
Faces and darkness separate us over and over.

Now I am a lake. A woman bends over me,
Searching my reaches for what she really is.
Then she turns to those liars, the candles or the moon.
I see her back, and reflect it faithfully.
She rewards me with tears and an agitation of hands.
I am important to her. She comes and goes.
Each morning it is her face that replaces the darkness.
In me she has drowned a young girl, and in me an old woman
Rises toward her day after day, like a terrible fish.

Sylvia Plath

The Mistake

With the mistake your life goes in reverse.
Now you can see exactly what you did
Wrong yesterday and wrong the day before
And each mistake leads back to something worse.

And every nuance of your hypocrisy
Towards yourself, and every excuse
Stands solidly on the perspective lines
And there is perfect visibility.

What an enlightenment. The colonnade
Rolls past on either side. You needn't move.
The statues of your errors brush your sleeve.
You watch the tale turn back – and you're dismayed.

And this dismay at this, this big mistake
Is made worse by the sight of all those who
Knew all along where the mistakes would lead –
Those frozen friends who watched the crisis break.

Why didn't they *say*? Oh, but they did indeed –
Said with a murmur when the time was wrong
Or by a mild refusal to assent
Or told you plainly but you would not heed.

Yes, you can hear them now. It hurts. It's worse
Than any sneer from any enemy.
Take this dismay. Lay claim to this mistake.
Look straight along the lines of this reverse.

James Fenton

The Mitchells

I am seeing this: two men are sitting on a pole
they have dug a hole for and will, after dinner, raise
I think for wires. Water boils in a prune tin.
Bees hum their shift in unthinning mists of white

bursaria blossom, under the noon of wattles.
The men eat big meat sandwiches out of a styrofoam
box with a handle. One is overheard saying:
drought that year. Yes. Like trying to farm the road.

The first man, if asked, would say *I'm one of the Mitchells.*
The other would gaze for a while, dried leaves in his palm,
and looking up, with pain and subtle amusement,

say *I'm one of the Mitchells*. Of the pair, one has been rich
but never stopped wearing his oil-stained felt hat. Nearly everything
they say is ritual. Sometimes the scene is an avenue.

Les Murray

Morning Birdsong

I didn't die – waking up I hear that.

Ko Un, translated by Clare You and Richard Silberg

Morning Song

Love set you going like a fat gold watch.
The midwife slapped your footsoles, and your bald cry
Took its place among the elements.

Our voices echo, magnifying your arrival. New statue.
In a drafty museum, your nakedness
Shadows our safety. We stand round blankly as walls.

I'm no more your mother
Than the cloud that distils a mirror to reflect its own slow
Effacement at the wind's hand.

All night your moth-breath
Flickers among the flat pink roses. I wake to listen:
A far sea moves in my ear.

One cry, and I stumble from bed, cow-heavy and floral
In my Victorian nightgown.
Your mouth opens clean as a cat's. The window square

Whitens and swallows its dull stars. And now you try
Your handful of notes;
The clear vowels rise like balloons.

Sylvia Plath

Mother

He fell from her knees like a ball of yarn.
He unwound in a hurry and ran blindly away.
She held the beginning of life. She would wind it
on her finger like a ring, she wanted to preserve him.
He was rolling down steep slopes, sometimes
he was climbing up. He would come back tangled, and be silent.
Never will he return to the sweet throne of her knees.

The stretched-out hands are alight in the darkness
like an old town.

Zbigniew Herbert, translated by John R. Carpenter and Bogdana Carpenter

The Mother

I do not grudge them; Lord, I do not grudge
My two strong sons that I have seen go out
To break their strength and die, they and a few,
In bloody protest for a glorious thing.
They shall be spoken of among their people,
The generations shall remember them,
And call them blessed;
But I will speak their names to my own heart
In the long nights;
The little names that were familiar once
Round my dead hearth.
Lord, thou art hard on mothers:
We suffer in their coming and their going;
And tho' I grudge them not, I weary, weary

Of the long sorrow – And yet I have my joy:
My sons were faithful, and they fought.

Pádraig Pearse

Musée des Beaux Arts

About suffering they were never wrong,
The Old Masters: how well they understood
Its human position; how it takes place
While someone else is eating or opening a window or just walking
dully along;
How, when the aged are reverently, passionately waiting
For the miraculous birth, there always must be
Children who did not specially want it to happen, skating
On a pond at the edge of the wood:
They never forgot
That even the dreadful martyrdom must run its course
Anyhow in a corner, some untidy spot
Where the dogs go on with their doggy life and the torturer's horse
Scratches its innocent behind on a tree.

In Brueghel's *Icarus*, for instance: how everything turns away
Quite leisurely from the disaster; the ploughman may
Have heard the splash, the forsaken cry,
But for him it was not an important failure; the sun shone
As it had to on the white legs disappearing into the green
Water; and the expensive delicate ship that must have seen
Something amazing, a boy falling out of the sky,
Had somewhere to get to and sailed calmly on.

W. H. Auden

Museum

Here are plates with no appetite.
And wedding rings, but the requited love
has been gone now for some three hundred years.

Here's a fan – where is the maiden's blush?
Here are swords – where is the ire?
Nor will the lute sound at the twilight hour.

Since eternity was out of stock,
ten thousand aging things have been amassed instead.
The moss-grown guard in golden slumber
props his mustache on Exhibit Number . . .

Eight. Metals, clay and feathers celebrate
their silent triumphs over dates.
Only some Egyptian flapper's silly hairpin giggles.

The crown has outlasted the head.
The hand has lost out to the glove.
The right shoe has defeated the foot.

As for me, I am still alive, you see.
The battle with my dress still rages on.
It struggles, foolish thing, so stubbornly!
Determined to keep living when I'm gone!

Wislawa Szymborska, translated by Stanislaw Baranczak and Clare Cavanagh

Mushrooms

Overnight, very
Whitely, discreetly,
Very quietly

Our toes, our noses
Take hold on the loam,
Acquire the air.

Nobody sees us,
Stops us, betrays us;
The small grains make room.

Soft fists insist on
Heaving the needles,
The leafy bedding,

Even the paving.
Our hammers, our rams,
Earless and eyeless,

Perfectly voiceless,
Widen the crannies,
Shoulder through holes. We

Diet on water,
On crumbs of shadow,
Bland-mannered, asking

Little or nothing.
So many of us!
So many of us!

We are shelves, we are
Tables, we are meek,
We are edible,

Nudgers and shovers
In spite of ourselves.
Our kind multiplies:

We shall by morning
Inherit the earth.
Our foot's in the door.

Sylvia Plath

My At-Last Lover

Your face sleeps
    illuminated
in the early morning
    warmth
        of my slack arm

you're my at-last sound asleep
        child
you're my cat
    with a dreaming paw
        flexing in my hand

you're my raw storm
        gorgeously spent

and what am I, darling?

Exhausted

and full of trapped bubbles
    like honeycomb.

Dorothy Porter

'My love is as a fever, longing still'

My love is as a fever, longing still
For that which longer nurseth the disease,
Feeding on that which doth preserve the ill,
Th' uncertain sickly appetite to please.
My reason, the physician to my love,
Angry that his prescriptions are not kept,
Hath left me, and I desperate now approve
Desire is death, which physic did except.
Past cure I am, now reason is past care,
And frantic-mad with evermore unrest;
My thoughts and my discourse as madmen's are,
At random from the truth vainly expressed:
    For I have sworn thee fair, and thought thee bright,
    Who art as black as hell, as dark as night.

Sonnet 147, William Shakespeare

My True Love Hath My Heart

My true love hath my heart and I have his,
By just exchange one for the other given:
I hold his dear, and mine he cannot miss;
There never was a bargain better driven.
His heart in me keeps me and him in one;
My heart in him his thoughts and senses guides:
He loves my heart, for once it was his own;
I cherish his because in me it bides.
His heart his wound received from my sight;
My heart was wounded with his wounded heart;
For as from me on him his hurt did light,
So still, methought, in me his hurt did smart:
  Both equal hurt, in this change sought our bliss,
  My true love hath my heart and I have his.

From Arcadia*, Sir Philip Sidney*

Nativity

Immensity cloistered in thy dear womb,
Now leaves His well-belov'd imprisonment,
There He hath made Himself to His intent
Weak enough, now into the world to come;
But O, for thee, for Him, hath the inn no room?
Yet lay Him in this stall, and from the Orient,
Stars and wise men will travel to prevent
The effect of Herod's jealous general doom.
Seest thou, my soul, with thy faith's eyes, how He
Which fills all place, yet none holds Him, doth lie?

Was not His pity towards thee wondrous high,
That would have need to be pitied by thee?
Kiss Him, and with Him into Egypt go,
With His kind mother, who partakes thy woe.

John Donne

Never Give All the Heart

Never give all the heart, for love
Will hardly seem worth thinking of
To passionate women if it seem
Certain, and they never dream
That it fades out from kiss to kiss;
For everything that's lovely is
But a brief, dreamy, kind delight.
O never give the heart outright,
For they, for all smooth lips can say,
Have given their hearts up to the play.
And who could play it well enough
If deaf and dumb and blind with love?
He that made this knows all the cost,
For he gave all his heart and lost.

W. B. Yeats

The New Colossus

Not like the brazen giant of Greek fame,
With conquering limbs astride from land to land;
Here at our sea-washed, sunset gates shall stand
A mighty woman with a torch, whose flame

Is the imprisoned lightning, and her name
Mother of Exiles. From her beacon-hand
Glows world-wide welcome; her mild eyes command
The air-bridged harbor that twin cities frame.
'Keep, ancient lands, your storied pomp!' cries she
With silent lips. 'Give me your tired, your poor,
Your huddled masses yearning to breathe free,
The wretched refuse of your teeming shore.
Send these, the homeless, tempest-tost to me,
I lift my lamp beside the golden door!'

Emma Lazarus

'Night deepens'

Night deepens
with the sound
of a calling deer,
and I hear
my own one-sided love.

Ono No Komachi, translated by Jane Hirshfield with Mariko Aratani

Night Mail

I

This is the Night Mail crossing the Border,
Bringing the cheque and the postal order,

Letters for the rich, letters for the poor,
The shop at the corner, the girl next door.

Pulling up Beattock, a steady climb:
The gradient's against her, but she's on time.

Past cotton-grass and moorland boulder
Shovelling white steam over her shoulder,

Snorting noisily, she passes
Silent miles of wind-bent grasses.

Birds turn their heads as she approaches,
Stare from bushes at her blank-faced coaches.

Sheep-dogs cannot turn her course;
They slumber on with paws across.
In the farm she passes no one wakes,
But a jug in a bedroom gently shakes.

II

Dawn freshens, Her climb is done.
Down towards Glasgow she descends,
Towards the steam tugs yelping down a glade of cranes
Towards the fields of apparatus, the furnaces
Set on the dark plain like gigantic chessmen.
All Scotland waits for her:
In dark glens, beside pale-green lochs
Men long for news.

III

Letters of thanks, letters from banks,
Letters of joy from girl and boy,
Receipted bills and invitations
To inspect new stock or to visit relations,
And applications for situations,
And timid lovers' declarations,
And gossip, gossip from all the nations,
News circumstantial, news financial,
Letters with holiday snaps to enlarge in,
Letters with faces scrawled on the margin,
Letters from uncles, cousins, and aunts,
Letters to Scotland from the South of France,
Letters of condolence to Highlands and Lowlands
Written on paper of every hue,
The pink, the violet, the white and the blue,
The chatty, the catty, the boring, the adoring,
The cold and official and the heart's outpouring,
Clever, stupid, short and long,
The typed and the printed and the spelt all wrong.

IV

Thousands are still asleep,
Dreaming of terrifying monsters
Or of friendly tea beside the band in Cranston's or Crawford's
Asleep in working Glasgow, asleep in well-set Edinburgh,
Asleep in granite Aberdeen,
They continue their dreams,
But shall wake soon and hope for letters,
And none will hear the postman's knock

Without a quickening of the heart,
For who can bear to feel himself forgotten?

W. H. Auden

The Night of the Dance

The cold moon hangs to the sky by its horn,
    And centres its gaze on me;
The stars, like eyes in reverie,
Their westering as for a while forborne,
    Quiz downward curiously.

Old Robert draws the backbrand in,
    The green logs steam and spit;
The half-awakened sparrows flit
From the riddled thatch; and owls begin
    To whoo from the gable-slit.

Yes; far and nigh things seem to know
    Sweet scenes are impending here;
That all is prepared; that the hour is near
For welcomes, fellowships, and flow
    Of sally, song, and cheer;

That spigots are pulled and viols strung;
    That soon will arise the sound
Of measures trod to tunes renowned;
That She will return in Love's low tongue
    My vows as we wheel around.

Thomas Hardy

The Night-Ride

Gas flaring on the yellow platform; voices running up and down;
Milk-tins in cold dented silver; half-awake I stare,
Pull up the blind, blink out – all sounds are drugged;
The slow blowing of passengers asleep;
Engines yawning; water in heavy drips;
Black, sinister travellers, lumbering up the station,
One moment in the window, hooked over bags;
Hurrying, unknown faces – boxes with strange labels –
All groping clumsily to mysterious ends,
Out of the gaslight, dragged by private Fates,
Their echoes die. The dark train shakes and plunges;
Bells cry out, the night-ride starts again.
Soon I shall look out into nothing but blackness,
Pale, windy fields. The old roar and knock of the rails
Melts in dull fury. Pull down the blind. Sleep. Sleep.
Nothing but grey, rushing rivers of bush outside.
Gaslight and milk-cans. Of Rapptown I recall nothing else.

Kenneth Slessor

'No different, really'

No different, really –
a summer moth's
visible burning
and this body,
transformed by love.

Izumi Shikibu, translated by Jane Hirshfield with Mariko Aratani

No End of Fun

So he's got to have happiness,
he's got to have truth, too,
he's got to have eternity –
did you ever!

He has only just learned to tell dreams from waking;
only just realized that he is he;
only just whittled with his hand né fin
a flint, a rocket ship;
easily drowned in the ocean's teaspoon,
not even funny enough to tickle the void;
sees only with his eyes;
hears only with his ears;
his speech's personal best is the conditional;
he uses his reason to pick holes in reason.
In short, he's next to no one,
but his head's full of freedom, omniscience, and the Being
beyond his foolish meat –
did you ever!

For he does apparently exist.
He genuinely came to be
beneath one of the more parochial stars.
He's lively and quite active in his fashion.
His capacity for wonder is well advanced
for a crystal's deviant descendant.
And considering his difficult childhood
spent kowtowing to the herd's needs,

he's already quite an individual indeed –
did you ever!

Carry on, then, if only for the moment
that it takes a tiny galaxy to blink!
One wonders what will become of him,
since he does in fact seem to be.
And as far as being goes, he really tries quite hard.
Quite hard indeed – one must admit.
With that ring in his nose, with that toga, that sweater.
He's no end of fun, for all you say.
Poor little beggar.
A human, if ever we saw one.

Wislawa Szymborska, translated by Stanislaw Baranczak and Clare Cavanagh

No, Thank You, John

I never said I loved you, John:
    Why will you tease me, day by day,
And wax a weariness to think upon
    With always 'do' and 'pray'?

You know I never loved you, John;
    No fault of mine made me your toast:
Why will you haunt me with a face as wan
    As shows an hour-old ghost?

I dare say Meg or Moll would take
    Pity upon you, if you'd ask:

And pray don't remain single for my sake
    Who can't perform that task.

I have no heart? – Perhaps I have not;
    But then you're mad to take offence
That I don't give you what I have not got:
    Use your common sense.

Let bygones be bygones:
    Don't call me false, who owed not to be true:
I'd rather answer 'No' to fifty Johns
    Than answer 'Yes' to you.

Let's mar our pleasant days no more,
    Song-birds of passage, days of youth:
Catch at today, forget the days before:
    I'll wink at your untruth.

Let us strike hands as hearty friends;
    No more, no less: and friendship's good:
Only don't keep in view ulterior ends,
    And points not understood

In open treaty. Rise above
    Quibbles and shuffling off and on:
Here's friendship for you if you like; but love, –
    No, thank you, John.

Christina Rossetti

'Now from his breast into the eyes the ache'

Now from his breast into the eyes the ache
of longing mounted, and he wept at last,
his dear wife, clear and faithful, in his arms,
longed for as the sunwarmed earth is longed for by a swimmer
spent in rough water where his ship went down
under Poseidon's blows, gale winds and tons of sea.
Few men can keep alive through a big surf
to crawl, clotted with brine, on kindly beaches
in joy, in joy, knowing the abyss behind:
and so she too rejoiced, her gaze upon her husband,
her white arms round him pressed as though forever.

The rose Dawn might have found them weeping still
had not grey-eyed Athena slowed the night
when night was most profound, and held the Dawn
under the Ocean of the East. That glossy team,
Firebright and Daybright, the Dawn's horses
that draw her heavenward for men – Athena
stayed their harnessing.

Homer, The Odyssey, *from Book 23, translated by Robert Fitzgerald*

'O Lord, thou hast searched me, and known me'

O Lord, thou hast searched me, and known me.
Thou knowest my downsitting and mine uprising, thou
  understandest my thought afar off.
Thou compassest my path and my lying down, and art acquainted
  with all my ways.

For there is not a word in my tongue, but, lo, O Lord, thou knowest
it altogether.
Thou hast beset me behind and before, and laid thine hand upon me.
Such knowledge is too wonderful for me; it is high, I cannot attain
unto it.
Whither shall I go from thy spirit? or whither shall I flee from
thy presence?
If I ascend up into heaven, thou art there: if I make my bed in hell,
behold, thou art there.
If I take the wings of the morning, and dwell in the uttermost parts
of the sea;
Even there shall thy hand lead me, and thy right hand shall hold me.
If I say, Surely the darkness shall cover me; even the night shall be
light about me.
Yea, the darkness hideth not from thee; but the night shineth as the
day: the darkness and the light are both alike to thee.
For thou hast possessed my reins: thou hast covered me in my
mother's womb.
I will praise thee; for I am fearfully and wonderfully made:
marvellous are thy works; and that my soul knoweth right well.
My substance was not hid from thee, when I was made in secret, and
curiously wrought in the lowest parts of the earth.
Thine eyes did see my substance, yet being unperfect; and in thy
book all my members were written, which in continuance were
fashioned, when as yet there was none of them.
How precious also are thy thoughts unto me, O God! how great is
the sum of them!
If I should count them, they are more in number than the sand:
when I awake, I am still with thee.

Psalm 139:1–18, King James Bible

'O mistress mine'

O mistress mine, where are you roaming?
O stay and hear, your true love's coming,
That can sing both high and low.
Trip no further, pretty sweeting.
Journeys end in lovers' meeting,
Every wise man's son doth know.

What is love, 'tis not hereafter,
Present mirth hath present laughter
What's to come is still unsure.
In delay there lies no plenty,
Then come kiss me, sweet and twenty:
Youth's a stuff will not endure.

Feste's song in Twelfth Night, *William Shakespeare*

'O, pardon me, thou bleeding piece of earth'

O, pardon me, thou bleeding piece of earth,
That I am meek and gentle with these butchers!
Thou art the ruins of the noblest man
That ever lived in the tide of times.
Woe to the hand that shed this costly blood!
Over thy wounds now do I prophesy,
Which, like dumb mouths, do ope their ruby lips,
To beg the voice and utterance of my tongue –
A curse shall light upon the limbs of men;
Domestic fury and fierce civil strife
Shall cumber all the parts of Italy;

Blood and destruction shall be so in use
And dreadful objects so familiar
That mothers shall but smile when they behold
Their infants quarter'd with the hands of war;
All pity choked with custom of fell deeds:
And Caesar's spirit, ranging for revenge,
With Até by his side come hot from hell,
Shall in these confines with a monarch's voice
Cry 'Havoc,' and let slip the dogs of war;
That this foul deed shall smell above the earth
With carrion men, groaning for burial.

Antony in Julius Caesar, *William Shakespeare*

Ode on Melancholy

No, no, go not to Lethe, neither twist
  Wolf's-bane, tight-rooted, for its poisonous wine;
Nor suffer thy pale forehead to be kiss'd
  By nightshade, ruby grape of Proserpine;
Make not your rosary of yew-berries,
  Nor let the beetle, nor the death-moth be
    Your mournful Psyche, nor the downy owl
A partner in your sorrow's mysteries;
  For shade to shade will come too drowsily,
    And drown the wakeful anguish of the soul.

But when the melancholy fit shall fall
  Sudden from heaven like a weeping cloud,
That fosters the droop-headed flowers all,
  And hides the green hill in an April shroud;

Then glut thy sorrow on a morning rose,
Or on the rainbow of the salt sand-wave,
Or on the wealth of globed peonies;
Or if thy mistress some rich anger shows,
Emprison her soft hand, and let her rave,
And feed deep, deep upon her peerless eyes.

She dwells with Beauty – Beauty that must die;
And Joy, whose hand is ever at his lips
Bidding adieu; and aching Pleasure nigh,
Turning to poison while the bee-mouth sips:
Ay, in the very temple of Delight
Veil'd Melancholy has her sovran shrine,
Though seen of none save him whose strenuous tongue
Can burst Joy's grape against his palate fine;
His soul shalt taste the sadness of her might,
And be among her cloudy trophies hung.

John Keats

Ode to a Nightingale

My heart aches, and a drowsy numbness pains
My sense, as though of hemlock I had drunk,
Or emptied some dull opiate to the drains
One minute past, and Lethe-wards had sunk:
'Tis not through envy of thy happy lot,
But being too happy in thine happiness –
That thou, light-wingèd Dryad of the trees,
In some melodious plot

Of beechen green, and shadows numberless,
Singest of summer in full-throated ease.

O, for a draught of vintage! that hath been
Cool'd a long age in the deep-delved earth,
Tasting of Flora and the country green,
Dance, and Provençal song, and sunburnt mirth!
O for a beaker full of the warm South,
Full of the true, the blushful Hippocrene,
With beaded bubbles winking at the brim,
And purple-stained mouth;
That I might drink, and leave the world unseen,
And with thee fade away into the forest dim:

Fade far away, dissolve, and quite forget
What thou among the leaves hast never known,
The weariness, the fever, and the fret
Here, where men sit and hear each other groan;
Where palsy shakes a few, sad, last grey hairs,
Where youth grows pale, and spectre-thin, and dies;
Where but to think is to be full of sorrow
And leaden-eyed despairs,
Where Beauty cannot keep her lustrous eyes,
Or new Love pine at them beyond tomorrow.

Away! away! for I will fly to thee,
Not charioted by Bacchus and his pards,
But on the viewless wings of Poesy,
Though the dull brain perplexes and retards:
Already with thee! tender is the night,

And haply the Queen-Moon is on her throne,
Cluster'd around by all her starry Fays;
But here there is no light,
Save what from heaven is with the breezes blown
Through verdurous glooms and winding mossy ways.

I cannot see what flowers are at my feet,
Nor what soft incense hangs upon the boughs,
But, in embalmed darkness, guess each sweet
Wherewith the seasonable month endows
The grass, the thicket, and the fruit-tree wild;
White hawthorn, and the pastoral eglantine;
Fast-fading violets cover'd up in leaves;
And mid-May's eldest child,
The coming musk-rose, full of dewy wine,
The murmurous haunt of flies on summer eves.

Darkling I listen; and, for many a time
I have been half in love with easeful Death,
Call'd him soft names in many a mused rhyme,
To take into the air my quiet breath;
Now more than ever seems it rich to die,
To cease upon the midnight with no pain,
While thou art pouring forth thy soul abroad
In such an ecstasy!
Still wouldst thou sing, and I have ears in vain –
To thy high requiem become a sod.

Thou wast not born for death, immortal Bird!
No hungry generations tread thee down;

The voice I hear this passing night was heard
  In ancient days by emperor and clown:
Perhaps the self-same song that found a path
  Through the sad heart of Ruth, when, sick for home,
    She stood in tears amid the alien corn;
        The same that ofttimes hath
  Charm'd magic casements, opening on the foam
    Of perilous seas, in faery lands forlorn.

Forlorn! the very word is like a bell
  To toll me back from thee to my sole self!
Adieu! the fancy cannot cheat so well
  As she is famed to do, deceiving elf.
Adieu! adieu! thy plaintive anthem fades
  Past the near meadows, over the still stream,
    Up the hill-side; and now 'tis buried deep
        In the next valley-glades:
  Was it a vision, or a waking dream?
    Fled is that music: – do I wake or sleep?

John Keats

Ode to the Clitoris

Little eagerness;
flower-girl basket of soft thorn
and petal, near the entry of the satin
column of the inner aisle;
scout in the wilderness; wild ear
which perks up; tender dowser, which points;

imp; shape-shifter; bench-pressing biceps of a
teeny goddess who is buff; lotus
for grief; weentsy Minerva who springs
full-armored, molten – I did not know you,
at seven, I thought you were God's way
of addressing me, when I kept swinging
on the rings, after the bell had rung . . .
He didn't use his words, he used
you to get my attention, he wrenched me
and wrenched me, then, in six or seven
wrenches of my body and brain, you
the living wrench which winched the wrenches.
Later, you would do that without God –
with boys, with kisses, and later you'd become
an instrument of love's music. Today,
I saw your portrait for the first time, your
dorsal vein, your artery, your
cavernous body, your vestibular bulb,
your suspensory ligament – and I
could see how evolution got
the idea from you, to invent an organ
something like you but a lot bigger.
You were named for a Greek hill, *klinein*,
a slope – you are the ground of our being, the tiny
figure of the human, the hooded stranger who
comes to the door, and if we bless her we will be blessed.

Sharon Olds

Ode to the Hymen

I don't know when you came into being,
inside me, when I was inside my mother –
maybe when the involuntary
muscles were setting, like rose jello.
I love to think of you then, so whole, so
impervious, you and the clitoris as
safe as the lives in which you were housed, they would have
had to kill both my mother and me
to get at either of you. I love her, at this
moment, as the big fortress around me, the
matronhead around the sweetmeat
of my maidenhead. I don't know who
invented you – to keep a girl's inwards
clean and well-cupboarded. Dear wall,
dear gate, dear stile, dear Dutch door, not a
cat-slap nor a swinging door
but a one-time piñata. How many places in the
body were made to be destroyed
once? You were very sturdy, weren't you,
you took your job seriously – I'd never
felt such pain – you were the hourglass lady
the magician saws in two. I was proud of you,
turning to a cupful of the bright arterial
ingredient. And how lucky we were,
you and I, that we got to choose
when, and with whom, and where, and why – plush
pincushion, somehow related
to statues that wept. It happened on the rug

of a borrowed living room, but I felt
as if we were in Diana's woods –
he, and I, and you, together,
or as if we were where the magma from the core of the
earth burst up through the floor of the sea.
Thank you for your life and death,
thank you for your flower-girl walk
before me, throwing down your scarlet
petals. It would be years before
I married – years before I carried, within me,
a tiny, baby hymen, near the
eggs with other teentsy hymens
within them – but you unscrolled the carpet,
leading me into the animal life
of a woman. You were a sort of blood
mother to me: first you held me
close, for eighteen years, and then
you let me go.

Sharon Olds

'Of comfort no man speak'

Of comfort no man speak:
Let's talk of graves, of worms, and epitaphs;
Make dust our paper and with rainy eyes
Write sorrow on the bosom of the earth,
Let's choose executors and talk of wills:
And yet not so, for what can we bequeath
Save our deposed bodies to the ground?
Our lands, our lives and all are Bolingbroke's,

And nothing can we call our own but death
And that small model of the barren earth
Which serves as paste and cover to our bones.
For God's sake, let us sit upon the ground
And tell sad stories of the death of kings;
How some have been deposed; some slain in war,
Some haunted by the ghosts they have deposed;
Some poison'd by their wives: some sleeping kill'd;
All murder'd: for within the hollow crown
That rounds the mortal temples of a king
Keeps Death his court and there the antic sits,
Scoffing his state and grinning at his pomp,
Allowing him a breath, a little scene,
To monarchize, be fear'd and kill with looks,
Infusing him with self and vain conceit,
As if this flesh which walls about our life,
Were brass impregnable, and humor'd thus
Comes at the last and with a little pin
Bores through his castle wall, and farewell king!
Cover your heads and mock not flesh and blood
With solemn reverence: throw away respect,
Tradition, form and ceremonious duty,
For you have but mistook me all this while:
I live with bread like you, feel want,
Taste grief, need friends: subjected thus,
How can you say to me, I am a king?

King Richard in Richard II, *William Shakespeare*

Old Love and New

In my heart the old love
Struggled with the new,
It was ghostly waking
All night through.

Dear things, kind things
That my old love said,
Ranged themselves reproachfully
Round my bed.

But I could not heed them,
For I seemed to see
Dark eyes of my new love
Fixed on me.

Old love, old love,
How can I be true?
Shall I be faithless to myself
Or to you?

Sara Teasdale

On His Blindness

When I consider how my light is spent
  Ere half my days in this dark world and wide,
  And that one Talent which is death to hide,
  Lodg'd with me useless, though my soul more bent
To serve therewith my Maker, and present

My true account, lest He returning chide,
'Doth God exact day-labour, light denied?'
I fondly ask. But Patience to prevent
That murmur, soon replies, 'God doth not need
Either man's work or his own gifts. Who best
Bear his mild yoke, they serve him best. His state
Is kingly. Thousands at his bidding speed
And post o'er land and ocean without rest:
They also serve who only stand and wait.'

John Milton

On Seeing the First Flasher

Grey-coated, solitary stranger, hail!
Thou harbinger of summer's lusty days,
tracing through country parks thy mazy trail,
or lingering by some brook to catch the gaze
of passing schoolgirl, who, with scornful eye,
remarks upon thy manhood's lack of length,
then vanishing, before her angry cry
shall summon to her aid the studded strength
of forty skinheads, or, with deadly aim,
her dainty foot shall plunge into thy crotch –
when shalt thou find a partner to thy game,
a maid whose pleasure is to stand and watch?
As soon, alas, as poets shall enthrall
commuter crowds, or fill the Albert Hall.

Vicki Raymond

'Once I pass'd through a populous city'

Once I pass'd through a populous city, imprinting my brain, for
  future use, with its shows, architecture, customs, and traditions;
Yet now, of all that city, I remember only a woman I casually met
  there, who detain'd me for love of me;
Day by day and night by night we were together – all else has long
  been forgotten by me;
I remember, I say, only that woman who passionately clung to me;
Again we wander – we love – we separate again;
Again she holds me by the hand – I must not go!
I see her close beside me, with silent lips, sad and tremulous.

Walt Whitman

Once in a Lifetime, Snow

For Chris and Mary Sharah

Winters at home brought wind,
black frost and raw
grey rain in barbed-wire fields,
but never more

until the day my uncle
rose at dawn
and stepped outside – to find
his paddocks gone,

his cattle to their hocks
in ghostly ground

and unaccustomed light
for miles around.

And he stopped short, and gazed
lit from below,
and half his wrinkles vanished
murmuring *Snow*.

A man of farm and fact
he stared to see
the facts of weather raised
to a mystery

white on the world he knew
and all he owned.
Snow? Here? he mused. I see.
High time I learned.

Here, guessing what he meant
had much to do
with that black earth dread old men
are given to,

he stooped to break the sheer
crust with delight
at finding the cold unknown
so deeply bright,

at feeling it take his prints
so softly deep,

as if it thought he knew
enough to sleep,

or else so little he
might seek to shift
its weight of wintry light
by a single drift,

perceiving this much, he scuffed
his slippered feet
and scooped a handful up
to taste, and eat

in memory of the fact
that even he
might not have seen the end
of reality . . .

Then, turning, he tiptoed in
to a bedroom, smiled,
and wakened a murmuring child
and another child.

Les Murray

One need not be a chamber to be haunted

One need not be a chamber to be haunted,
One need not be a house;
The brain has corridors surpassing
Material place.

Far safer, of a midnight meeting
External ghost,
Than its interior confronting
That cooler host.

Far safer through an abbey gallop,
The stones a-chase,
Than, unarmed, one's own self encounter
In lonesome place.

Ourself behind ourself, concealed,
Should startle most;
Assassin, hid in our apartment,
Be horror's least.

The body carries a revolver,
He bolts the door,
O'erlooking a superior spectre
Or more.

Emily Dickinson

1:30 AM

The light went out in Unit 506 on the 18th floor.
Across
on the 19th floor, the light in 706 went out soon after.

Sleep well.
Get to know each other tomorrow.

Ko Un, translated by Clare You and Richard Silberg

'Or I shall live your epitaph to make'

Or I shall live your epitaph to make,
Or you survive when I in earth am rotten,
From hence your memory death cannot take,
Although in me each part will be forgotten.
Your name from hence immortal life shall have,
Though I, once gone, to all the world must die:
The earth can yield me but a common grave
When you entombed in men's eyes shall lie.
Your monument shall be my gentle verse,
Which eyes not yet created shall o'er-read,
And tongues to be your being shall rehearse
When all the breathers of this world are dead;
   You still shall live – such virtue hath my pen –
   Where breath most breathes, even in the mouths of men.

Sonnet 81, William Shakespeare

Ordinance on Arrival

Welcome to you
who have managed to get here.
It's been a terrible trip;
you should be happy you have survived it.
Statistics prove that not many do.
You would like a bath, a hot meal,
a good night's sleep. Some of you
need medical attention.
None of this is available.
These things have always been

in short supply; now
they are impossible to obtain.

                    This is not
a temporary situation;
it is permanent.
Our condolences on your disappointment.
It is not our responsibility
everything you have heard about this place
is false. It is not our fault
you have been deceived,
ruined your health getting here.
For reasons beyond our control
there is no vehicle out.

Naomi Lazard

Ordinary People's Lithograph

Heavy, huge, honey-filled figs weighted down
the blazing noonday. The man hitched his horse to the fig tree.
He ate figs and licked his fingers. He stripped –
fierce, solitary, hirsute. He plunged into the river.
The two daughters of the field guard, complicitous, silent,
were watching from behind the willows. Inside their mouths
they felt the tiny seeds from the figs
that the horseman had eaten a short while ago. Then,
right above their heads, a bird let out
a wicked cry. The girls, alarmed, ran off.
The man emerged from the water all gold and got dressed.

Yannis Ritsos, translated by Edmund Keeley

The Oxen

Christmas Eve, and twelve of the clock.
    'Now they are all on their knees,'
An elder said as we sat in a flock
    By the embers in hearthside ease.

We pictured the meek mild creatures where
    They dwelt in their strawy pen,
Nor did it occur to one of us there
    To doubt they were kneeling then.

So fair a fancy few would weave
    In these years! Yet, I feel,
If someone said on Christmas Eve,
    'Come; see the oxen kneel,

'In the lonely barton by yonder coomb
    Our childhood used to know,'
I should go with him in the gloom,
    Hoping it might be so.

Thomas Hardy

Ozymandias

I met a traveller from an antique land,
Who said – 'Two vast and trunkless legs of stone
Stand in the desert . . . Near them, on the sand,
Half sunk a shattered visage lies, whose frown,
And wrinkled lip, and sneer of cold command,

Tell that its sculptor well those passions read
Which yet survive, stamped on these lifeless things,
The hand that mocked them, and the heart that fed;
And on the pedestal, these words appear:
"My name is Ozymandias, King of Kings,
Look on my Works ye Mighty, and despair!"
No thing beside remains. Round the decay
Of that colossal wreck, boundless and bare
The lone and level sands stretch far away.' –

Percy Bysshe Shelley

The Panther

In the Jardin des Plantes, Paris

His vision, from the constantly passing bars,
has grown so weary that it cannot hold
anything else. It seems to him there are
a thousand bars; and behind the bars, no world.

As he paces in cramped circles, over and over,
the movement of his powerful soft strides
is like a ritual dance around a center
in which a mighty will stands paralysed.

Only at times, the curtain of the pupils
lifts, quietly–. An image enters in,
rushes down through the tensed, arrested muscles,
plunges into the heart and is gone.

Rainer Maria Rilke, translated by Stephen Mitchell

The Past

I used to see her in a sandwich shop
On Brunswick Road. She made me toasted cheese.
I liked her ponytail and gypsy scarf,

I liked her running shoes and sawn off jeans,
I liked a little bruise beneath her knee,
And so my sandwiches got high with ham:

They dripped with mayonnaise and frayed with sprouts
While I just gazed at her and murmured, 'Swiss;
Tomatoes; onion; lettuce; pepper; salt.'

I had to ask her out: my sandwiches
Had got too big to eat. We lived off Smith,
I did Philosophy, and wrote all day –

'Is Death Impossible?' – and jumped on her
The moment she was home from work at five.
Our neighbour was a Physicist, and yarned

Of flavoured quarks and tachions, those things
That speed into the past, and wrote SF
About a 'Tachion Machine': a burst

Would put you with the apes or dinosaurs
While very few would nudge you back a week.
'What would you like on that?' Susanna asked

When kissing me in bed. 'The lot,' I'd say.
Some nights I'd wake up scared to hell by time.
Susanna was still there in white whipped sheets,

And sleepily I'd hold her tight, and hold
Our evening tight, and whisper to the dark,
'Release a tachion – just one, just one.'

Kevin Hart

Pied Beauty

Glory be to God for dappled things –
  For skies of couple-colour as a brinded cow;
    For rose-moles all in stipple upon trout that swim;
Fresh-firecoal chestnut-falls; finches' wings;
  Landscape plotted and pieced – fold, fallow, and plough;
    And áll trádes, their gear and tackle and trim.

All things counter, original, spare, strange;
  Whatever is fickle, freckled (who knows how?)
    With swift, slow; sweet, sour; adazzle, dim;
He fathers-forth whose beauty is past change:
        Praise him.

Gerard Manley Hopkins

Pillow Talk

The hot midsummer nights I whisper
assignations, trysts, heather beds
I'd like to lay you down in, remote beaches

we could escape to, watch
bonfire sparks mix with stars.
I want you to stay alive till we two
meet again, to hold the line, to ignore
the gossip traded about me in the marketplace.
I fall back on cliché, the small
change of an adulterous summer,
plots of half-hatched movies, theories
of forked lightning, how you make
the soles of my feet burn when I come.

What you don't hear is the other voice
when she speaks through me
beyond human pity and mercy. She wants you.
Put her eye on you the first time
she saw you. And I'm powerless,
a slave to her whim. She shall
have you. What can I do
when she speaks of white river stones,
elfin grots, her sacred birds?
I know she once tore a man apart,
limb from limb with her bare hands
in some rite in her bloody past.
My stomach turns at the hot
relentless stench of her history.

Nights you stare out
panic-stricken through the mask.
I think you may have heard her speak:
you realize that you ride a demon
that the dark has no end to it.

Though I mean you no grief,
I cannot vouchsafe her intent. I fear
not all my healing arts can salve
the wound she has in store for you.

Paula Meehan

A Pity, We Were Such a Good Invention

They amputated
Your thighs off my hips.
As far as I'm concerned
They are all surgeons. All of them.

They dismantled us
Each from the other.
As far as I'm concerned
They are all engineers. All of them.

A pity. We were such a good
And loving invention.
An aeroplane made from a man and wife.
Wings and everything.
We hovered a little above the earth.

We even flew a little.

Yehuda Amichai, translated by Assia Gutmann

The Planter's Daughter

When night stirred at sea
And the fire brought a crowd in,
They say that her beauty
Was music in mouth
And few in the candlelight
Thought her too proud,
For the house of the planter
Is known by the trees.

Men that had seen her
Drank deep and were silent,
The women were speaking
Wherever she went –
As a bell that is rung
Or a wonder told shyly,
And O she was the Sunday
In every week.

Austin Clarke

Pleasures

First look from morning's window
The rediscovered book
Fascinated faces
Snow, the change of the seasons
The newspaper
The dog
Dialectics

Showering, swimming
Old music
Comfortable shoes
Comprehension
New music
Writing, planting
Traveling
Singing
Being friendly

Bertolt Brecht, translated by Marcy Jarvis

A Poem on the Assassination of Robert F. Kennedy

Trees are never felled . . . in summer . . . Not when the fruit . . .
is yet to be borne . . . Never before the promise . . . is fulfilled . . .
Not when their cooling shade . . . has yet to comfort . . .

Yet there are those . . . unheeding of nature . . . indifferent to
ecology . . . ignorant of need . . . who . . . with ax and sharpened
saw . . . would . . . in boots . . . step forth damaging . . .

Not the tree . . . for it falls . . . But those who would . . . in
summer's heat . . . or winter's cold . . . contemplate . . . the
beauty . . .

Nikki Giovanni

A Poison Tree

I was angry with my friend;
I told my wrath, my wrath did end.
I was angry with my foe:
I told it not, my wrath did grow.

And I waterd it in fears,
Night & morning with my tears:
And I sunned it with smiles,
And with soft deceitful wiles.

And it grew both day and night.
Till it bore an apple bright.
And my foe beheld it shine,
And he knew that it was mine.

And into my garden stole,
When the night had veild the pole;
In the morning glad I see;
My foe outstretched beneath the tree.

William Blake

Postscript

And some time make the time to drive out west
Into County Clare, along the Flaggy Shore,
In September or October, when the wind
And the light are working off each other
So that the ocean on one side is wild
With foam and glitter, and inland among stones

The surface of a slate-grey lake is lit
By the earthed lightning of a flock of swans,
Their feathers roughed and ruffling, white on white,
Their fully grown headstrong-looking heads
Tucked or cresting or busy underwater.
Useless to think you'll park and capture it
More thoroughly. You are neither here nor there,
A hurry through which known and strange things pass
As big soft buffetings come at the car sideways
And catch the heart off guard and blow it open.

Seamus Heaney

Prayer Before Birth

I am not yet born; O hear me.
Let not the bloodsucking bat or the rat or the stoat or the
club-footed ghoul come near me.

I am not yet born, console me.
I fear that the human race may with tall walls wall me,
with strong drugs dope me, with wise lies lure me,
on black racks rack me, in blood-baths roll me.

I am not yet born; provide me
With water to dandle me, grass to grow for me, trees to talk
to me, sky to sing to me, birds and a white light
in the back of my mind to guide me.

I am not yet born; forgive me
For the sins that in me the world shall commit, my words

when they speak me, my thoughts when they think me,
my treason engendered by traitors beyond me,
my life when they murder by means of my
hands, my death when they live me.

I am not yet born; rehearse me
In the parts I must play and the cues I must take when
old men lecture me, bureaucrats hector me, mountains
frown at me, lovers laugh at me, the white
waves call me to folly and the desert calls
me to doom and the beggar refuses
my gift and my children curse me.

I am not yet born; O hear me,
Let not the man who is beast or who thinks he is God
come near me.

I am not yet born; O fill me
With strength against those who would freeze my
humanity, would dragoon me into a lethal automaton,
would make me a cog in a machine, a thing with
one face, a thing, and against all those
who would dissipate my entirety, would
blow me like thistledown hither and
thither or hither and thither
like water held in the
hands would spill me.

Let them not make me a stone and let them not spill me.
Otherwise kill me.

Louis MacNeice

Proud Songsters

The thrushes sing as the sun is going,
And the finches whistle in ones and pairs,
And as it gets dark loud nightingales
In bushes
Pipe, as they can when April wears,
As if all Time were theirs.

These are brand new birds of twelvemonths' growing,
Which a year ago, or less than twain,
No finches were, nor nightingales,
Nor thrushes,
But only particles of grain,
And earth, and air, and rain.

Thomas Hardy

'The quality of mercy is not strained'

The quality of mercy is not strained.
It droppeth as the gentle rain from heaven
Upon the place beneath. It is twice blessed:
It blesseth him that gives and him that takes.
'Tis mightiest in the mightiest. It becomes
The throned monarch better than his crown.
His scepter shows the force of temporal power,
The attribute to awe and majesty
Wherein doth sit the dread and fear of kings,
But mercy is above this sceptered sway.
It is enthroned in the hearts of kings.

It is an attribute to God himself.
And earthly power doth then show likest God's
When mercy seasons justice.

Portia in **The Merchant of Venice,** *William Shakespeare*

Quarantine

In the worst hour of the worst season
    of the worst year of a whole people
a man set out from the workhouse with his wife.
He was walking – they were both walking – north.

She was sick with famine fever and could not keep up.
    He lifted her and put her on his back.
He walked like that west and west and north.
Until at nightfall under freezing stars they arrived.

In the morning they were both found dead.
    Of cold. Of hunger. Of the toxins of a whole history.
But her feet were held against his breastbone.
The last heat of his flesh was his last gift to her.

Let no love poem ever come to this threshold.
    There is no place here for the inexact
praise of the easy graces and sensuality of the body.
There is only time for this merciless inventory:

Their death together in the winter of 1847.
    Also what they suffered. How they lived.

And what there is between a man and woman.
And in which darkness it can best be proved.

Eavan Boland

The Railroad Station

My nonarrival in the city of N.
took place on the dot.

You'd been alerted
in my unmailed letter.

You were able not to be there
at the agreed-upon time.

The train pulled up at Platform 3.
A lot of people got out.

My absence joined the throng
as it made its way toward the exit.

Several women rushed
to take my place
in all that rush.

Somebody ran up to one of them.
I didn't know him,
but she recognized him
immediately.

While they kissed
with not our lips,
a suitcase disappeared,
not mine.

The railroad station in the city of N.
passed its exam
in objective existence
with flying colors.

The whole remained in place.
Particulars scurried
along the designated tracks.

Even a rendezvous
took place as planned.

Beyond the reach
of our presence.

In the paradise lost
of probability.

Somewhere else.
Somewhere else.
How these little words ring.

Wislawa Szymborska, translated by Stanislaw Baranczak and Clare Cavanagh

Recalling the Past at T'ung Pass

As if gathered together,
the peaks of the ranges.
As if raging,
the waves on these banks.
Winding along
these mountains & rivers,
the road to the T'ung Pass.
I look west
& hesitant I lament
here where
opposing armies passed through.
Palaces
of countless rulers
now but dust.
Empires rise:
people suffer.
Empires fall:
people suffer.

Chang Yang-Hao, 'made new' by C. H. Knock and Gary Gach

Resumé

Razors pain you;
Rivers are damp;
Acids stain you;
And drugs cause cramp.
Guns aren't lawful;
Nooses give;

Gas smells awful;
You might as well live.

Dorothy Parker

Riddle 25 from the Anglo-Saxon Riddle Hoard

I am a wonderful help to women
The hope of something to come. I harm
No citizen except my slayer.
Rooted I stand on a high bed.
I am shaggy below. Sometimes the beautiful
Peasant's daughter, an eager-armed,
Proud woman grabs my body
Rushes my red skin, holds me hard,
Claims my head. The curly haired
Woman who catches me fast will feel
Our meeting. Her eye will be wet.

Anonymous

Rider's Song

Córdoba,
Far and lonely,

Black pony, fat moon,
And olives in my pocket:
Although I know the roads
I'll never reach Córdoba.

Across the plain, against the wind
Black pony, red moon.
And death is watching me
From the towers of Córdoba.

Oh, the long, long road
Oh, my brave pony
Oh, death has me covered
Before I reach Córdoba.

Córdoba,
Far and lonely.

Federico García Lorca, translated by Alex McGregor and Paul Kelly

'Ring out, wild bells'

Ring out, wild bells, to the wild sky,
  The flying cloud, the frosty light:
  The year is dying in the night;
Ring out, wild bells, and let him die.

Ring out the old, ring in the new,
  Ring, happy bells, across the snow:
  The year is going, let him go;
Ring out the false, ring in the true.

Ring out the grief that saps the mind,
  For those that here we see no more;
  Ring out the feud of rich and poor,
Ring in redress to all mankind.

Ring out a slowly dying cause,
And ancient forms of party strife;
Ring in the nobler modes of life,
With sweeter manners, purer laws.

Ring out the want, the care, the sin,
The faithless coldness of the times;
Ring out, ring out thy mournful rhymes,
But ring the fuller minstrel in.

Ring out false pride in place and blood,
The civic slander and the spite;
Ring in the love of truth and right,
Ring in the common love of good.

Ring out old shapes of foul disease,
Ring out the narrowing lust of gold;
Ring out the thousand wars of old,
Ring in the thousand years of peace.

Ring in the valiant man and free,
The larger heart, the kindlier hand;
Ring out the darkness of the land,
Ring in the Christ that is to be.

In Memoriam, *106, Alfred, Lord Tennyson*

The Rubáiyát of Omar Khayyám

VII

Come, fill the Cup, and in the Fire of Spring
The Winter Garment of Repentance fling:
The Bird of Time has but a little way
To fly – and Lo! the Bird is on the Wing.

XII

A Book of Verses underneath the Bough,
A Jug of Wine, a Loaf of Bread – and Thou
Beside me singing in the Wilderness
Oh, Wilderness were Paradise enow!

XXII

For some we loved, the loveliest and the best
That from his Vintage rolling Time hath pressed,
Have drunk their Cup a Round or two before,
And one by one crept silently to rest.

XXIV

Ah, make the most of what we yet may spend,
Before we too into the Dust descend;
Dust into Dust, and under Dust to lie,
Sans Wine, sans Song, sans Singer, and – sans End!

LXXI

The Moving Finger writes, and, having writ,
Moves on; nor all your Piety nor Wit
Shall lure it back to cancel half a Line,
Nor all your Tears wash out a Word of it.

Omar Khayyám, translated by Edward FitzGerald

Said Hanrahan

'We'll all be rooned,' said Hanrahan,
In accents most forlorn,
Outside the church, ere Mass began,
One frosty Sunday morn.

The congregation stood about,
Coat-collars to the ears,
And talked of stock, and crops, and drought,
As it had done for years.

'It's lookin' crook,' said Daniel Croke;
'Bedad, it's cruke, me lad,
For never since the banks went broke
Has seasons been so bad.'

'It's dry, all right,' said young O'Neil,
With which astute remark
He squatted down upon his heel
And chewed a piece of bark.

And so around the chorus ran
'It's keepin' dry, no doubt.'
'We'll all be rooned,' said Hanrahan,
'Before the year is out.

'The crops are done; ye'll have your work
To save one bag of grain;
From here way out to Back-o'-Bourke
They're singin' out for rain.

'They're singin' out for rain,' he said,
'And all the tanks are dry.'
The congregation scratched its head,
And gazed around the sky.

'There won't be grass, in any case,
Enough to feed an ass;
There's not a blade on Casey's place
As I came down to Mass.'

'If rain don't come this month,' said Dan,
And cleared his throat to speak –
'We'll all be rooned,' said Hanrahan,
'If rain don't come this week.'

A heavy silence seemed to steal
On all at this remark;
And each man squatted on his heel,
And chewed a piece of bark.

'We want a inch of rain, we do,'
O'Neil observed at last;
But Croke 'maintained' we wanted two
To put the danger past.

'If we don't get three inches, man,
Or four to break this drought,
We'll all be rooned,' said Hanrahan,
'Before the year is out.'

In God's good time down came the rain;
And all the afternoon
On iron roof and window-pane
It drummed a homely tune.

And through the night it pattered still,
And lightsome, gladsome elves
On dripping spout and window-sill
Kept talking to themselves.

It pelted, pelted all day long,
A-singing at its work,
Till every heart took up the song
Way out to Back-o'-Bourke.

And every creek a banker ran,
And dams filled overtop;
'We'll all be rooned,' said Hanrahan,
'If this rain doesn't stop.'

And stop it did, in God's good time;
And spring came in to fold
A mantle o'er the hills sublime
Of green and pink and gold.

And days went by on dancing feet,
With harvest-hopes immense,
And laughing eyes beheld the wheat
Nid-nodding o'er the fence.

And, oh, the smiles on every face,
As happy lad and lass
Through grass knee-deep on Casey's place
Went riding down to Mass.

While round the church in clothes genteel
Discoursed the men of mark,
And each man squatted on his heel,
And chewed his piece of bark.

'There'll be bush-fires for sure, me man,
There will, without a doubt;
We'll all be rooned,' said Hanrahan,
'Before the year is out.'

P. J. Hartigan

Sailing to Byzantium

That is no country for old men. The young
In one another's arms, birds in the trees,
– Those dying generations – at their song,
The salmon-falls, the mackerel-crowded seas,
Fish, flesh, or fowl, commend all summer long
Whatever is begotten, born, and dies.
Caught in that sensual music all neglect
Monuments of unageing intellect.

An aged man is but a paltry thing,
A tattered coat upon a stick, unless
Soul clap its hands and sing, and louder sing
For every tatter in its mortal dress,
Nor is there singing school but studying
Monuments of its own magnificence;
And therefore I have sailed the seas and come
To the holy city of Byzantium.

O sages standing in God's holy fire
As in the gold mosaic of a wall,
Come from the holy fire, perne in a gyre,
And be the singing-masters of my soul.
Consume my heart away; sick with desire
And fastened to a dying animal
It knows not what it is; and gather me
Into the artifice of eternity.

Once out of nature I shall never take
My bodily form from any natural thing,

But such a form as Grecian goldsmiths make
Of hammered gold and gold enamelling
To keep a drowsy Emperor awake;
Or set upon a golden bough to sing
To lords and ladies of Byzantium
Of what is past, or passing, or to come.

W. B. Yeats

The Second Coming

Turning and turning in the widening gyre
The falcon cannot hear the falconer;
Things fall apart; the centre cannot hold;
Mere anarchy is loosed upon the world,
The blood-dimmed tide is loosed, and everywhere
The ceremony of innocence is drowned;
The best lack all conviction, while the worst
Are full of passionate intensity.

Surely some revelation is at hand;
Surely the Second Coming is at hand.
The Second Coming! Hardly are those words out
When a vast image out of *Spiritus Mundi*
Troubles my sight: somewhere in sands of the desert
A shape with lion body and the head of a man,
A gaze blank and pitiless as the sun,
Is moving its slow thighs, while all about it
Reel shadows of the indignant desert birds.
The darkness drops again; but now I know
That twenty centuries of stony sleep

Were vexed to nightmare by a rocking cradle,
And what rough beast, its hour come round at last,
Slouches towards Bethlehem to be born?

W. B. Yeats

Seduction Poem

I want the slew of muscle, a less
cerebral meeting place; no word
but your male shout, the shirred
unpublic face and honest skin
crying to me, yes,
the mouthless, eyeless tenderness
crying to be let in.

Unbutton all your weight, like a bird
flying the night's starred nakedness:
put down your grammatical tongue, undress
your correct and social skin:
come white and absurd
all your language one word
crying to be let in.

Alison Croggon

Sermon on the Mount

And seeing the multitudes, he went up into a mountain: and when he was set, his disciples came unto him:
And he opened his mouth, and taught them, saying,

Blessed are the poor in spirit: for theirs is the kingdom of heaven.
Blessed are they that mourn: for they shall be comforted.
Blessed are the meek: for they shall inherit the earth.
Blessed are they which do hunger and thirst after righteousness: for they shall be filled.
Blessed are the merciful: for they shall obtain mercy.
Blessed are the pure in heart: for they shall see God.
Blessed are the peacemakers: for they shall be called the children of God.
Blessed are they which are persecuted for righteousness' sake: for theirs is the kingdom of heaven.
Blessed are ye, when men shall revile you, and persecute you, and shall say all manner of evil against you falsely, for my sake.
Rejoice, and be exceeding glad: for great is your reward in heaven: for so persecuted they the prophets which were before you.
Ye are the salt of the earth: but if the salt have lost his savour, wherewith shall it be salted? it is thenceforth good for nothing, but to be cast out, and to be trodden under foot of men.
Ye are the light of the world. A city that is set on an hill cannot be hid.
Neither do men light a candle, and put it under a bushel, but on a candlestick; and it giveth light unto all that are in the house.
Let your light so shine before men, that they may see your good works, and glorify your Father which is in heaven.
Think not that I am come to destroy the law, or the prophets: I am not come to destroy, but to fulfil.
For verily I say unto you, Till heaven and earth pass, one jot or one tittle shall in no wise pass from the law, till all be fulfilled.

Matthew 5:1–18, King James Bible

Sex Without Love

How do they do it, the ones who make love
without love? Beautiful as dancers,
gliding over each other like ice-skaters
over the ice, fingers hooked
inside each other's bodies, faces
red as steak, wine, wet as the
children at birth whose mothers are going to
give them away. How do they come to the
come to the   come to the   God   come to the
still waters, and not love
the one who came there with them, light
rising slowly as steam off their joined
skin? These are the true religious,
the purists, the pros, the ones who will not
accept a false Messiah, love the
priest instead of the God. They do not
mistake the lover for their own pleasure,
they are like great runners – they know they are alone
with the road surface, the cold, the wind,
the fit of their shoes, their over-all cardio-
vascular health – just factors, like the partner
in the bed, and not the truth, which is the
single body alone in the universe
against its own best time.

Sharon Olds

'Shall I compare thee to a summer's day?'

Shall I compare thee to a summer's day?
Thou art more lovely and more temperate:
Rough winds do shake the darling buds of May,
And summer's lease hath all too short a date:
Sometime too hot the eye of heaven shines,
And often is his gold complexion dimm'd;
And every fair from fair sometime declines,
By chance or nature's changing course untrimm'd:
But thy eternal summer shall not fade
Nor lose possession of that fair thou owest;
Nor shall Death brag thou wanderest in his shade,
When in eternal lines to time thou growest:
    So long as men can breathe, or eyes can see,
    So long lives this, and this gives life to thee.

Sonnet 18, William Shakespeare

She Hears the Storm

There was a time in former years
    While my rooftree was his
When I should have been distressed by fears
    At such a night as this!

I should have murmured anxiously,
    'The prickling rain strikes cold;
His road is bare of hedge or tree,
    And he is getting old.'

But now the fitful chimney-roar,
    The drone of Thorncombe trees,
The Froom in flood upon the moor,
    The mud of Mellstock Leaze,

The candle slanting sooty-wick'd,
    The thuds upon the thatch,
The eaves drops on the window flicked,
    The clanking garden-hatch,

And what they mean to wayfarers,
    I scarcely heed or mind;
He has won that storm-tight roof of hers
    Which Earth grants all her kind.

Thomas Hardy

She Walks in Beauty

She walks in beauty, like the night
Of cloudless climes and starry skies;
And all that's best of dark and bright
Meet in her aspect and her eyes;
Thus mellowed to that tender light
Which heaven to gaudy day denies.

One shade the more, one ray the less,
Had half impaired the nameless grace
Which waves in every raven tress,
Or softly lightens o'er her face;

Where thoughts serenely sweet express,
How pure, how dear their dwelling-place.

And on that cheek, and o'er that brow,
So soft, so calm, yet eloquent,
The smiles that win, the tints that glow,
But tell of days in goodness spent,
A mind at peace with all below,
A heart whose love is innocent!

George Gordon, Lord Byron

Shooting the Dogs

There wasn't much else we could do
that final day on the farm.
We couldn't take them with us into town,
no one round the district needed them
and the new people had their own.
It was one of those things.

You sometimes hear of dogs
who know they're about to be put down
and who look up along the barrel of the rifle
into responsible eyes that never forget
that look and so on,
but our dogs didn't seem to have a clue.

They only stopped for a short while
to look at the Bedford stacked with furniture
not hay

and then cleared off towards the swamp,
plunging through the thick paspalum
noses up, like speedboats.

They weren't without their faults.
The young one liked to terrorize the chooks
and eat the eggs.
Whenever he started doing this
we'd let him have an egg full of chilli paste
and then the chooks would get some peace.

The old one's weakness was rolling in dead sheep.
Sometimes after this he'd sit outside
the kitchen window at dinner time.
The stink would hit us all at once
and we'd grimace like the young dog
discovering what was in the egg.

But basically they were pretty good.
They worked well and added life to the place.
I called them back enthusiastically
and got the old one as he bounded up
and then the young one as he shot off
for his life.

I buried them behind the tool shed.
It was one of the last things I did before we left.
Each time the gravel slid off the shovel
it sounded like something
trying to hang on by its nails.

Philip Hodgins

The Sick Rose

O Rose, thou art sick:
The invisible worm
That flies in the night,
In the howling storm,

Has found out thy bed
Of crimson joy;
And his dark secret love
Does thy life destroy.

William Blake

Sign of Love

Lesbia always speaks ill of me, never shuts up
about me: damn me if she doesn't love me.
What's the sign? Because it's the same with me: I'm
continually complaining, but damn me if I don't love her.

Catullus, translated by A. S. Kline

A Simple Story

A visiting conductor
    when I was seventeen,
took me back to his hotel room
    to cover the music scene.

I'd written a composition.
    Would wonders never cease –
here was a real musician
    prepared to hold my piece.

He spread my score on the counterpane
    with classic casualness,
and put one hand on the manuscript
    and the other down my dress.

It was hot as hell in The Windsor.
    I said I'd like a drink.
We talked across gin and grapefruit,
    and I heard the ice go clink

as I gazed at the lofty forehead
    of one who led the band,
and guessed at the hoarded sorrows
    no wife could understand.

I dreamed of a soaring passion
    as an egg might dream of flight,
while he read my crude sonata.
    If he'd said, 'That bar's not right,'

or, 'Have you thought of a coda?'
    or, 'Watch that first repeat,'
or, 'Modulate to the dominant,'
    he'd have had me at his feet.

But he shuffled it all together,
    and said, 'That's *lovely*, dear,'
as he put it down on the washstand
    in a way that made it clear

that I was no composer.
    And I being young and vain,
removed my lovely body
    from one who'd scorned my brain.

I swept off like Miss Virtue
    down dusty Roma Street,
and heard the goods trains whistle
    WHO? WHOOOOOO? in aching heat.

Gwen Harwood

'Since brass, nor stone, nor earth, nor boundless sea'

Since brass, nor stone, nor earth, nor boundless sea
But sad mortality o'er-sways their power,
How with this rage shall beauty hold a plea,
Whose action is no stronger than a flower?
O, how shall summer's honey breath hold out
Against the wrackful siege of batt'ring days,
When rocks impregnable are not so stout,
Nor gates of steel so strong, but Time decays?
O fearful meditation! Where, alack,
Shall Time's best jewel from Time's chest lie hid?
Or what strong hand can hold his swift foot back?
Or who his spoil of beauty can forbid?

O, none, unless this miracle have might,
That in black ink my love may still shine bright.

Sonnet 65, William Shakespeare

'Sing a song of sixpence'

Sing a song of sixpence,
A pocket full of rye,
Four and twenty blackbirds
Baked in a pie.

When the pie was opened
The birds began to sing –
Wasn't that a dainty dish
To set before the king?

The king was in the counting-house
Counting out his money,
The queen was in the parlor
Eating bread and honey,

The maid was in the garden
Hanging out the clothes.
Along came a blackbird
And snipped off her nose.

Sing a song of sixpence,
A pocket full of rye,
Four and twenty blackbirds
Baked in a pie.

When the pie was opened
The birds began to sing –
Wasn't that a dainty dish
To set before the king?

Anonymous

Sir from Biology

I cannot even remember
his face

he stood high above me
on long widely spread legs
I saw
a gold chain
ash-grey waistcoat
and thin neck
to which was pinned
a lifeless tie

he the first to show us
the leg of a dead frog
which touched by a needle
contracted suddenly

he led us
through a golden eyepiece
into the intimate life
of our ancestor
slipper

he brought
a dark grain
and said: a spore

through his encouragement
when ten
I became a father
when after a long wait
from a chestnut immersed in water
emerged a yellow sprout
and everything burst into song
all around

in the second year of the war
the rascals from history
killed sir from biology

if he went up to heaven –

perhaps he now is walking
down long sunrays
clad in grey stockings
with a great net
and green box
gaily flopping behind him

but if he had not gone up –

when on a forest path
I encounter a beetle struggling
on a heap of sand

I approach
shuffle my feet
and say
– good morning sir professor
would you allow me to assist –

carry him carefully
and long gaze after him
until he disappears
in the dark teachers' room
at the end of the corridor of leaves

Zbigniew Herbert, translated by Marcel Weyland

Song of Solomon

1

The song of songs, which is Solomon's.
Let him kiss me with the kisses of his mouth: for thy love is better than wine.
Because of the savour of thy good ointments thy name is as ointment poured forth, therefore do the virgins love thee.
Draw me, we will run after thee: the king hath brought me into his chambers: we will be glad and rejoice in thee, we will remember thy love more than wine: the upright love thee.
I am black, but comely, O ye daughters of Jerusalem, as the tents of Kedar, as the curtains of Solomon.
Look not upon me, because I am black, because the sun hath looked upon me: my mother's children were angry with me; they made me the keeper of the vineyards; but mine own vineyard have I not kept.

Tell me, O thou whom my soul loveth, where thou feedest, where thou makest thy flock to rest at noon: for why should I be as one that turneth aside by the flocks of thy companions?

If thou know not, O thou fairest among women, go thy way forth by the footsteps of the flock, and feed thy kids beside the shepherds' tents.

I have compared thee, O my love, to a company of horses in Pharaoh's chariots.

Thy cheeks are comely with rows of jewels, thy neck with chains of gold.

We will make thee borders of gold with studs of silver.

While the king sitteth at his table, my spikenard sendeth forth the smell thereof.

A bundle of myrrh is my well-beloved unto me; he shall lie all night betwixt my breasts.

My beloved is unto me as a cluster of camphire in the vineyards of Engedi.

Behold, thou art fair, my love; behold, thou art fair; thou hast doves' eyes.

Behold, thou art fair, my beloved, yea, pleasant: also our bed is green.

The beams of our house are cedar, and our rafters of fir.

2

I am the rose of Sharon, and the lily of the valleys.

As the lily among thorns, so is my love among the daughters.

As the apple tree among the trees of the wood, so is my beloved among the sons. I sat down under his shadow with great delight, and his fruit was sweet to my taste.

He brought me to the banqueting house, and his banner over me was love.

Stay me with flagons, comfort me with apples: for I am sick of love.

His left hand is under my head, and his right hand doth embrace me.

I charge you, O ye daughters of Jerusalem, by the roes, and by the hinds of the field, that ye stir not up, nor awake my love, till he please.

The voice of my beloved! behold, he cometh leaping upon the mountains, skipping upon the hills.

My beloved is like a roe or a young hart: behold, he standeth behind our wall, he looketh forth at the windows, shewing himself through the lattice.

My beloved spake, and said unto me, Rise up, my love, my fair one, and come away.

For, lo, the winter is past, the rain is over and gone;

The flowers appear on the earth; the time of the singing of birds is come, and the voice of the turtle is heard in our land;

The fig tree putteth forth her green figs, and the vines with the tender grape give a good smell. Arise, my love, my fair one, and come away.

O my dove, that art in the clefts of the rock, in the secret places of the stairs, let me see thy countenance, let me hear thy voice; for sweet is thy voice, and thy countenance is comely.

Take us the foxes, the little foxes, that spoil the vines: for our vines have tender grapes.

My beloved is mine, and I am his: he feedeth among the lilies.

Until the day break, and the shadows flee away, turn, my beloved, and be thou like a roe or a young hart upon the mountains of Bether.

3

By night on my bed I sought him whom my soul loveth: I sought him, but I found him not.

I will rise now, and go about the city in the streets, and in the broad ways I will seek him whom my soul loveth: I sought him, but I found him not.

The watchmen that go about the city found me: to whom I said, Saw ye him whom my soul loveth?

It was but a little that I passed from them, but I found him whom my soul loveth: I held him, and would not let him go, until I had brought him into my mother's house, and into the chamber of her that conceived me.

I charge you, O ye daughters of Jerusalem, by the roes, and by the hinds of the field, that ye stir not up, nor awake my love, till he please.

Who is this that cometh out of the wilderness like pillars of smoke, perfumed with myrrh and frankincense, with all powders of the merchant?

Behold his bed, which is Solomon's; threescore valiant men are about it, of the valiant of Israel.

They all hold swords, being expert in war: every man hath his sword upon his thigh because of fear in the night.

King Solomon made himself a chariot of the wood of Lebanon.

He made the pillars thereof of silver, the bottom thereof of gold, the covering of it of purple, the midst thereof being paved with love, for the daughters of Jerusalem.

Go forth, O ye daughters of Zion, and behold king Solomon with the crown wherewith his mother crowned him in the day of his espousals, and in the day of the gladness of his heart.

4

Behold, thou art fair, my love; behold, thou art fair; thou hast doves' eyes within thy locks: thy hair is as a flock of goats, that appear from mount Gilead.

Thy teeth are like a flock of sheep that are even shorn, which came up from the washing; whereof every one bear twins, and none is barren among them.

Thy lips are like a thread of scarlet, and thy speech is comely: thy temples are like a piece of a pomegranate within thy locks.

Thy neck is like the tower of David builded for an armoury, whereon there hang a thousand bucklers, all shields of mighty men.

Thy two breasts are like two young roes that are twins, which feed among the lilies.

Until the day break, and the shadows flee away, I will get me to the mountain of myrrh, and to the hill of frankincense.

Thou art all fair, my love; there is no spot in thee.

Come with me from Lebanon, my spouse, with me from Lebanon: look from the top of Amana, from the top of Shenir and Hermon, from the lions' dens, from the mountains of the leopards.

Thou hast ravished my heart, my sister, my spouse; thou hast ravished my heart with one of thine eyes, with one chain of thy neck.

How fair is thy love, my sister, my spouse! how much better is thy love than wine! and the smell of thine ointments than all spices!

Thy lips, O my spouse, drop as the honeycomb: honey and milk are under thy tongue; and the smell of thy garments is like the smell of Lebanon.

A garden inclosed is my sister, my spouse; a spring shut up, a fountain sealed.

Thy plants are an orchard of pomegranates, with pleasant fruits; camphire, with spikenard,

Spikenard and saffron; calamus and cinnamon, with all trees of frankincense; myrrh and aloes, with all the chief spices:

A fountain of gardens, a well of living waters, and streams from Lebanon.

Awake, O north wind; and come, thou south; blow upon my garden, that the spices thereof may flow out. Let my beloved come into his garden, and eat his pleasant fruits.

5

I am come into my garden, my sister, my spouse: I have gathered my myrrh with my spice; I have eaten my honeycomb with my honey; I have drunk my wine with my milk: eat, O friends; drink, yea, drink abundantly, O beloved.

I sleep, but my heart waketh: it is the voice of my beloved that knocketh, saying, Open to me, my sister, my love, my dove, my undefiled: for my head is filled with dew, and my locks with the drops of the night.

I have put off my coat; how shall I put it on? I have washed my feet; how shall I defile them?

My beloved put in his hand by the hole of the door, and my bowels were moved for him.

I rose up to open to my beloved; and my hands dropped with myrrh, and my fingers with sweet smelling myrrh, upon the handles of the lock.

I opened to my beloved; but my beloved had withdrawn himself, and was gone: my soul failed when he spake: I sought him, but I could not find him; I called him, but he gave me no answer.

The watchmen that went about the city found me, they smote me, they wounded me; the keepers of the walls took away my veil from me.

I charge you, O daughters of Jerusalem, if ye find my beloved, that ye tell him, that I am sick of love.

What is thy beloved more than another beloved, O thou fairest among women? what is thy beloved more than another beloved, that thou dost so charge us?

My beloved is white and ruddy, the chiefest among ten thousand.
His head is as the most fine gold, his locks are bushy, and black
as a raven.
His eyes are as the eyes of doves by the rivers of waters, washed with
milk, and fitly set.
His cheeks are as a bed of spices, as sweet flowers: his lips like lilies,
dropping sweet smelling myrrh.
His hands are as gold rings set with the beryl: his belly is as bright
ivory overlaid with sapphires.
His legs are as pillars of marble, set upon sockets of fine gold: his
countenance is as Lebanon, excellent as the cedars.
His mouth is most sweet: yea, he is altogether lovely. This is my
beloved, and this is my friend, O daughters of Jerusalem.

Song of Solomon 1–5, King James Bible

Songs for a Woman

3

If you open your coat
my love must widen

if you wear that round white beret
my blood must redden

wherever you love
furniture must be removed from the room

trees, mountains, seas – all of it
gone from the narrow world.

4

When you smile
serious ideas suddenly get drowsy

all night the mountains keep silent at your side –
at morning, the sand goes out with you, to sea

when you do nice things to me
all heavy industry shuts down.

Yehuda Amichai, translated by David Rosenberg

Songs of Grass

A shoe's idiot gape
tells no one the story of its footless
uncoupling in these tussocks of silence

And a beetle climbs a single spine of grass
towards delirious skies that shovel him back
earthwards under his weight

Tomorrow's grass will be yellow and voiceless
apart from the small green spear in its heart
shouting tomorrow and tomorrow

Alison Croggon

Sonnets 44 and 45

If the dull substance of my flesh were thought,
Injurious distance should not stop my way;
For then despite of space I would be brought,
From limits far remote where thou dost stay.
No matter then although my foot did stand
Upon the farthest earth removed from thee;
For nimble thought can jump both sea and land
As soon as think the place where he would be.
But ah! thought kills me that I am not thought,
To leap large lengths of miles when thou art gone,
But that so much of earth and water wrought
I must attend time's leisure with my moan,
    Receiving nought by elements so slow
    But heavy tears, badges of either's woe.

The other two, slight air and purging fire,
Are both with thee, wherever I abide;
The first my thought, the other my desire,
These present-absent with swift motion slide.
For when these quicker elements are gone
In tender embassy of love to thee,
My life, being made of four, with two alone
Sinks down to death, oppress'd with melancholy;
Until life's composition be recured
By those swift messengers return'd from thee,
Who even but now come back again, assured
Of thy fair health, recounting it to me:
    This told, I joy; but then no longer glad,
    I send them back again and straight grow sad.

William Shakespeare

Sorcery

I'm a witch who lost all her powers, then
    in place of my powers, I got the coiled beauty
of seashells and sleeping infants. The coiled
beauty of eardrums, and the sound wave
of bells. The bells! This is the country of clouds.
        The molten body, the Floridian pinks,
        and centuries of sand dollars examining
the arcing waves. New territory
of interiority and I'm in the middle of this.
    White like a negative belt.
I am an airless thing. When I get high, I get low.
            But I'm real and airless and love you.

Sandra Simonds

Spleen

I am like the king of a rainy land,
Wealthy but powerless, both young and very old,
Who contemns the fawning manners of his tutors
And is bored with his dogs and other animals.
Nothing can cheer him, neither the chase nor falcons,
Nor his people dying before his balcony.
The ludicrous ballads of his favorite clown
No longer smooth the brow of this cruel invalid;
His bed, adorned with fleurs-de-lis, becomes a grave;
The lady's maids, to whom every prince is handsome,
No longer can find gowns shameless enough
To wring a smile from this young skeleton.

The alchemist who makes his gold was never able
To extract from him the tainted element,
And in those baths of blood come down from Roman times,
And which in their old age the powerful recall,
He failed to warm this dazed cadaver in whose veins
Flows the green water of Lethe in place of blood.

Charles Baudelaire, translated by William Aggeler

'The spotted hawk swoops by and accuses me'

The spotted hawk swoops by and accuses me, he complains of my gab
and my loitering.

I too am not a bit tamed, I too am untranslatable,
I sound my barbaric yawp over the roofs of the world.

The last scud of day holds back for me,
It flings my likeness after the rest and true as any on the shadow'd wilds,
It coaxes me to the vapor and the dusk.

I depart as air, I shake my white locks at the runaway sun,
I effuse my flesh in eddies, and drift it in lacy jags.

I bequeath myself to the dirt to grow from the grass I love,
If you want me again look for me under your boot-soles.

You will hardly know who I am or what I mean,
But I shall be good health to you nevertheless,
And filter and fibre your blood.

Failing to fetch me at first keep encouraged,
Missing me one place search another,
I stop somewhere waiting for you.

Song of Myself*: 52, Walt Whitman*

Spring and Fall

To a young child

Márgarét, áre you gríeving
Over Goldengrove unleaving?
Leáves like the things of man, you
With your fresh thoughts care for, can you?
Ah! ás the heart grows older
It will come to such sights colder
By and by, nor spare a sigh
Though worlds of wanwood leafmeal lie;
And yet you wíll weep and know why.
Now no matter, child, the name:
Sórrow's spríngs áre the same.
Nor mouth had, no nor mind, expressed
What heart heard of, ghost guessed:
It ís the blight man was born for,
It is Margaret you mourn for.

Gerard Manley Hopkins

The Statue of the Virgin at Granard Speaks

It can be bitter here at times like this,
November wind sweeping across the border.
Its seeds of ice would cut you to the quick.
The whole town tucked up safe and dreaming,
even wild things gone to earth, and I
stuck up here in this grotto, without as much as
star or planet to ease my vigil.

The howling won't let up. Trees
cavort in agony as if they would be free
and take off – ghost voyagers
on the wind that carries intimations
of garrison towns, walled cities, ghetto lanes
where men hunt each other and invoke
the various names of God as blessing
on their death tactics, their night manoeuvres.
Closer to home the wind sails over
dying lakes. I hear fish drowning.
I taste the stagnant water mingled
with turf smoke from outlying farms.

They call me Mary – Blessed, Holy, Virgin.
They fit me to a myth of a man crucified:
the scourging and the falling, and the falling again,
the thorny crown, the hammer blow of iron
into wrist and ankle, the sacred bleeding heart.
They name me Mother of all this grief
though mated to no mortal man.
They kneel before me and their prayers

fly up like sparks from a bonfire
that blaze a moment, then wink out.

It can be lovely here at times. Springtime,
early summer. Girls in Communion frocks
pale rivals to the riot in the hedgerows
of cow parsley and haw blossom, the perfume
from every rushy acre that's left for hay
when the light swings longer with the sun's push north.

Or the grace of a midsummer wedding
when the earth herself calls out for coupling
and I would break loose of my stony robes,
pure blue, pure white, as if they had robbed
a child's sky for their colour. My being
cries out to be incarnate, incarnate,
maculate and tousled in a honeyed bed.

Even an autumn burial can work its own pageantry.
The hedges heavy with the burden of fruiting
crab, sloe, berry, hip; clouds scud east
pear scented, windfalls secret in long
orchard grasses, and some old soul is lowered
to his kin. Death is just another harvest
scripted to the season's play.

But on this All Souls' Night there is
no respite from the keening of the wind.
I would not be amazed if every corpse came risen
from the graveyard to join in exaltation with the gale,
a cacophony of bone imploring sky for judgement
and release from being the conscience of the town.

On a night like this I remember the child
who came with fifteen summers to her name,
and she lay down alone at my feet
without midwife or doctor or friend to hold her hand
and she pushed her secret out into the night,
far from the town tucked up in little scandals,
bargains struck, words broken, prayers, promises,
and though she cried out to me in extremis
I did not move,
I didn't lift a finger to help her,
I didn't intercede with heaven,
nor whisper the charmed word in God's ear.

On a night like this I number the days to the solstice
and the turn back to the light.
                        O sun,
centre of our foolish dance,
burning heart of stone,
molten mother of us all,
hear me and have pity.

Paula Meehan

Stopping by Woods on a Snowy Evening

Whose woods these are I think I know.
His house is in the village though;
He will not see me stopping here
To watch his woods fill up with snow.

My little horse must think it queer
To stop without a farmhouse near
Between the woods and frozen lake
The darkest evening of the year.

He gives his harness bells a shake
To ask if there is some mistake.
The only other sound's the sweep
Of easy wind and downy flake.

The woods are lovely, dark and deep,
But I have promises to keep,
And miles to go before I sleep,
And miles to go before I sleep.

Robert Frost

The Streets of Laredo

As I walked out on the streets of Laredo,
As I walked out on Laredo one day,
I spied a young cowboy all wrapped in white linen,
Wrapped in white linen as cold as the clay.

'I can see by your outfit that you are a cowboy' –
These words he did say as I boldly stepped by,
'Come and sit down beside me and hear my sad story;
I'm shot in the breast and I know I must die.

'It was once in the saddle I used to go dashing
Once in the saddle I used to go gay;

First to the ale-house and then down to the jail-house,
Got shot in the breast and I'm dying today.

'Get six jolly cowboys to carry my coffin;
Get six pretty maidens to bear up my pall;
Put bunches of roses all over my coffin,
Roses to deaden the clods as they fall.

'Oh, beat the drum slowly and play the fife lowly,
Play the dead march as you carry me along;
Take me to the green valley and lay the sod o'er me
For I'm a young cowboy and I know I've done wrong.

'Go gather around you a crowd of young cowboys
And tell them the story of this, my sad fate;
Tell one and the other before they go further
To stop their wild roving before it's too late.

'Go fetch me a cup, a cup of cold water
To cool my parched lips,' the cowboy then said.
Before I returned, the spirit had left him
And gone to its Maker – the cowboy was dead.

We beat the drum slowly and played the fife lowly,
And bitterly wept as we carried him along;
For we all loved our comrade, so brave, young and handsome,
We all loved our comrade although he'd done wrong.

Anonymous

The Summer Day

Who made the world?
Who made the swan, and the black bear?
Who made the grasshopper?
This grasshopper, I mean –
the one who has flung herself out of the grass,
the one who is eating sugar out of my hand,
who is moving her jaws back and forth instead of up and down–
who is gazing around with her enormous and complicated eyes.
Now she lifts her pale forearms and thoroughly washes her face.
Now she snaps her wings open, and floats away.
I don't know exactly what a prayer is.
I do know how to pay attention, how to fall down
into the grass, how to kneel down in the grass,
how to be idle and blessed, how to stroll through the fields,
which is what I have been doing all day.
Tell me, what else should I have done?
Doesn't everything die at last, and too soon?
Tell me, what is it you plan to do
with your one wild and precious life?

Mary Oliver

Summer Night

A beautiful summer night.
The tall houses leave
their balcony shutters open
to the wide plaza of the old village.
In the large deserted square,

stone benches, burning bush and acacias
trace their black shadows
symmetrically on the white sand.
In its zenith, the moon; in the tower,
the clock's illuminated globe.
I walk through this ancient village,
alone, like a ghost.

Antonio Machado, translated by Willis Barnstone

The Sun Rising

Busy old fool, unruly Sun,
Why dost thou thus,
Through windows, and through curtains, call on us?
Must to thy motions lovers' seasons run?
Saucy pedantic wretch, go chide
Late school-boys and sour prentices,
Go tell court-huntsmen that the king will ride,
Call country ants to harvest offices;
Love, all alike, no season knows nor clime,
Nor hours, days, months, which are the rags of time.

Thy beams, so reverend and strong
Why shouldst thou think?
I could eclipse and cloud them with a wink,
But that I would not lose her sight so long.
If her eyes have not blinded thine,
Look, and tomorrow late tell me,
Whether both th' Indias of spice and mine
Be where thou left'st them, or lie here with me.

Ask for those kings whom thou saw'st yesterday,
And thou shalt hear, 'All here in one bed lay.'

She's all states, and all princes I;
Nothing else is;
Princes do but play us; compared to this,
All honour's mimic, all wealth alchemy.
Thou, Sun, art half as happy as we,
In that the world's contracted thus;
Thine age asks ease, and since thy duties be
To warm the world, that's done in warming us.
Shine here to us, and thou art everywhere;
This bed thy center is, these walls thy sphere.

John Donne

Sunset

Sunset glitters on the beads
Of the curtains. Spring flowers
Bloom in the valley. The gardens
Along the river are filled
With perfume. Smoke of cooking
Fires drifts over the slow barges.
Sparrows hop and tumble in
The branches. Whirling insects
Swarm in the air. Who discovered
That one cup of thick wine
Will dispel a thousand cares?

Tu Fu, translated by Kenneth Rexroth

Surely God Was a Lover

Surely God was a lover when He bade the day begin
Soft as a woman's eyelid – white as a woman's skin.

Surely God was a lover, with a lover's faults and fears,
When He made the sea as bitter as a wilful woman's tears.

Surely God was a lover, with the madness love will bring:
He wrought while His love was singing, and put her soul in the Spring.

Surely God was a lover, by a woman's wile controlled,
When He made the Summer a woman thirsty and unconsoled.

Surely God was a lover when He made the trees so fair;
In every leaf is a glory caught from a woman's hair.

Surely God was a lover – see, in the flowers He grows,
His love's eyes in the violet – her sweetness in the rose.

John Shaw Neilson

'Sweet is the breath of Morn'

Sweet is the breath of Morn; her rising sweet,
With charm of earliest birds: pleasant the sun,
When first on this delightful land he spreads
His orient beams, on herb, tree, fruit, and flower,
Glistering with dew; fragrant the fertile earth
After soft showers; and sweet the coming on
Of grateful Evening mild; then silent Night

With this her solemn bird and this fair moon,
And these the gems of Heaven, her starry train:
But neither breath of Morn when she ascends
With charm of earliest birds; nor rising sun
On this delightful land, nor herb, fruit, flower,
Glistering with dew; nor fragrance after showers;
Nor grateful Evening mild; nor silent Night,
With this her solemn bird; nor walk by moon,
Or glittering star-light without thee is sweet.

Eve to Adam in **Paradise Lost,** *Book IV, John Milton*

Swineherd

'When all this is over,' said the swineherd,
'I mean to retire, where
Nobody will have heard about my special skills
And conversation is mainly about the weather.

I intend to learn how to make coffee, at least as well
As the Portuguese lay-sister in the kitchen
And polish the brass fenders every day.
I want to lie awake at night
Listening to cream crawling to the top of the jug
And the water lying soft in the cistern.

I want to see an orchard where the trees grow in straight lines
And the yellow fox finds shelter between the navy-blue trunks,
Where it gets dark early in summer
And the apple-blossom is allowed to wither on the bough.'

Eiléan Ní Chuilleanáin

Taklamakan Desert

Why I'm going to the Taklamakan Desert:
the emptiness there.

Why I'm going to the Taklamakan Desert
at seventy-five, leaving all words behind: the cry
of the emptiness there.

Why I'm going to the Taklamakan Desert:
I can no longer stand
the world's greed
or mine.

There, in the Taklamakan Desert,
the silence of a thousand-year-old skull.

Ko Un, translated by Suji Kwock Kim and Sunja Kim Kwock

'That time of year thou may'st in me behold'

That time of year thou may'st in me behold
When yellow leaves, or none, or few, do hang
Upon those boughs which shake against the cold,
Bare ruin'd choirs, where late the sweet birds sang.
In me thou see'st the twilight of such day,
As after sunset fadeth in the west,
Which by-and-by black night doth take away,
Death's second self, that seals up all in rest.
In me thou see'st the glowing of such fire
That on the ashes of his youth doth lie,

As the death-bed whereon it must expire
Consum'd with that which it was nourish'd by.
　　This thou perceivest, which makes thy love more strong,
　　To love that well which thou must leave ere long.

Sonnet 73, William Shakespeare

Theatre Impressions

For me the tragedy's most important act is the sixth:
the raising of the dead from the stage's battlegrounds,
the straightening of wigs and fancy gowns,
removing knives from stricken breasts,
taking nooses from lifeless necks,
lining up among the living
to face the audience.

The bows, both solo and ensemble –
the pale hand on the wounded heart,
the curtsies of the hapless suicide,
the bobbing of the chopped-off head.

The bows in pairs –
rage extends its arm to meekness,
the victim's eyes smile at the torturer,
the rebel indulgently walks beside the tyrant.

Eternity trampled by the golden slipper's toe.
Redeeming values swept aside with the swish of a wide-brimmed hat.
The unrepentant urge to start all over tomorrow.

Now enter, single file, the hosts who died early on,
In Acts 3 and 4, or between scenes.
The miraculous return of all those lost without a trace.
The thought that they've been waiting patiently offstage
without taking off their makeup
or their costumes
moves me more than all the tragedy's tirades.

But the curtain's fall is the most uplifting part,
the things you see before it hits the floor:
here one hand quickly reaches for a flower,
there another hand picks up a fallen sword.
Only then, one last unseen hand
does its duty
and grabs me by the throat.

Wislawa Szymborska, translated by Stanislaw Baranczak and Clare Cavanagh

There Will Come Soft Rain

There will come soft rain and the smell of the ground,
And swallows circling with their shimmering sound;

And frogs in the pools singing at night,
And wild plum trees in tremulous white;

Robins will wear their feathery fire,
Whistling their whims on a low fence-wire;

And not one will know of the war, not one
Will care at last when it is done.

Not one would mind, neither bird nor tree,
If mankind perished utterly;

And Spring herself, when she woke at dawn
Would scarcely know that we were gone.

Sara Teasdale

There's No Place Like Home

It's the Lucky Country's closet; a dark interior with frontier skeletons. Whirly-winds run rampant, spawning red-sand mandalas of chaos. These frenetic twisters find easy prey on ochre-kissed Dorothys, carrying them off to Parallel Oz. In Parallel Oz, neither the Good witches nor the wicked afford these Dorothys little pairs of magic red shoes . . . there's no place like a broken home . . . there's no place like a broken home . . . there's no place like a broken home. The yellow-brick road is pock-marked with massacre sites and the Wizard, the Wizard of Parallel Oz; he holds Dorothy hostage to a mutual obligation agreement. The Straw Man has the grazing monopoly, the Tin Man has the mines, and the Lion waits in the spinifex, with the long-grass drinkers. Parallel Oz and it's rag-doll Dorothys; not just an Advance Australia Fairytale, but a reality spinning out of control, gaining catastrophic momentum . . .

Samuel Wagan Watson

'They say that time assuages'

They say that 'time assuages', –
    Time never did assuage;
An actual suffering strengthens,
    As sinews do, with age.
Time is a test of trouble,
    But not a remedy.
If such it prove, it prove too
    There was no malady.

Emily Dickinson

'They told me, Heraclitus'

They told me, Heraclitus, they told me you were dead,
They brought me bitter news to hear and bitter tears to shed.
I wept as I remembered how often you and I
Had tired the sun with talking and sent him down the sky.

And now that thou art lying, my dear old Carian guest,
A handful of grey ashes, long, long ago at rest,
Still are thy pleasant voices, thy nightingales, awake;
For Death, he taketh all away, but them he cannot take.

Callimachus, translated by William Johnson Cory

Things I Want Decided

Which shouldn't exist
in this world,
the one who forgets
or the one
who is forgotten?

Which is better,
to love
one who has died
or not to see
each other when you're alive?

Which is better,
the distant lover
you long for
or the one you see daily
without desire?

Which is the least unreliable
among fickle things –
the swift rapids,
a flowing river,
or this human world?

Izumi Shikibu, translated by Jane Hirshfield with Mariko Aratani

A Thirsty Fish

I don't get tired of you. Don't grow weary
of being compassionate toward me!

All this thirst equipment
must surely be *tired* of me,
the water jar, the water carrier.

I have a thirsty fish in me
that can never find enough
of what it's thirsty for!

Show me the way to the ocean!
Break these half-measures,
these small containers.

All this fantasy
and grief.

Let my house be drowned in the wave
that rose last night in the courtyard
hidden in the center of my chest.

Joseph fell like the moon into my well.
The harvest I expected was washed away.
But no matter.
A fire has risen above my tombstone hat.
I don't want learning, or dignity,
or respectability.

I want this music and this dawn
and the warmth of your cheek against mine.

The grief-armies assemble,
but I'm not going with them.

This is how it always is
when I finish a poem.

A great silence comes over me,
and I wonder why I ever thought
to use language.

Rumi, translated by Coleman Barks with John Moyne

Thornbills

Their tiny torrent of flight
sounds in the trees like rain,
flicking the leaves to the light –
a scattered handful of grain,
the thornbills little as bees.

I hear in the blowing trees
the sudden tune of their song.
Pray that the hawk not sees,
who has scanned the wind so long
for his small living food.

Oh let no enemies
drink the quick wine of blood
that leaps in their pulse of praise.

Wherever a trap is set
may they slip through the mesh of the net.
Nothing should do them wrong.

Judith Wright

'Thou, nature, art my goddess'

Thou, nature, art my goddess; to thy law
My services are bound. Wherefore should I
Stand in the plague of custom, and permit
The curiosity of nations to deprive me,
For that I am some twelve or fourteen moon-shines
Lag of a brother? Why bastard? wherefore base?
When my dimensions are as well compact,
My mind as generous, and my shape as true,
As honest madam's issue? Why brand they us
With base? with baseness? bastardy? base, base?
Who, in the lusty stealth of nature, take
More composition and fierce quality
Than doth, within a dull, stale, tired bed,
Go to the creating a whole tribe of fops,
Got 'tween asleep and wake? Well, then,
Legitimate Edgar, I must have your land:
Our father's love is to the bastard Edmund
As to the legitimate: fine word, 'legitimate!'
Well, my legitimate, if this letter speed,
And my invention thrive, Edmund the base
Shall top the legitimate: – I grow; I prosper:
Now, gods, stand up for bastards!

Edmund in King Lear, *William Shakespeare*

'Though I speak with the tongues of men and of angels'

Though I speak with the tongues of men and of angels, and have not charity, I am become as sounding brass, or a tinkling cymbal.

And though I have the gift of prophecy, and understand all mysteries, and all knowledge; and though I have all faith, so that I could remove mountains, and have not charity, I am nothing.

And though I bestow all my goods to feed the poor, and though I give my body to be burned, and have not charity, it profiteth me nothing.

Charity suffereth long, and is kind; charity envieth not; charity vaunteth not itself, is not puffed up,

Doth not behave itself unseemly, seeketh not her own, is not easily provoked, thinketh no evil;

Rejoiceth not in iniquity, but rejoiceth in the truth;

Beareth all things, believeth all things, hopeth all things, endureth all things.

Charity never faileth: but whether there be prophecies, they shall fail; whether there be tongues, they shall cease; whether there be knowledge, it shall vanish away.

For we know in part, and we prophesy in part.

But when that which is perfect is come, then that which is in part shall be done away.

When I was a child, I spake as a child, I understood as a child, I thought as a child: but when I became a man, I put away childish things.

For now we see through a glass, darkly; but then face to face: now I know in part; but then shall I know even as also I am known.

And now abideth faith, hope, charity, these three; but the greatest of these is charity.

The Thirteenth Chapter of St Paul's First Letter to the Corinthians, King James Bible

'Thought Is Surrounded by a Halo'

Ludwig Wittgenstein, Philosophical Investigations 97

Show me the order of the world,
the hard-edge light of this-is-so
prior to all experience
and common to both world and thought,
no model, but the truth itself.

Language is not a perfect game,
and if it were, how could we play?
The world's more than the sum of things
like moon, sky, centre, body, bed,
as all the singing masters know.

Picture two lovers side by side
who sleep and dream and wake to hold
the real and the imagined world
body by body, word by word
in the wild halo of their thought.

Gwen Harwood

The Three Fates

At the instant of drowning he invoked the three sisters.
It was a mistake, an aberration, to cry out for
Life everlasting.

He came up like a cork and back to the river-bank,
Put on his clothes in reverse order,
Returned to the house.

He suffered the enormous agonies of passion
Writing poems from the end backwards,
Brushing away tears that had not yet fallen.

Loving her wildly as the day regressed towards morning
He watched her swinging in the garden, growing younger,
Bare-foot, straw-hatted.

And when she was gone and the house and the swing and daylight
There was an instant's pause before it began all over,
The reel unrolling towards the river.

Rosemary Dobson

Tiresias

You wouldn't read about it:
all the women in black, and the flames like dragons
hissing down from the broken roof, and Oedipus
raining blood from his eyes like terrible tears
and his mother and wife in the bedroom, hanging herself.

I saw it coming, but no one listened, of course.
You can't cheat fate, I said, and those gods are buggers
if you try to outwit them – but with his usual hubris
Oedipus told me to shut my mouth unless I was going to say
something cheerful, so I just went away, saying
you can wander in the desert yourself, your majesty:
you can't say much to arrogance like that.

Not that I don't feel sorry for him. He wasn't bad,
a good king and usually fair, except when the famines
and starving people got to him. And he could have taken
Jocasta's way, shrugged the whole thing off his shoulders:
still, there's no satisfaction in being right. You can't say
I told you so to a man like that.

Alison Croggon

to a dark moses

you are the one
i am lit for.
come with your rod
that twists
and is a serpent.
i am the bush.
i am burning.
i am not consumed.

Lucille Clifton

To an Athlete Dying Young

The time you won your town the race
We chaired you through the market-place;
Man and boy stood cheering by,
And home we brought you shoulder-high.

Today, the road all runners come,
Shoulder-high we bring you home,

And set you at your threshold down,
Townsman of a stiller town.

Smart lad, to slip betimes away
From fields where glory does not stay,
And early though the laurel grows
It withers quicker than the rose.

Eyes the shady night has shut
Cannot see the record cut,
And silence sounds no worse than cheers
After earth has stopped the ears.

Now you will not swell the rout
Of lads that wore their honours out,
Runners whom renown outran
And the name died before the man.

So set, before its echoes fade,
The fleet foot on the sill of shade,
And hold to the low lintel up
The still-defended challenge-cup.

And round that early-laurelled head
Will flock to gaze the strengthless dead,
And find unwithered on its curls
The garland briefer than a girl's.

A. E. Housman

To Be a Slave of Intensity

Friend, hope for the Guest while you are alive.
Jump into experience while you are alive!
Think . . . and think . . . while you are alive.
What you call 'salvation' belongs to the time before death.

If you don't break your ropes while you're alive,
do you think
ghosts will do it after?

The idea that the soul will join the ecstatic
just because the body is rotten –
that is all fantasy.
What is found now is found then.
If you find nothing now,
you will simply end up with an apartment in the City of Death.
If you make love with the divine now, in the next life you will have the face of satisfied desire.

So plunge into the truth, find out who the Teacher is, believe in the Great Sound!

Kabir says this: When the Guest is being searched for, it is the intensity of the longing for the Guest that does all the work.

Look at me, and you will see a slave of that intensity.

Kabir, translated by Robert Bly

'To be or not to be'

To be, or not to be, that is the question:
Whether 'tis nobler in the mind to suffer
The slings and arrows of outrageous fortune,
Or to take arms against a sea of troubles,
And by opposing end them: to die, to sleep
No more; and by a sleep, to say we end
The heart-ache, and the thousand natural shocks
That flesh is heir to? 'Tis a consummation
Devoutly to be wished. To die, to sleep,
To sleep, perchance to dream; aye, there's the rub,
For in that sleep of death, what dreams may come,
When we have shuffled off this mortal coil,
Must give us pause. There's the respect
That makes calamity of so long life:
For who would bear the whips and scorns of time,
The oppressor's wrong, the proud man's contumely,
The pangs of dispriz'd love, the law's delay,
The insolence of office, and the spurns
That patient merit of the unworthy takes,
When he himself might his quietus make
With a bare bodkin? Who would fardels bear,
To grunt and sweat under a weary life,
But that the dread of something after death,
The undiscovered country, from whose bourn
No traveller returns, puzzles the will,
And makes us rather bear those ills we have,
Than fly to others that we know not of.
Thus conscience does make cowards of us all,
And thus the native hue of resolution

Is sicklied o'er, with the pale cast of thought,
And enterprises of great pitch and moment,
With this regard their currents turn awry,
And lose the name of action.

Hamlet in Hamlet, *William Shakespeare*

'To every thing there is a season'

To every thing there is a season, and a time to every purpose under the heaven:
A time to be born, and a time to die; a time to plant, and a time to pluck up that which is planted;
A time to kill, and a time to heal; a time to break down, and a time to build up;
A time to weep, and a time to laugh; a time to mourn, and a time to dance;
A time to cast away stones, and a time to gather stones together; a time to embrace, and a time to refrain from embracing;
A time to get, and a time to lose; a time to keep, and a time to cast away;
A time to rend, and a time to sew; a time to keep silence, and a time to speak;
A time to love, and a time to hate; a time of war, and a time of peace.

. . .

That which hath been is now; and that which is to be hath already been; and God requireth that which is past.
And moreover I saw under the sun the place of judgment, that wickedness was there; and the place of righteousness, that iniquity was there.

I said in mine heart, God shall judge the righteous and the wicked: for there is a time there for every purpose and for every work.
I said in mine heart concerning the estate of the sons of men, that God might manifest them, and that they might see that they themselves are beasts.
For that which befalleth the sons of men befalleth beasts; even one thing befalleth them: as the one dieth, so dieth the other; yea, they have all one breath; so that a man hath no preeminence above a beast: for all is vanity.
All go unto one place; all are of the dust, and all turn to dust again.

Ecclesiastes 3:1–8, 15–20, King James Bible

To His Mistress Going to Bed

Come, madam, come, all rest my powers defy;
Until I labour, I in labour lie.
The foe oft-times, having the foe in sight,
Is tired with standing, though he never fight.
Off with that girdle, like heaven's zone glittering,
But a far fairer world encompassing.
Unpin that spangled breast-plate, which you wear,
That th' eyes of busy fools may be stopp'd there.
Unlace yourself, for that harmonious chime
Tells me from you that now tis your bed-time.
Off with that happy busk, which I envy,
That still can be, and still can stand so nigh.
Your gown going off such beauteous state reveals,
As when from flowery meads th' hill's shadow steals.
Off with your wiry coronet, and show

The hairy diadem which on you doth grow.
Off with your hose and shoes; then softly tread
In this love's hallow'd temple, this soft bed.
In such white robes heaven's angels used to be
Revealed to men; thou, angel, bring'st with thee
A heaven-like Mahomet's paradise; and though
Ill spirits walk in white, we easily know
By this these angels from an evil sprite;
Those set our hairs, but these our flesh upright.
    Licence my roving hands, and let them go
Before, behind, between, above, below.
O, my America, my new-found-land,
My kingdom, safest when with one man mann'd,
My mine of precious stones, my empery;
How am I blest in thus discovering thee!
To enter in these bonds, is to be free;
Then, where my hand is set, my soul shall be.
    Full nakedness! All joys are due to thee;
As souls unbodied, bodies unclothed must be
To taste whole joys. Gems which you women use
Are like Atlanta's ball cast in men's views;
That, when a fool's eye lighteth on a gem,
His earthly soul might covet that, not them.
Like pictures, or like books' gay coverings made
For laymen, are all women thus array'd.
Themselves are only mystic books, which we
– Whom their imputed grace will dignify –
Must see reveal'd. Then, since that I may know,
As liberally as to thy midwife show
Thyself; cast all, yea, this white linen hence;

There is no penance, much less innocence:
    To teach thee, I am naked first; why then,
What needst thou have more covering than a man?

John Donne

To My Dear and Loving Husband

If ever two were one, then surely we.
If ever man were lov'd by wife, then thee.
If ever wife was happy in a man,
Compare with me, ye women, if you can.
I prize thy love more than whole mines of gold
Or all the riches that the East doth hold.
My love is such that rivers cannot quench,
Nor ought but love from thee give recompense.
Thy love is such I can no way repay.
The heavens reward thee manifold, I pray.
Then while we live, in love let's so persever,
That when we live no more, we may live ever.

Anne Bradstreet

To Those Born After

I

To the cities I came in a time of disorder
That was ruled by hunger.
I sheltered with the people in a time of uproar

And then I joined in their rebellion.
That's how I passed my time that was given to me on this Earth.

I ate my dinners between the battles,
I lay down to sleep among the murderers,
I didn't care much for love
And for nature's beauties I had little patience.
That's how I passed my time that was given to me on this Earth.

The city streets all led to foul swamps in my time,
My speech betrayed me to the butchers.
I could do only little
But without me those that ruled might sleep more easily:
That's what I hoped.
That's how I passed my time that was given to me on this Earth.

Our forces were slight and small,
Our goal lay in the far distance
Clearly in our sights,
If for me myself beyond my reaching.
That's how I passed my time that was given to me on this Earth.

II

You who will come to the surface
From the flood that's overwhelmed us and drowned us all
Must think, when you speak of our weakness in times of darkness
That you've not had to face:

Days when we were used to changing countries
More often than shoes,

Through the war of the classes despairing
That there was only injustice and no outrage.

Even so we realised
Hatred of oppression still distorts the features,
Anger at injustice still makes voices raised and ugly.
Oh we, who wished to lay the foundations for peace
 and friendliness,
Could never be friendly ourselves.

And in the future when no longer
Do human beings still treat themselves as animals,
Look back on us with indulgence.

Bertolt Brecht, translated by Des de Moor

Today we are in a hospital ward

I lie on a gurney, we all do, like brides. I don't know any of the others
but there is a certain amount I do know, at this point, that you don't.

We are all pregnant and we are waiting for this to leave
we have all been given the right combination of pills before you
 even got here
you saw nothing of that.

There is no turning back at this juncture
with expectation and fear
much like a wedding night, in fact.

The pain is terrific
the others move through this much quicker than I do
some even leave their beds, it is done for them.

There is no one waving the reddened sheet in the street or ululating
but they are done and I am still sweating or screaming

through this labour to nothing
while women continue to pass in and out of this room stripping
    their beds
and taking their linen with them.

Tusiata Avia

'Tomorrow, and tomorrow, and tomorrow'

Tomorrow, and tomorrow, and tomorrow,
Creeps in this petty pace from day to day,
To the last syllable of recorded time;
And all our yesterdays have lighted fools
The way to dusty death. Out, out, brief candle!
Life's but a walking shadow, a poor player,
That struts and frets his hour upon the stage,
And then is heard no more. It is a tale
Told by an idiot, full of sound and fury,
Signifying nothing.

Macbeth in Macbeth, *William Shakespeare*

Took the Children Away

This story's right, this story's true
I would not tell lies to you
Like the promises they did not keep
And how they fenced us in like sheep
Said to us come take our hand
Set us up on mission land
Taught us to read, to write and pray
Then they took the children away
Took the children away
The children away
Snatched from their mother's breast
Said this is for the best
Took them away

The welfare and the policeman
Said you've got to understand
We'll give them what you can't give
Teach them how to really live
Teach them how to live they said
Humiliated them instead
Taught them that and taught them this
And others taught them prejudice
You took the children away
The children away
Breaking their mother's heart
Tearing us all apart
Took them away

One dark day on Framlingham
Came and didn't give a damn

My mother cried 'Go get their dad!'
He came running, fighting mad
Mother's tears were falling down
Dad shaped up and stood his ground
He said 'You touch my kids and you fight me'
Then they took us from our family
Took us away
They took us away
Snatched from our mother's breast
Said this was for the best
Took us away

Told us what to do and say
Taught us all the white man's ways
Then they split us up again
And gave us gifts to ease the pain
Sent us off to foster homes
As we grew up we felt alone
Cause we were acting white
Yet feeling black
One sweet day all the children came back

The children came back
The children came back
Back where their hearts grow strong
Back where they all belong
The children came back
Said the children came back
The children came back
Back where they understand
Back to their mother's land
The children came back

Back to their mother
Back to their father
Back to their sister
Back to their brother
Back to their people
Back to their land
All the children came back
The children came back
The children came back
Yes I came back

Archie Roach

Torture

If you're tortured
you know a human is inhuman.
Both the torturer
and the tortured
deep at night in the second basement room.

Ko Un, translated by Clare You and Richard Silberg

The Trees

The trees are coming into leaf
Like something almost being said;
The recent buds relax and spread,
Their greenness is a kind of grief.

Is it that they are born again
And we grow old? No, they die too.
Their yearly trick of looking new
Is written down in rings of grain.

Yet still the unresting castles thresh
In fullgrown thickness every May.
Last year is dead, they seem to say,
Begin afresh, afresh, afresh.

Philip Larkin

Triads

3 Things not to be expected

Patience from a drunk woman
Humour from a drunk man
Understanding from armies

3 Things to be forgotten

A stillborn sister
A grandmother's long hair
A nubile mother

3 Impossible things

To shape the air
To civilise money
To comfort a paranoiac

3 Fragile things

The cool of sunrise
Peace in the fowlyard
The throat of a statesman

3 Unacceptable things

A dirty dentist
A timid bookie
A prayerless priest

3 Lost things

Poems by heart
Water without acid
Sleep without fear.

Vincent Buckley

Try to Remember Some Details

Try to remember some details. Remember the clothing
of the one you love
so that on the day of loss you'll be able to say: last seen
wearing such-and-such, brown jacket, white hat.
Try to remember some details. For they have no face
and their soul is hidden and their crying
is the same as their laughter,
and their silence and their shouting rise to one height
and their body temperature is between 98 and 104 degrees

and they have no life outside this narrow space
and they have no graven image, no likeness, no memory
and they have paper cups on the day of their rejoicing
and disposable paper plates.

Try to remember some details. For the world
is filled with people who were torn from their sleep
with no one to mend the tear,
and unlike wild beasts they live
each in his lonely hiding place and they die
together on battlefields
and in hospitals.
And the earth will swallow all of them,
good and evil together, like the followers of Korah,
all of them in their rebellion against death,
their mouths open till the last moment,
praising and cursing in a single
howl. Try, try
to remember some details.

Yehuda Amichai, translated by Chana Bloch

'Twenty-eight young men'

Twenty-eight young men bathe by the shore,
Twenty-eight young men and all so friendly;
Twenty-eight years of womanly life and all so lonesome.

She owns the fine house by the rise of the bank,
She hides handsome and richly drest aft the blinds of the window.

Which of the young men does she like the best?
Ah the homeliest of them is beautiful to her.

Where are you off to, lady? for I see you,
You splash in the water there, yet stay stock still in your room.

Dancing and laughing along the beach came the twenty-ninth bather,
The rest did not see her, but she saw them and loved them.

The beards of the young men glisten'd with wet, it ran from
their long hair,
Little streams pass'd all over their bodies.

An unseen hand also pass'd over their bodies,
It descended tremblingly from their temples and ribs.

The young men float on their backs, their white bellies bulge
to the sun, they do not ask who seizes fast to them,
They do not know who puffs and declines with pendant
and bending arch,
They do not think whom they souse with spray.

Song of Myself: ***11, Walt Whitman***

The Tyger

Tyger! Tyger! burning bright,
In the forests of the night;
What immortal hand or eye,
Could frame thy fearful symmetry?

In what distant deeps or skies,
Burnt the fire of thine eyes?
On what wings dare he aspire?
What the hand, dare seize the fire?

And what shoulder, & what art,
Could twist the sinews of thy heart?
And when thy heart began to beat,
What dread hand? & what dread feet?

What the hammer? what the chain?
In what furnace was thy brain?
What the anvil? what dread grasp,
Dare its deadly terrors clasp?

When the stars threw down their spears,
And watered heaven with their tears,
Did he smile his work to see?
Did he who made the Lamb make thee?

Tyger! Tyger! burning bright
In the forests of the night,
What immortal hand or eye,
Dare frame thy fearful symmetry?

William Blake

Uluru Statement from the Heart

We, gathered at the 2017 National Constitutional Convention, coming from all points of the southern sky, make this statement from the heart:

Our Aboriginal and Torres Strait Islander tribes were the first sovereign Nations of the Australian continent and its adjacent islands, and possessed it under our own laws and customs. This our ancestors did, according to the reckoning of our culture, from the Creation, according to the common law from 'time immemorial', and according to science more than 60,000 years ago.

This sovereignty is *a spiritual notion: the ancestral tie between the land, or 'mother nature', and the Aboriginal and Torres Strait Islander peoples who were born therefrom, remain attached thereto, and must one day return thither to be united with our ancestors. This link is the basis of the ownership of the soil, or better, of sovereignty.* It has never been ceded or extinguished, and co-exists with the sovereignty of the Crown.

How could it be otherwise? That peoples possessed a land for sixty millennia and this sacred link disappears from world history in merely the last two hundred years?

With substantive constitutional change and structural reform, we believe this ancient sovereignty can shine through as a fuller expression of Australia's nationhood.

Proportionally, we are the most incarcerated people on the planet. We are not an innately criminal people. Our children are aliened from their families at unprecedented rates. This cannot be because we have no love for them. And our youth languish in detention in obscene numbers. They should be our hope for the future.

These dimensions of our crisis tell plainly the structural nature of our problem. This is *the torment of our powerlessness.*

We seek constitutional reforms to empower our people and take *a rightful place* in our own country. When we have power over our destiny our children will flourish. They will walk in two worlds and their culture will be a gift to their country.

We call for the establishment of a First Nations Voice enshrined in the Constitution.

Makarrata is the culmination of our agenda: *the coming together after a struggle.* It captures our aspirations for a fair and truthful relationship with the people of Australia and a better future for our children based on justice and self-determination.

We seek a Makarrata Commission to supervise a process of agreement-making between governments and First Nations and truth-telling about our history.

In 1967 we were counted, in 2017 we seek to be heard. We leave base camp and start our trek across this vast country. We invite you to walk with us in a movement of the Australian people for a better future.

250 Aboriginal and Torres Strait Islander delegates from all around Australia

Us

I was wrapped in black
fur and white fur and
you undid me and then
you placed me in gold light
and then you crowned me,
while snow fell outside
the door in diagonal darts.
While a ten-inch snow
came down like stars
in small calcium fragments,
we were in our own bodies
(that room that will bury us)
and you were in my body
(that room that will outlive us)
and at first I rubbed your
feet dry with a towel
because I was your slave
and then you called me princess.
Princess!

Oh then
I stood up in my gold skin
and I beat down the psalms
and I beat down the clothes
and you undid the bridle
and you undid the reins
and I undid the buttons,
the bones, the confusions,
the New England postcards,

the January ten o'clock night,
and we rose up like wheat,
acre after acre of gold,
and we harvested,
we harvested.

Anne Sexton

La Vie C'est La Vie

On summer afternoons I sit
Quiescent by you in the park,
And idly watch the sunbeams gild
And tint the ash-trees' bark.

Or else I watch the squirrels frisk
And chaffer in the grassy lane;
And all the while I mark your voice
Breaking with love and pain.

I know a woman who would give
Her chance of heaven to take my place;
To see the love-light in your eyes,
The love-glow on your face!

And there's a man whose lightest word
Can set my chilly blood afire;
Fulfilment of his least behest
Defines my life's desire.

But he will none of me, nor I
Of you. Nor you of her. 'Tis said
The world is full of jests like these.–
I wish that I were dead.

Jessie Redmon Fauset

Waiting for the Barbarians

What are we waiting for, assembled in the forum?

    The barbarians are due here today.

Why isn't anything going on in the senate?
Why are the senators sitting there without legislating?

    Because the barbarians are coming today.
    What's the point of senators making laws now?
    Once the barbarians are here, they'll do the legislating.

Why did our emperor get up so early,
and why is he sitting enthroned at the city's main gate,
in state, wearing the crown?

    Because the barbarians are coming today
    and the emperor's waiting to receive their leader.
    He's even got a scroll to give him,
    loaded with titles, with imposing names.

Why have our two consuls and praetors come out today
wearing their embroidered, their scarlet togas?

Why have they put on bracelets with so many amethysts,
rings sparkling with magnificent emeralds?
Why are they carrying elegant canes
beautifully worked in silver and gold?

    Because the barbarians are coming today
    and things like that dazzle the barbarians.

Why don't our distinguished orators turn up as usual
to make their speeches, say what they have to say?

    Because the barbarians are coming today
    and they're bored by rhetoric and public speaking.

Why this sudden bewilderment, this confusion?
(How serious people's faces have become.)
Why are the streets and squares emptying so rapidly,
everyone going home lost in thought?

    Because night has fallen and the barbarians haven't come.
    And some of our men just in from the border say
    there are no barbarians any longer.

Now what's going to happen to us without barbarians?
Those people were a kind of solution.

C. P. Cavafy, translated by Edmund Keeley and Philip Sherrard

Watching six seasons of the Nanny while my long-term relationship slowly fell apart

Watching six seasons of the Nanny while my long-term relationship
fell apart
Was more self-inflicted boredom than nostalgia
As Maxwell chased Fran up and down the staircase with a frying pan
And I lay in bed, listening to the distant sound of trains
Pulling their shit-for-brains cargo through the dark

There are some months when all art feels worthless
And life feels thin, and weak and full of spite
And the pastel hysteria of spring outside the window
Just makes me wince with disappointment and rage
And the total, mind-numbing futility of it all
Often, I think about the man who walked into the National Gallery
And punched a hole straight into a ten million-dollar Monet painting
Of a sailboat, drifting down a river of autumn leaves
And got sent to prison for five years

There's nothing in this world more boring than heartbreak
It's like a tax audit of the soul
And what once seemed rare and poignant
And full of emotional promise
Just makes me want to dose myself to the brim with horse tranquilizers
And take a long vacation to skeleton town

There's only so much sitting by the window
Begging the moon for punishment
You can take, before you have to get mad
And stride up and down the toiletries aisles of the grocery store

Wishing every old woman painstakingly reading the back of a
   Listerine packet
An expedient journey to hell
And all the poets you loved
Reveal themselves to be little bitches
Whose constant need to reupholster their pain
Seems sad & extravagant
Like grief factories, polluting the local waterways with pathos and nuance

The present has overflowed and turned the whole past bad
Ancient Greece, art nouveau, the entire Italian renaissance
All ruined
Monet too, with his surfeit of waterlilies
Wilting in the heat like a loose-leaf salad

I sit like Nostradamus
In my kingdom of disappointment
Burning down the cities of the future
Going through my google calendar
Listing all the bad things to come

Hera Lindsay Bird

We Did It

We did it in front of the mirror
and in the light. We did it in darkness,
in the water and the high grass.

We did it in honor of man
and in honor of beast and in honor of God.

But they didn't want to know about us,
they had already seen that sort of thing.

We did it with flair and in colors,
with the mingling of reddish hair and brown
and with difficult exercises
gladdening the heart. We did it
like the wheel-shaped angels and the holy beasts
and the divine chariot of the prophets.
We did it with six wings
and six legs, but the heavens
were hard above us
like the summer earth beneath us.

Yehuda Amichai, translated by Robert Alter

We grow accustomed to the Dark

We grow accustomed to the Dark –
When Light is put away –
As when the Neighbor holds the Lamp
To witness her Good bye –

A Moment – We uncertain step
For newness of the night –
Then – fit our Vision to the Dark –
And meet the Road – erect –

And so of larger – Darknesses –
Those Evenings of the Brain –

When not a Moon disclose a sign –
Or Star – come out – within –

The Bravest – grope a little –
And sometimes hit a Tree
Directly in the Forehead –
But as they learn to see –

Either the Darkness alters –
Or something in the sight
Adjusts itself to Midnight –
And Life steps almost straight.

Emily Dickinson

'Well, say there is no kingdom then for Richard'

Well, say there is no kingdom then for Richard;
What other pleasures can the world afford?
I'll make my heaven in a lady's lap,
And deck my body in gay ornaments,
And witch sweet ladies with my words and looks.
O miserable thought! and more unlikely
Than to accomplish twenty golden crowns!
Why, love forswore me in my mother's womb:
And, for I should not deal in her soft laws,
She did corrupt frail nature with some bribe,
To shrink mine arm up like a wither'd shrub;
To make an envious mountain on my back,
Where sits deformity to mock my body;

To shape my legs of an unequal size;
To disproportion me in every part,
Like to a chaos, or an unlick'd bear-whelp
That carries no impression like the dam.
And am I then a man to be beloved?
O monstrous fault, to harbour such a thought!
Then, since this earth affords no joy to me,
But to command, to cheque, to o'erbear such
As are of better person than myself,
I'll make my heaven to dream upon the crown,
And, whiles I live, to account this world but hell,
Until my mis-shaped trunk that bears this head
Be round impaled with a glorious crown.
And yet I know not how to get the crown,
For many lives stand between me and home:
And I – like one lost in a thorny wood,
That rends the thorns and is rent with the thorns,
Seeking a way and straying from the way;
Not knowing how to find the open air,
But toiling desperately to find it out, –
Torment myself to catch the English crown:
And from that torment I will free myself,
Or hew my way out with a bloody axe.
Why, I can smile, and murder while I smile,
And cry 'Content' to that which grieves my heart,
And wet my cheeks with artificial tears,
And frame my face to all occasions.
I'll drown more sailors than the mermaid shall;
I'll slay more gazers than the basilisk;
I'll play the orator as well as Nestor,
Deceive more slily than Ulysses could,

And, like a Sinon, take another Troy.
I can add colours to the chameleon,
Change shapes with Proteus for advantages,
And set the murderous Machiavel to school.
Can I do this, and cannot get a crown?
Tut, were it farther off, I'll pluck it down.

Richard III in Henry VI, *William Shakespeare*

Western Arrernte rain poem

Among the rippling waters he sits without a move, –
It is Kantjia himself who is sitting without a move.
Moveless like a boulder he is sitting;
His hair bedewed with rain he is sitting.
On the fissured rock-plates he is sitting;
On rock-plates welling with water he is sitting.
Bedrizzled with rain he sits without a move;
Among the rippling waters he sits without a move.
Bedrizzled with rain, a reddish glow overspreads him;
Among the rippling waters a reddish glow overspreads him.
The sky is clouded with water-moss;
The sky sends down scattered showers.
Over the rock-plates the flow is echoing, –
Over the rock-plates green with moss.
'Moss-covered one,
Spread forth your waters!'
'Come, moss-covered one,
Pour forth your waters!'
'Come, foam-crests,
Come, spread over the waters!'

'Come, drifting twigs,
Come, spread over the waters!'
Over the sun-darkened river sands calls the voice of the thunder,
the voice of the thunder;
From billowing storm-clouds calls the voice of the thunder, the
voice of the thunder.
The first storm-showers, –
The first storm showers are falling here and there, are falling
here and there.
The first storm-showers, –
The first storm showers are pouring down in torrents, are
pouring down in torrents.
A flash of lightning
Shivers trees in pieces.
A flash of lightning
Shocks and terrifies.
Overflowing its banks into side-channels
The flood rolls down its waves.

Anonymous, recorded and translated by T. G. H. Strehlow

What Kind of a Person

'What kind of a person are you,' I heard them say to me.
I'm a person with a complex plumbing of the soul,
Sophisticated instruments of feeling and a system
Of controlled memory at the end of the twentieth century,
But with an old body from ancient times
And with a God even older than my body.

I'm a person for the surface of the earth.
Low places, caves and wells
Frighten me. Mountain peaks
And tall buildings scare me.

I'm not like an inserted fork,
Not a cutting knife, not a stuck spoon.
I'm not flat and sly
Like a spatula creeping up from below.
At most I am a heavy and clumsy pestle
Mashing good and bad together
For a little taste
And a little fragrance.

Arrows do not direct me. I conduct
My business carefully and quietly
Like a long will that began to be written
The moment I was born.

Now I stand at the side of the street
Weary, leaning on a parking meter.
I can stand here for nothing, free.

I'm not a car, I'm a person,
A man-god, a god-man
Whose days are numbered. Hallelujah.

Yehuda Amichai, translated by Barbara and Benjamin Harshav

'When all the others were away at Mass'

When all the others were away at Mass
I was all hers as we peeled potatoes.
They broke the silence, let fall one by one
Like solder weeping off the soldering iron:
Cold comforts set between us, things to share
Gleaming in a bucket of clean water.
And again let fall. Little pleasant splashes
From each other's work would bring us to our senses.

So while the parish priest at her bedside
Went hammer and tongs at the prayers for the dying
And some were responding and some crying
I remembered her head bent towards my head,
Her breath in mine, our fluent dipping knives –
Never closer the whole rest of our lives.

Section III, Clearances, *Seamus Heaney*

When I Am With You

When I am with you, we stay up all night.
When you're not here, I can't go to sleep.

Praise God for these two insomnias!
And the difference between them.

The minute I heard my first love story
I started looking for you, not knowing
how blind that was.

Lovers don't finally meet somewhere.
They're in each other all along.

We are the mirror as well as the face in it.
We are tasting the taste this minute
of eternity. We are pain
and what cures pain, both. We are
the sweet cold water and the jar that pours.

I want to hold you close like a lute,
so we can cry out with loving.

You would rather throw stones at a mirror?
I am your mirror, and here are the stones.

Rumi, translated by Coleman Barks with John Moyne

'When my love swears that she is made of truth'

When my love swears that she is made of truth,
I do believe her, though I know she lies,
That she might think me some untutored youth,
Unlearnèd in the world's false subtleties.
Thus vainly thinking that she thinks me young,
Although she knows my days are past the best,
Simply I credit her false-speaking tongue;
On both sides thus is simple truth suppressed.
But wherefore says she not she is unjust?
And wherefore say not I that I am old?
Oh, love's best habit is in seeming trust,
And age in love loves not to have years told.

Therefore I lie with her and she with me,
And in our faults by lies we flattered be.

Sonnet 138, William Shakespeare

'When to the sessions of sweet silent thought'

When to the sessions of sweet silent thought
I summon up remembrance of things past,
I sigh the lack of many a thing I sought,
And with old woes new wail my dear time's waste;
Then can I drown an eye, unused to flow,
For precious friends hid in death's dateless night,
And weep afresh love's long since cancelled woe,
And moan th'expense of many a vanished sight;
Then can I grieve at grievances foregone,
And heavily from woe to woe tell o'er
The sad account of fore-bemoanèd moan,
Which I new pay as if not paid before.
But if the while I think on thee, dear friend,
All losses are restored and sorrows end.

Sonnet 30, William Shakespeare

When You Are Old

When you are old and grey and full of sleep,
And nodding by the fire, take down this book,
And slowly read, and dream of the soft look
Your eyes had once, and of their shadows deep;

How many loved your moments of glad grace,
And loved your beauty with love false or true,
But one man loved the pilgrim soul in you,
And loved the sorrows of your changing face;

And bending down beside the glowing bars,
Murmur, a little sadly, how Love fled
And paced upon the mountains overhead
And hid his face amid a crowd of stars.

W. B. Yeats

Where Does Such Tenderness Come From?

Where does such tenderness come from?
These aren't the first curls
I've wound around my finger –
I've kissed lips darker than yours.

The sky is washed and dark
(Where does such tenderness come from?)
Other eyes have known
and shifted away from my eyes.

But I've never heard words like this
in the night
(Where does such tenderness come from?)
with my head on your chest, rest.

Where does this tenderness come from?
And what will I do with it? Young

stranger, poet, wandering through town,
you and your eyelashes – longer than anyone's.

Marina Tsvetaeva, translated by Ilya Kaminsky and Jean Valentine

White Sunday/Lotu Tamaiti

We are soft with our hangovers
as they march like plastic angels over the hard floor
this is the day we love them

and let them eat first and don't yell at them
too much or hit them.
One of my cousins talks quietly

about the letter from school about the marks
on her son's legs and how he told the teacher
his parents hit him and how embarrassing that was.

The children sing 'Amazing Grace' and 'Nearer to Thee'
and act out the stories of Meshach, Shadrach and Abednego,
the golden idol is a mannequin in a lamé dress and a wig. The
    babies cry

so, in the kitchen we talk about the two women
who cornered each other in the church toilets
and beat the hell out of each other

and the girl who called her uncle *Dad*
and then got caught at the airport trying
to run off with him to Wellington

and the woman who slept with her cousin's husband
and then did it again and then again
and how it served her right when her niece did it right back to her.

After the play about Sodom and Gomorrah
the fattest faifeau in the world stands up and says the words
homosexual and lesbian, homosexual and lesbian

in English, so many times it sounds like welts
and we watch the face of our sister on the other side
who has come to church today for the first time in years.

After the service our sister tells us what our father told her
when her heart was breaking –
the story of our mother's cousin who was in love with a girl

and flew all the way to New Zealand to win her back.
But when she saw the girl was married
she went back to Samoa and hung herself.

He said, there are lots of other people out there for me.
People, our sister says again to us, *He said 'people'*.
The food is tasteless; we all remark on it, but we eat anyway.

Tusiata Avia

'Who killed Cock Robin?'

Who killed Cock Robin?
I, said the Sparrow,
with my bow and arrow,
I killed Cock Robin.

Who saw him die?
I, said the Fly,
with my little eye,
I saw him die.

Who caught his blood?
I, said the Fish,
with my little dish,
I caught his blood.

Who'll make the shroud?
I, said the Beetle,
with my thread and needle,
I'll make the shroud.

Who'll dig his grave?
I, said the Owl,
with my little trowel,
I'll dig his grave.

Who'll be the parson?
I, said the Rook,
with my little book,
I'll be the parson.

Who'll be the clerk?
I, said the Lark,
if it's not in the dark,
I'll be the clerk.

Who'll carry the link?
I, said the Linnet,
I'll fetch it in a minute,
I'll carry the link.

Who'll be chief mourner?
I, said the Dove,
I mourn for my love,
I'll be chief mourner.

Who'll carry the coffin?
I, said the Kite,
if it's not through the night,
I'll carry the coffin.

Who'll bear the pall?
We, said the Wren,
both the cock and the hen,
We'll bear the pall.

Who'll sing a psalm?
I, said the Thrush,
as she sat on a bush,
I'll sing a psalm.

Who'll toll the bell?
I, said the Bull,
because I can pull,
I'll toll the bell.

All the birds of the air
fell a-sighing and a-sobbing,
when they heard the bell toll
for poor Cock Robin.

Anonymous

Why I Love Your Body

I put your body
    between me
        and the history of horrors

your sweet tongue
snaking through my lips

your heavy breasts
thudding ripe on my ribs

your thin legs climbing mine
like twin grape vines

your creamy wetness
creeping through my fingers

when your body bursts over me
my mind goes almost quiet
faintly squeaking to itself
like a fruit bat dozing
        upside down.

I put your body
  between me
    and the terrifying future
      of my body

tonight I'm a noisy swamp
squelching under your bare toes.

Dorothy Porter

Wild Swans

I looked in my heart while the wild swans went over.
And what did I see I had not seen before?
Only a question less or a question more;
Nothing to match the flight of wild birds flying.
Tiresome heart, forever living and dying,
House without air, I leave you and lock your door.
Wild swans, come over the town, come over
The town again, trailing your legs and crying!

Edna St. Vincent Millay

The Windhover

To Christ our Lord

I caught this morning morning's minion, king-
  dom of daylight's dauphin, dapple-dawn-drawn Falcon, in his riding
  Of the rolling level underneath him steady air, and striding
High there, how he rung upon the rein of a wimpling wing
In his ecstasy! then off, off forth on swing,

As a skate's heel sweeps smooth on a bow-bend: the hurl and gliding
Rebuffed the big wind. My heart in hiding
Stirred for a bird, – the achieve of; the mastery of the thing!

Brute beauty and valour and act, oh, air, pride, plume, here
Buckle! AND the fire that breaks from thee then, a billion
Times told lovelier, more dangerous, O my chevalier!

No wonder of it: shéer plód makes plough down sillion
Shine, and blue-bleak embers, ah my dear,
Fall, gall themselves, and gash gold-vermillion.

Gerard Manley Hopkins

Windy Mick and the Falcon

He'd seen enough of the Nightcliffe
He'd had enough of his friends
If he didn't get out of Darwin
The grog'd do him in
So staggerin' home from another show
He falls down in someone's yard – no problem it's happened before
At least the dog's tied up

When he sees before him all neat and clean
An XB Falcon ute, V8 four speed,
Roo bar, spotties, brand new boots, CB, stereo
Well all you want really if you have a look
Keys in the ignition
Never had a second thought, rolled her out of the drive
Crescent moon looked in on him from away up in the sky

She starts first kick, and up the street the you-beaut's idlin' sweet
And he's sneakin' out a town now away from the Timor sea

A bogey in the Katherine river, a pie and sauce at Mataranka
He camps in the scrub till he's feelin' better – waitin' for the day to end
He'll be sober and right to drive all night
When all good caravans are in bed.

And when he drove, he drove alone right up to the dawn
Just him and all the interstate truckies
With their CB crackle talk, he says;

'You got a copy there southbound? – I'm in the Falcon comin' past'
'Yeah mate'
'Come from Darwin – got away from the grog at last'
'Well you never had enough' they said n' that's how they get their laughs.

But he overtakes them all, puts their circus lights behind
Till it's just him, the moon and the Falcon
Under a thousand miles of sky
Sweepin' over flood plains with an eye out for a bullock
Along the side of rivers where insects hit the screen
And when that crescent moon again dips low towards the ground
Mick gives a little shiver
But the Falcon's runnin' well

Shifting gears out of Elliott the country it peels back
Shedding trees all the way down south along the track
At daybreak the sky it opens – he's back in the desert again
The tug of a range further out, his right arm gettin' red
The windows open wide and the wind is in his hair

He smells every desert fragrance, feels every dreamtime lair
The familiar landscape burstin' forth, the memories alive
Of all the old time camps stretched out under starlit nights
A hundred campfires lit and died with a girl in his arms he held
But he puts it all behind him now cause the Falcon's runnin' well

He smelt a beer at Ti-Tree so he pulls in for a charge
Grabs a carton for the road, spins the wheels in a cloud of dust
The MacDonnell Ranges crack the sky same time the sun goes down
Alice Springs is up ahead he knows it's not far now
And the stereo is wound right up – some old country tune
Mick's laughin' and singin' along he don't worry about the moon
He don't worry about any cops that might be lookin' for him too
He lets the Falcon have its head and guzzles on a can
'No bastard'll stop me now' he says 'the Falcon's runnin' well'

Maybe some old roo leans back on his tail
And sees the headlights comin' fast and tail lights disappearin'
Off the road out in the scrub it over shot a turn
And in a single bound the Falcon leaps and takes off in the air

Mick looks out and shits himself to see he's left the ground
'Jesus Christ I must've died, help me if you can!'
He pulls his head in, checks the gauges, tries the tape for sound
The earth falls back behind him
But by geez the Falcon's runnin' well

Over the great salt pan basins far above the gibber plains
Where dusty men scratch holes in the ground
And end up sad and dazed
On and on and on by night

Till it seems that the earth just turns
Mick keeps his seatbelt fastened tight
And steers toward the moon

Far below he spies the lights of a road train crawlin' slow
'Geez mate have ya got a copy I'm not sure where I am?'
And in the cab below the driver hears a desperate hand
'You got a copy there mate, I'm above ya in the sky!'
'Well tell that airliner to dip his lights' says the disbelieving driver

Windy Mick came back to earth on the good side of Port Augusta
The Falcon hit the road again on its shock absorbers
'Thank you God for that' Mick says 'me drinkin' days are over'
And he whips the ute through Horrocks pass and onto the
Barrier Highway
And guns it for the rabbits all the way through Broken Hill
Puttoh, puttoh, their heads they hit the Falcon runnin' well
Dodgin' roos and sheep through Wilcannia onto Cobar
Pointin' east to Nyngan, where the farms and fences start
In Narromine or Dubbo there's nowhere to toss a swag
So Mick plants it through to Orange and the miles they just fell
From Bathurst to Katoomba you know the Falcon's runnin' well!

Up and over the great divide and there at last it spreads below
The great old Sydney urban sprawl, snoozing in a smog of grey
pink dawn
Pacific Ocean lappin' at her shores, jets cruisin' in with tourists galore
You might well wonder what Mick came here for

Well he drove around for an hour or two and couldn't find a park
So he hung a Uey in George Street and was back on the plains by dark

And the drinkers in the pubs en route
This is what they tell,
How can you put it all behind ya,
With a Falcon, runnin' well.

Neil Murray

Wine

Reading a life of Alexander the Great, Alexander
whose rough father, Philip, hired Aristotle to tutor
the young scion and warrior, to put some polish
on his smooth shoulders. Alexander who, later
on the campaign trail into Persia, carried a copy of
The Iliad in a velvet-lined box, he loved that book so
much. He loved to fight and drink, too.
I came to that place in the life where Alexander, after
a long night of carousing, a wine-drunk (the worst kind of drunk –
hangovers you don't forget), threw the first brand
to start a fire that burned Persepolis, capital of the Persian Empire
(ancient even in Alexander's day).
Razed it right to the ground. Later, of course,
next morning – maybe even while the fire roared – he was
remorseful. But nothing like the remorse felt
the next evening when, during a disagreement that turned ugly
and, on Alexander's part, overbearing, his face flushed
from too many bowls of uncut wine, Alexander rose drunkenly to
his feet,
grabbed a spear and drove it through the breast
of his friend, Cletus, who'd saved his life at Granicus.

For three days Alexander mourned. Wept. Refused food. 'Refused
to see to his bodily needs.' He even promised
to give up wine forever.
(I've heard such promises and the lamentations that go with them.)
Needless to say, life for the army came to a full stop
as Alexander gave himself over to his grief.
But at the end of those three days, the fearsome heat
beginning to take its toll on the body of his dead friend,
Alexander was persuaded to take action. Pulling himself together
and leaving his tent, he took out his copy of Homer, untied it,
began to turn the pages. Finally he gave orders that the funeral
rites described for Patroklos be followed to the letter:
he wanted Cletus to have the biggest possible send-off.
And when the pyre was burning and the bowls of wine were
passed his way during the ceremony? Of course, what do you
think? Alexander drank his fill and passed
out. He had to be carried to his tent. He had to be lifted, to be put
into his bed.

Raymond Carver

Woman to Child

You who were darkness warmed my flesh
where out of darkness rose the seed.
Then all a world I made in me;
all the world you hear and see
hung upon my dreaming blood.

There moved the multitudinous stars,
and coloured birds and fishes moved.

There swam the sliding continents.
All time lay rolled in me, and sense,
and love that knew not its beloved.

O node and focus of the world;
I hold you deep within that well
you shall escape and not escape –
that mirrors still your sleeping shape;
that nurtures still your crescent cell.

I wither and you break from me;
yet though you dance in living light
I am the earth, I am the root,
I am the stem that fed the fruit,
the link that joins you to the night.

Judith Wright

Woman to Man

The eyeless labourer in the night,
the selfless, shapeless seed I hold,
builds for its resurrection day –
silent and swift and deep from sight
foresees the unimagined light.

This is no child with a child's face;
this has no name to name it by:
yet you and I have known it well.
This is our hunter and our chase,
the third who lay in our embrace.

This is the strength that your arm knows,
the arc of flesh that is my breast,
the precise crystals of our eyes.
This is the blood's wild tree that grows
the intricate and folded rose.

This is the maker and the made;
this is the question and reply;
the blind head butting at the dark,
the blaze of light along the blade.
Oh hold me, for I am afraid.

Judith Wright

'Women of Corinth'

Women of Corinth, I have come out of the house,
so that you will not hold anything against me. I know that many people
are standoffish, some in the privacy of home
and others in the public sphere. Some people, because they are shy,
have acquired the ill repute of indifference.
There is no justice in people's perception:
there are some who, before they know a person inside out,
hate him on sight, even if they have never been wronged by him.
An outsider in particular must conform to the city.
A native too: I do not condone self-absorbed people
who through insensitivity irritate their neighbours.
But for me this unexpected disaster
has wrecked my life. I am cast adrift. I have lost
all pleasure in living and I want to die, my friends.
The man who was everything to me, try to understand this,

has turned out to be the vilest man alive, my own husband.
Of all creatures that have life and reason
we women are the sorriest lot:
first we must at a great expenditure of money
buy a husband and even take on a master
over our body: this evil is more galling than the first.
Here is the most challenging contest, whether we will get a bad man
or a good one. Besides, divorce is unsavoury
for a woman and it is not possible to say no to one's husband.
And when she comes into new customs and rules
a woman must be a prophet of what she could never learn at home:
how best to deal with her marriage partner;
and if we get it worked out well and a husband shares
our life with us, and he bears the yoke without violence,
life is to be envied. Otherwise we are better off dead.
But the man, when he is bored with things at home
he can go out to ease the weariness of his heart.
But we have just one person to look to.
They say that we live a life free of danger
at home while they face battle with the spear.
How wrong they are. I would rather stand three times
in the line of battle than once bear a child.

Medea in Medea, *Euripides, translated by Cecelia Eaton Luschnig*

'Your children are not your children'

Your children are not your children.
They are the sons and daughters of Life's longing for itself.
They come through you but not from you,
And though they are with you, they belong not to you.

You may give them your love but not your thoughts.
For they have their own thoughts.
You may house their bodies but not their souls,
For their souls dwell in the house of tomorrow,
  which you cannot visit, not even in your dreams.
You may strive to be like them, but seek not to make them like you.
For life goes not backward nor tarries with yesterday.
You are the bows from which your children as living arrows are
  sent forth.
The archer sees the mark upon the path of the infinite,
  and He bends you with His might that His arrows may go
  swift and far.
Let your bending in the archer's hands be for gladness;
For even as He loves the arrow that flies, so He loves also the bow
  that is stable.

The Prophet, ***Kahlil Gibran***

Your Feet

When I can not look at your face
I look at your feet.

Your feet of arched bone,
your hard little feet.

I know that they support you,
and that your gentle weight
rises upon them.

Your waist and your breasts,
the doubled purple
of your nipples,
the sockets of your eyes
that have just flown away,
your wide fruit mouth,
your red tresses,
my little tower.

But I love your feet
only because they walked
upon the earth and upon
the wind and upon the waters,
until they found me.

Pablo Neruda, translated by Donald D. Walsh

Your Kiss

I feel your nakedness inside your kiss
(And once I nearly died inside your kiss)

All day the sky just lazes on the sea
And I am swimming in that tide, your kiss

How everything I see is soaked with time
(But in your arms I've always sighed 'Your kiss!')

It's summer and the days peel off their skin
And naked half the day I ride your kiss

At night my walnut tree soaks up the dark
(Just as one night in bed you lied your kiss)

Death has its fundamentalists as well
But I shall take another guide: your kiss!

The heart is ringing in its spire of bone
(Then pushes time aside – just for your kiss)

Kevin Hart

Youth

Your unhappy and silly youth.
Your arrival from the provinces to the city.
Misted-over windowpanes of streetcars,
Restless misery of the crowd.
Your dread when you entered a place too expensive.
But everything was too expensive. Too high.
Those people must have noticed your crude manners,
Your outmoded clothes, and your awkwardness.

There were none who would stand by you and say,

You are a handsome boy,
You are strong and healthy,
Your misfortunes are imaginary.

You would not have envied a tenor in an overcoat of camel hair
Had you guessed his fear and known how he would die.

She, the red-haired, because of whom you suffered tortures,
So beautiful she seemed to you, is a doll in fire,
You don't understand what she screams with her lips of a clown.

The shapes of hats, the cut of robes, faces in the mirrors,
You will remember unclearly like something from long ago
Or like what remains from a dream.

The house you approached trembling,
The apartment that dazzled you –
Look, on this spot the cranes clear the rubble.

In your turn you will have, possess, secure,
Able to be proud at last, when there is no reason.

Your wishes will be fulfilled, you will gape then
At the essence of time, woven of smoke and mist,

An iridescent fabric of lives that last one day,
Which rises and falls like an unchanging sea.

Books you have read will be of use no more.
You searched for an answer but lived without answer.

You will walk in the streets of southern cities,
Restored to your beginnings, seeing again in rapture
The whiteness of a garden after the first night of snow.

Czeslaw Milosz, translated by the author

Index of Poets and Their Works

ABORIGINAL DELEGATES
Uluru Statement from the Heart 340

ROBERT ADAMSON 1943–
Elegy from Balmoral Beach 89
Eurydice and the Tawny Frogmouth 91

ANNA AKHMATOVA 1889–1966
Everything Is Plundered 92
In Dream 156

YEHUDA AMICHAI 1924–2000
Advice for Good Love 10
The Diameter of the Bomb 63
In the Middle of This Century 161
A Letter of Recommendation 178
A Pity, We Were Such a Good Invention 253
Songs for a Woman 293
Try to Remember Some Details 336
We Did It 347
What Kind of a Person 352

MAYA ANGELOU 1928–2014
Men 204

ANONYMOUS
Donal Og 79
The Hag of Beare 116
Katie Cruel 170
Riddle 25 from the Anglo-Saxon Riddle Hoard 264
'Sing a song of sixpence' 284
The Streets of Laredo 302
Western Arrernte rain poem 351
'Who killed Cock Robin?' 359

MATTHEW ARNOLD 1822–1888
Dover Beach 81

W. H. AUDEN 1907–1973
The Composer 51
Funeral Blues 111
Lullaby 188
Musée des Beaux Arts 213
Night Mail 220

TUSIATA AVIA 1966–
House 131
Today we are in a hospital ward 330
White Sunday/Lotu Tamaiti 358

CHARLES BAUDELAIRE 1821–1867
Spleen 296

JOHN BERRYMAN 1914–1972
The Ball Poem 24

KING JAMES BIBLE
'The Lord is my shepherd' (Psalm 23) 184
'O Lord, thou hast searched me, and known me' (Psalm 139) 228
Sermon on the Mount (Matthew) 274
Song of Solomon 1–5 287
'Though I speak with the tongues of men and of angels' (Corinthians) 318
'To every thing there is a season' (Ecclesiastes) 325

HERA LINDSAY BIRD 1987–
Keats Is Dead So Fuck Me From Behind 171
Watching six seasons of the Nanny . . . 346

WILLIAM BLAKE 1757–1827
The Garden of Love 111
A Poison Tree 256
The Sick Rose 281
The Tyger 338

EAVAN BOLAND 1944–
Quarantine 260

JORGE LUIS BORGES 1899–1986
In Praise of Darkness 157

ANNE BRADSTREET c. 1612–1672
To My Dear and Loving Husband 328

BERTOLT BRECHT 1898–1956
I Never Loved You More 143
I Want to Go with the One I Love 145
In Praise of Doubt 159
Pleasures 254
To Those Born After 328

MAHOGANY L. BROWNE
Inevitable 164

ELIZABETH BARRETT BROWNING 1806–1861
'I think of thee!' (Sonnet 29) 145
'If thou must love me' (Sonnet 14) 147

VINCENT BUCKLEY 1925–1988
Triads 335

ROBERT BURNS 1759–1796
A Man's a Man for A' That 195

GEORGE GORDON, LORD BYRON 1788–1824
She Walks in Beauty 278

CALLIMACHUS c. 305 BCE–c. 240 BCE
'They told me, Heraclitus' 313

KEV CARMODY 1946–
I've Been Moved 153

RAYMOND CARVER 1938–1988
Wine 368

CATULLUS c. 84 BCE–c. 54 BCE
Sign of Love 281

C. P. CAVAFY 1863–1933
Days of 1903 60
The God Abandons Antony 113
Ithaka 165
Waiting for the Barbarians 344

CHANG YANG-HAO 1270–1329
Recalling the Past at T'ung Pass 263

AUSTIN CLARKE 1896–1974
The Planter's Daughter 254

MAXINE BENEBA CLARKE 1979–
Brown 41

LUCILLE CLIFTON 1936–2010
to a dark moses 321

ALISON CROGGON 1962–
The Elwood Organic Fruit and Vegetable Shop 90
Lyric 189
Seduction Poem 274
Songs of Grass 294
Tiresias 320

E. E. CUMMINGS 1894–1962
i carry your heart with me 134

MAHMOUD DARWISH 1941–2008
Earth Presses Against Us 88
I Belong There 133

BRUCE DAWE 1930–
Drifters 83
Life-cycle 179

EMILY DICKINSON 1830–1886
'Hope' is the thing with feathers 130
'I'm nobody! Who are you?' 152
'One need not be a chamber to be haunted' 244
'They say that time assuages' 313
'We grow accustomed to the Dark' 348

ROSEMARY DOBSON 1920–2012
The Three Fates 319

JOHN DONNE 1572–1631
'Death, be not proud' (Holy Sonnet 10) 61
Nativity 218
The Sun Rising 305
To His Mistress Going to Bed 326

EIBHLÍN DUBH NÍ CHONAILL (DARK EILEEN) 1743–1800
Dirge on the Death of Art O'Leary 70

ALI COBBY ECKERMANN 1963–
Canoe 43
First Time (I Met My Grandmother) 98
Little Bit Long Time 183

T. S. ELIOT 1888–1965
The Journey of the Magi 168

ANSEL ELKINS 1982–
Autobiography of Eve 22

EURIPIDES c. 485 BCE–c. 406 BCE
'Women of Corinth' (*Medea*) 371

MICHEL FABER 1960–
Cute 57

JESSIE REDMON FAUSET 1882–1961
La Vie C'est La Vie 343

JAMES FENTON 1949–
In Paris with You 156
The Mistake 209

CAROLINE FINKELSTEIN 1940–2016
Conjecture Number One Thousand 52

ROBERT FROST 1874–1963
Stopping by Woods on a Snowy Evening 301

KAHLIL GIBRAN 1883–1931
'Your children are not your children' (*The Prophet*) 372

DANA GIOIA 1950–
Finding a Box of Family Letters 95

NIKKI GIOVANNI 1943–
A Poem on the Assassination of Robert F. Kennedy 255

DENIS GLOVER 1912–1980
The Magpies 190

ROBERT GRAY 1945–
Diptych 65

HAFIZ 1315–1390
The Great Secret 115

THOMAS HARDY 1840–1928
Afterwards 12
The Darkling Thrush 59
Heredity 127
The Night of the Dance 223
The Oxen 248
Proud Songsters 259
She Hears the Storm 277

KEVIN HART 1954–
The Members of the Orchestra 203
The Past 250
Your Kiss 374

P. J. HARTIGAN 1878–1952
Said Hanrahan 268

GWEN HARWOOD 1920–1995
Barn Owl 28
In the Park 162
A Simple Story 281
'Thought Is Surrounded by a Halo' 319

SEAMUS HEANEY 1939–2013
Act of Union 9
Digging 64
Follower 106
Postscript 256
'When all the others were away at Mass' (*Clearances*) 354

ZBIGNIEW HERBERT 1924–1998
Mother 212
Sir from Biology 285

F. R. HIGGINS 1896–1941
Father and Son 94

PHILIP HODGINS 1959–1995
Country Football 54
Milk Cream Butter 206
Shooting the Dogs 279

MIROSLAV HOLUB 1923–1998
The fly 103

HOMER c. 800–c. 750 BCE
'And so their spirits soared' (*The Iliad*) 15
'Now from his breast into the eyes the ache' (*The Odyssey*) 228

A. D. HOPE 1907–2000
The Death of the Bird 61

GERARD MANLEY HOPKINS 1844–1889
Binsey Poplars 35
God's Grandeur 114
Pied Beauty 251
Spring and Fall 298
The Windhover 363

A. E. HOUSMAN 1859–1936
'From far, from eve and morning' 110
To an Athlete Dying Young 321

LANGSTON HUGHES 1902–1967
Life Is Fine 181

TED HUGHES 1930–1998
Bride and Groom Lie Hidden for Three Days 38

SAM HUNT 1946–
Coming to It 49

MOUSHEGH ISHKHAN 1913–1990
The Armenian Language Is the Home of the Armenian 15

IZUMI SHIKIBU 974–1034
'In this world' 163
'No different, really' 224
Things I Want Decided 314

CLIVE JAMES 1939–
Japanese Maple 167

KABIR 1440–1518
To Be a Slave of Intensity 323

JOHN KEATS 1795–1821
La Belle Dame sans Merci 33
'Bright star, would I were stedfast as thou art' 39
Ode on Melancholy 231
Ode to a Nightingale 232

OMAR KHAYYÁM 1048–1131
The Rubáiyát of Omar Khayyám 267

GALWAY KINNELL 1927–2014
Man Splitting Wood in the Daybreak 194

JOHN KINSELLA 1963–
Drowning in Wheat 85

RUDYARD KIPLING 1865–1936
If 146

KO UN 1933–
Asking the Way 16
Morning Birdsong 210
1:30 AM 245
Taklamakan Desert 309
Torture 334

ONO NO KOMACHI c. 825–c. 900
'Night deepens' 220

MAXINE KUMIN 1925–2014
After Love 11
The Excrement Poem 92

PHILIP LARKIN 1922–1985
At Grass 16
Broadcast 40
Dublinesque 86
First Sight 97
The Trees 334

NAOMI LAZARD 1936–
Ordinance on Arrival 246

EMMA LAZARUS 1849–1887
The New Colossus 219

LI-YOUNG LEE 1957–
I Ask My Mother to Sing 133
Immigrant Blues 154

HENRY WADSWORTH LONGFELLOW 1807–1882
Loss and Gain 185

FEDERICO GARCÍA LORCA 1898–1936
Rider's Song 264

NORMAN MacCAIG 1910–1996
Aunt Julia 20
Basking Shark 31

DONAGH MacDONAGH 1912–1968
The Hungry Grass 132

ANTONIO MACHADO 1875–1939
Summer Night 304

LOUIS MacNEICE 1907–1963
Prayer Before Birth 257

PAULA MEEHAN 1955–
Child Burial 45
Pillow Talk 251
The Statue of the Virgin at Granard Speaks 299

MÁIRE MHAC AN tSAOI 1922–
Man for whom I endured . . . 191
Mary Hogan's Quatrains 198

EDNA ST. VINCENT MILLAY 1892–1950
God's World 115
Wild Swans 363

CZESLAW MILOSZ 1911–2004
Gift 112
Incantation 163
Love 185
Youth 375

JOHN MILTON 1608–1674
On His Blindness 240
'Sweet is the breath of Morn' (*Paradise Lost*) 307

SINÉAD MORRISSEY 1972–
Driving Alone on a Snowy Evening (After Frost) 84

LES MURRAY 1938–2019
An Absolutely Ordinary Rainbow 7
The Cows on Killing Day 55
Folklore 105
The Last Hellos 173
The Mitchells 210
Once in a Lifetime, Snow 242

NEIL MURRAY 1956–
Windy Mick and the Falcon 364

JOHN SHAW NEILSON 1872–1942
May 202
Surely God Was a Lover 307

PABLO NERUDA 1904–1973
I'm Explaining a Few Things 149
Your Feet 373

JOHN HENRY NEWMAN 1801–1890
'Lead, kindly Light, amid th'encircling gloom' 176

EILÉAN NÍ CHUILLEANÁIN 1942–
Swineherd 308

OODGEROO NOONUCCAL 1920–1993
Gifts 112

SHARON OLDS 1942–
Celibate's Ode to Balls 44
Ode to the Clitoris 235
Ode to the Hymen 237
Sex Without Love 276

MARY OLIVER 1935–2019
The Summer Day 304

OVID 43 BCE–c. 17 CE
Corinna 53

WILFRED OWEN 1893–1918
Dulce et Decorum Est 87

DOROTHY PARKER 1893–1967
Resumé 263

BANJO PATERSON 1864–1941
Clancy of the Overflow 47
The Man from Ironbark 192

OCTAVIO PAZ 1914–1998
Last Dawn 172

PADRAIG PEARSE 1879–1916
The Mother 212

SYLVIA PLATH 1932–1963
Hardcastle Crags 121
Mirror 208
Morning Song 211
Mushrooms 215

PO CHÜ-I 772–846
A Dream of Mountaineering 82

DOROTHY PORTER 1954–2008
Lucky 187
My At-Last Lover 216
Why I Love Your Body 362

VICKI RAYMOND 1949–
On Seeing the First Flasher 241

RAINER MARIA RILKE 1875–1926
The Panther 249

ARTHUR RIMBAUD 1854–1891
Departure 63

YANNIS RITSOS 1909–1990
Ordinary People's Lithograph 247

ARCHIE ROACH 1956–
Took the Children Away 332

CHRISTINA ROSSETTI 1830–1894
A Birthday 36
'Many in aftertimes will say of you' 198
No, Thank You, John 226

RUMI 1207–1273
A Thirsty Fish 315
When I Am With You 354

SAPPHO C. 620 BCE–C. 550 BCE
'He is more than a hero' 125

ANNE SEXTON 1928–1974
The Ballad of the Lonely Masturbator 25
Her Kind 126
Us 342

WILLIAM SHAKESPEARE 1564–1616
'All the world's a stage' (*As You Like It*) 13
'The barge she sat in, like a burnish'd throne' (*Antony and Cleopatra*) 27
'Be absolute for death' (*Measure for Measure*) 31
'But I do think it is their husbands' faults' (*Othello*) 42
'Come, you spirits' (*Macbeth*) 49
'Th' expense of spirit in a waste of shame' (Sonnet 129) 93
'Friends, Romans, countrymen' (*Julius Caesar*) 109
'I dream'd there was an Emperor Antony' (*Antony and Cleopatra*) 142
'If we are mark'd to die, we are enow' (*Henry V*) 148
'Like as the waves make towards the pebbled shore' (Sonnet 60) 183
'Methought I heard a voice cry' (*Macbeth*) 206
'My love is as a fever, longing still' (Sonnet 147) 217
'O mistress mine' (*Twelfth Night*) 230
'O, pardon me, thou bleeding piece of earth' (*Julius Caesar*) 230
'Of comfort no man speak' (*Richard II*) 238
'Or I shall live your epitaph to make' (Sonnet 81) 246
'The quality of mercy is not strained' (*The Merchant of Venice*) 259
'Shall I compare thee to a summer's day?' (Sonnet 18) 277
'Since brass, nor stone, nor earth, nor boundless sea' (Sonnet 65) 283
Sonnets 44 and 45 295
'That time of year thou may'st in me behold' (Sonnet 73) 309
'Thou, nature, art my goddess' (*King Lear*) 317
'To be or not to be' (*Hamlet*) 324
'Tomorrow, and tomorrow, and tomorrow' (*Macbeth*) 331
'Well, say there is no kingdom then for Richard' (*Henry VI*) 349
'When my love swears that she is made of truth' (Sonnet 138) 355
'When to the sessions of sweet silent thought' (Sonnet 30) 356

PERCY BYSSHE SHELLEY 1792–1822
Ozymandias 248

WARSAN SHIRE 1988–
Backwards 23
Home 128

SIR PHILIP SIDNEY 1554–1586
'My true love hath my heart' (*Arcadia*) 218

SANDRA SIMONDS 1977–
Sorcery 296

KENNETH SLESSOR 1901–1971
Five Bells 99
The Night-Ride 224

SOPHOCLES c. 496 BCE–c. 406 BCE
'I go, but first will tell thee why I came' (*Oedipus Rex*) 143
'Love, never conquered in battle' (*Antigone*) 186

WISLAWA SZYMBORSKA 1923–2012
Four A.M. 108
Hatred 123
The Letters of the Dead 179
A Man's Household 197
Museum 214
No End of Fun 225
The Railroad Station 261
Theatre Impressions 310

RABINDRANATH TAGORE 1861–1941
Closed Path 48

SARA TEASDALE 1884–1933
Old Love and New 240
There Will Come Soft Rain 311

ALFRED, LORD TENNYSON 1809–1892
'Ring out, wild bells' (*In Memoriam*) 265

DYLAN THOMAS 1914–1953
And death shall have no dominion' 14
Do not go gentle into that good night 78
The force that through the green fuse drives the flower 107

MARINA TSVETAEVA 1892–1941
Where Does Such Tenderness Come From? 357

TU FU 712–770
Sunset 306

OCEAN VUONG 1988–
Aubade with Burning City 18

SAMUEL WAGAN WATSON 1972–
There's No Place Like Home 312

FREDERIC E. WEATHERLY 1848–1929
Danny Boy 58

WALT WHITMAN 1819–1892
'I celebrate myself' (*Song of Myself*: 1–6) 135
'I think I could turn and live with animals' (*Song of Myself*: 32) 144
Once I Pass'd Through a Populous City 242
'The spotted hawk swoops by and accuses me' (*Song of Myself*: 52) 297
'Twenty-eight young men' (*Song of Myself*: 11) 337

ALISON WHITTAKER
beneviolence 35

RICHARD WILBUR 1921–2017
A Barred Owl 30

WILLIAM WORDSWORTH 1770–1850
Composed upon Westminster Bridge, September 3, 1802 50

JUDITH WRIGHT 1915–2000
Black Cockatoos 37
Thornbills 316

Woman to Child 369
Woman to Man 370

W. B. YEATS 1865–1939
An Irish Airman Foresees His Death 165
The Lake Isle of Innisfree 172
Leda and the Swan 177
Never Give All the Heart 219
Sailing to Byzantium 272
The Second Coming 273
When You Are Old 356

ADAM ZAGAJEWSKI 1945–
Auto Mirror 22

Index of First Lines

A beach. Small waves and a shark net 89
A beautiful summer night 304
A Book of Verses underneath the Bough 267
A cold coming we had of it 168
A day so happy 112
a girl watches a bead of sweat roll 43
A shoe's idiot gape 294
A sudden blow: the great wings beating still 177
A visiting conductor 281
About suffering they were never wrong 213
Advice for good love: Don't love 10
Afterward, the compromise 11
Ah, make the most of what we yet may spend 267
All me are standing on feed. The sky is shining 55
All the others translate: the painter sketches 51
All the world's a stage 13
Among the rippling waters he sits without a move,– 351
And death shall have no dominion 14
And seeing the multitudes, he went up into a mountain 274
And so their spirits soared 15
And some time make the time to drive out west 256
As brazen as the naked day 189
As I walked out on the streets of Laredo 302
As if gathered together 263
As you set out for Ithaka 165
Ask the god to open the house of your chest 131
At night, in my dream, I stoutly climbed a mountain 82
At the instant of drowning he invoked the three sisters 319
Aunt Julia spoke Gaelic 20
Be absolute for death; either death or life 31
Bent double, like old beggars under sacks 87
Between my finger and my thumb 64
Black and enduring separation 156
Bright star, would I were stedfast as thou art – 39
Busy old fool, unruly Sun 305
But I do think it is their husbands' faults 42

Christmas Eve, and twelve of the clock 248
Come, fill the Cup, and in the Fire of Spring 267
Come, madam, come, all rest my powers defy 326
Come, you spirits 49
Córdoba 264
Crossing the shallow holdings high above sea 132
Daybreak: the household slept 28
Death, be not proud, though some have called thee 61
Do not go gentle into that good night 78
Don't die, Dad – 173
Don't talk to me of love. I've had an earful 156
Down stucco sidestreets 86
Each certain kind of weather or of light 37
Earth has not any thing to show more fair 50
Earth is pressing against us, trapping us in the final passage 88
Ebb tide has come for me 116
Enough seen. The vision has been encountered in all skies 63
Everything is plundered, betrayed, sold 92
First look from morning's window 254
Flintlike, her feet struck 121
For every bird there is this last migration 61
For me the tragedy's most important act is the sixth 310
For some we loved, the loveliest and the best 267
Friend, hope for the Guest while you are alive 323
Friends, Romans, countrymen, lend me your ears 109
From far, from eve and morning 110
Gas flaring on the yellow platform; voices running up and down 224
Giant whispering and coughing from 40
Glory be to God for dappled things – 251
God was full of Wine last night 115
Grey-coated, solitary stranger, hail! 241
Heavy, huge, honey-filled figs weighted down 247
He'd get up every morning before the sun 206
He'd seen enough of the Nightcliffe 364
He fell from her knees like a ball of yarn 212
He is more than a hero 125
He's one of those men who want to do everything by themselves 197
Here are plates with no appetite 214
His vision, from the constantly passing bars 249
'Hope' is the thing with feathers – 130

How do they do it, the ones who make love 276
Human reason is beautiful and invincible 163
I'm a witch who lost all her powers, then 296
I am a wonderful help to women 264
I am like the king of a rainy land 296
I am not yet born; O hear me 257
I am seeing this: two men are sitting on a pole 210
I am silver and exact. I have no preconceptions 208
I am the family face 127
I'm nobody! Who are you? 152
I belong there. I have many memories. I was born as everyone is born 133
I cannot even remember 285
i carry your heart with me(i carry it in 134
I caught this morning morning's minion, king- 363
I celebrate myself, and sing myself 135
I didn't die – waking up I hear that 210
I do not grudge them; Lord, I do not grudge 212
I don't get tired of you. Don't grow weary 315
I don't know when you came into being 237
I dream'd there was an Emperor Antony 142
I feel your nakedness inside your kiss 374
I go, but first will tell thee why I came 143
I had written him a letter which I had, for want of better 47
I have gone out, a possessed witch 126
I know that I shall meet my fate 165
I leant upon a coppice gate 59
I lie on a gurney, we all do, like brides. I don't know any of the others 330
I looked in my heart while the wild swans went over 363
I met a traveller from an antique land 248
I never found them again – all lost so quickly . . . 60
I never loved you more, ma soeur 143
I never said I loved you, John 226
I put your body 362
I think I could turn and live with animals, they are so placid and self-contain'd 144
I think of thee! – my thoughts do twine and bud 145
I thought that my voyage had come to its end 48
I used to see her in a sandwich shop 250
I've been moved by the wind upon the waters 153
I want the slew of muscle, a less 274

I want to go with the one I love 145
I was angry with my friend 256
I was wrapped in black 342
I went down to the river 181
I went to the Garden of Love 111
I will arise and go now, and go to Innisfree 172
'I will bring you love,' said the young lover 112
I will go walking in Elwood with my mind as smooth as a marrow 90
If ever two were one, then surely we 328
If I loved him – I loved him – 52
If the dull substance of my flesh were thought 295
If thou must love me, let it be for naught 147
If we are mark'd to die, we are enow 148
If you can keep your head when all about you 146
If you open your coat 293
If you're tortured 334
Immensity cloistered in thy dear womb 218
In my heart the old love 240
In the middle of this century we turned to each other 161
In the rear-view mirror suddenly 22
In the worst hour of the worst season 260
In this world 163
Is there for honest Poverty 195
It can be bitter here at times like this 299
It is done by us all, as God disposes, from 92
It is late last night the dog was speaking of you 79
It's the Lucky Country's closet; a dark interior with frontier 312
It was hot – the day already more than half gone 53
It was the man from Ironbark who struck the Sydney town 192
Keats is dead so fuck me from behind 171
Lambs that learn to walk in snow 97
Lay your sleeping head, my love 188
Lead, kindly Light, amid th'encircling gloom 176
Lesbia always speaks ill of me, never shuts up 281
Like as the waves make towards the pebbled shore 183
Little eagerness 235
Love, never conquered in battle 186
Love means to learn to look at yourself 185
Love set you going like a fat gold watch 211
Man, for whom I suffered love 191

Many in aftertimes will say of you 198
Márgarét, áre you gríeving 298
Methought I heard a voice cry, 'Sleep no more! 206
Milkflower petals on the street 18
My aspens dear, whose airy cages quelled 35
My closest and dearest! 70
My father worked with a horse-plough 106
My heart aches, and a drowsy numbness pains 232
My heart is like a singing bird 36
My love is as a fever, longing still 217
My mother told me she had often stayed awake 65
My nonarrival in the city of N 261
My true love hath my heart and I have his 218
Never give all the heart, for love 219
Night deepens 220
No different, really – 224
No, no, go not to Lethe, neither twist 231
No one leaves home 128
Not like the brazen giant of Greek fame 219
Now from his breast into the eyes the ache 228
O Lord, thou hast searched me, and known me 228
O mistress mine, where are you roaming? 230
O, pardon me, thou bleeding piece of earth 230
O Rose thou art sick 281
O to be disentangled from this net – 198
O what can ail thee, knight-at-arms 33
O world, I cannot hold thee close enough! 115
Of comfort no man speak 238
Oh, Danny boy, the pipes, the pipes are calling 58
Old age (the name that others give it) 157
On summer afternoons I sit 343
On summer nights I sleep naked 178
On the low arch 91
Once I pass'd through a populous city 242
One day soon he'll tell her it's time to start packing 83
One need not be a chamber to be haunted 244
Only last week, walking the hushed fields 94
Or I shall live your epitaph to make 246
Overnight, very 215
People have been trying to kill me since I was born 154

Praised be doubt! I advise you to greet 159
Razors pain you 263
Reading a life of Alexander the Great, Alexander 368
Ring out, wild bells, to the wild sky 265
See how efficient it still is 123
Shall I compare thee to a summer's day? 277
She begins, and my grandmother joins her 133
She gives him his eyes, she found them 38
She sat on a willow-trunk 103
She sits in the park. Her clothes are out of date 162
She walks in beauty, like the night 278
Show me the order of the world 319
Shyly the silver-hatted mushrooms make 202
Since brass, nor stone, nor earth, nor boundless sea 283
Sing a song of sixpence 284
Sit down in the dirt and brush away the flies 98
So he's got to have happiness 225
sometimes 41
stay here 183
Stop all the clocks, cut off the telephone 111
Sunset glitters on the beads 306
Surely God was a lover when He bade the day begin 307
Sweet is the breath of Morn; her rising sweet 307
That is no country for old men. The young 272
That time of year thou may'st in me behold 309
The Armenian language is the home 15
The barge she sat in, like a burnish'd throne 27
The cold moon hangs to the sky by its horn 223
The dead say little in their letters 95
The diameter of the bomb was thirty centimeters 63
The ellipse, Hindu symbol of fertility 54
The end of the affair is always death 25
Th' expense of spirit in a waste of shame 93
The eye can hardly pick them out 16
The eyeless labourer in the night 370
The force that through the green fuse drives the flower 107
The hot midsummer nights I whisper 251
The hour between night and day 108
The light went out in Unit 506 on the 18th floor 245
The Lord is my shepherd; I shall not want 184

The man splitting wood in the daybreak 194
The Moving Finger writes, and, having writ 268
The other two, slight air and purging fire 295
The poem can start with him walking backwards into a room 23
The quality of mercy is not strained 259
The sea is calm tonight 81
The song of songs, which is Solomon's 287
The spotted hawk swoops by and accuses me, he complains of my gab 297
The thrushes sing as the sun is going 259
The time you won your town the race 321
The trees are coming into leaf 334
The warping night air having brought the boom 30
The word goes round Repins 7
The world is charged with the grandeur of God 114
Their tiny torrent of flight 316
There is no reason that I know 84
There's a damp melancholy 187
There was a time in former years 277
There wasn't much else we could do 279
There will come soft rain and the smell of the ground 311
They amputated 253
They'd been warned 85
They say that 'time assuages', – 313
They told me, Heraclitus, they told me you were dead 313
THIS IS *GOOD* FOR YOU! 35
This is the Night Mail crossing the Border 220
This story's right, this story's true 332
Thou, nature, art my goddess; to thy law 317
Though I speak with the tongues of men and of angels 318
Three kids down at the front gate 49
3 Things not to be expected 335
Time that is moved by little fidget wheels 99
To be, or not to be, that is the question 324
To every thing there is a season, and a time to every purpose under the heaven 325
To stub an oar on a rock where none should be 31
To the cities I came in a time of disorder 328
Tomorrow, and tomorrow, and tomorrow 331
Tonight, a first movement, a pulse 9
Trees are never felled . . . in summer . . . Not when the fruit . . . 255

Try to remember some details. Remember the clothing 336
Turning and turning in the widening gyre 273
Twenty-eight young men bathe by the shore 337
Tyger! Tyger! burning bright 338
Walk onto the dark stage dressed for a funeral 203
Watching six seasons of the Nanny while my long-term relationship fell apart 346
We are soft with our hangovers 358
We did it in front of the mirror 347
We, gathered at the 2017 National Constitutional Convention 340
We grow accustomed to the Dark – 348
We read the letters of the dead like helpless gods 179
Wearing nothing but snakeskin 22
Welcome to you 246
'We'll all be rooned,' said Hanrahan 268
Well, say there is no kingdom then for Richard 349
What are the sights of our town? 105
What are we waiting for, assembled in the forum? 344
What is the boy now, who has lost his ball 24
'What kind of a person are you,' I heard them say to me 352
When all the others were away at Mass 354
'When all this is over,' said the swineherd 308
When children are born in Victoria 179
When I am with you, we stay up all night 354
When I can not look at your face 373
When I compare 185
When I consider how my light is spent 240
when I dropped my 12-year-old off at her first 164
When I first came to town 170
When I first saw a naked man 44
When I was young, I used to 204
When my love swears that she is made of truth 355
When night stirred at sea 254
When suddenly, at midnight, you hear 113
When the Present has latched its postern behind my tremulous stay 12
When to the sessions of sweet silent thought 356
When Tom and Elizabeth took the farm 190
When you are old and grey and full of sleep 356
When you smile 294
Where does such tenderness come from? 357

Which shouldn't exist 314
Who killed Cock Robin? 359
Who made the world? 304
Whose woods these are I think I know 301
Why I'm going to the Taklamakan Desert 309
Winters at home brought wind 242
With the mistake your life goes in reverse 209
Women of Corinth, I have come out of the house 371
You are going to ask: and where are the lilacs? 149
you are the one 321
You cannot feel your toes, and so 57
You fools who ask what god is 16
You who were darkness warmed my flesh 369
You wouldn't read about it 320
Your children are not your children 372
Your coffin looked unreal 45
Your death, near now, is of an easy sort 167
Your face sleeps 216
Your hair is lost in the forest 172
Your unhappy and silly youth 375

Index of Paul Kelly's Musical Arrangements

'And death shall have no dominion', Dylan Thomas, from *Nature*★ 14
Barn Owl, Gwen Harwood, from *Thirteen Ways to Look at Birds*★ 28
A Barred Owl, Richard Wilbur, from *Thirteen Ways to Look at Birds* 30
Basking Shark, Norman MacCaig, from *Conversations with Ghosts* 31
Black Cockatoos, Judith Wright, from *Thirteen Ways to Look at Birds* 37
The Darkling Thrush, Thomas Hardy, from *Thirteen Ways to Look at Birds*★ 59
The Death of the Bird, A. D. Hope, from *Thirteen Ways to Look at Birds* 61
Eurydice and the Tawny Frogmouth, Robert Adamson★ 91
Five Bells, Kenneth Slessor, from *Conversations with Ghosts* 99
The fly, Miroslav Holub, from *Thirteen Ways to Look at Birds* 103
God's Grandeur, Gerard Manley Hopkins, from *Nature* 114
'Hope' is the thing with feathers, Emily Dickinson, from *Thirteen Ways to Look at Birds* 130
The Hungry Grass, Donagh MacDonagh, unreleased 132
'I think I could turn and live with animals', adapted to 'With Animals', from *Song of Myself*: 32, Walt Whitman, from *Nature*★ 144
An Irish Airman Foresees His Death, W. B. Yeats★ 165
The Lake Isle of Innisfree, W. B. Yeats, from *Conversations with Ghosts* 172
Leda and the Swan, W. B. Yeats, from *Thirteen Ways to Look at Birds* 177
Life Is Fine, Langston Hughes, from *Life Is Fine* 181
'Like as the waves make towards the pebbled shore', Sonnet 60, William Shakespeare, from *Seven Sonnets and a Song* 183
'The Lord is my shepherd', Psalm 23, adapted to 'To Meet Me in the Middle of the Air', from *Foggy Highway* 184
The Magpies, Denis Glover, from *Thirteen Ways to Look at Birds*★ 190
The Mother, Pádraig Pearse, unreleased 212
Mushrooms, Sylvia Plath, from *Nature*★ 215
My True Love Hath My Heart, Sir Philip Sidney, from *Seven Sonnets and a Song* 218
'O mistress mine', William Shakespeare, from *Seven Sonnets and a Song* 230
Ode to a Nightingale, John Keats, from *Thirteen Ways to Look at Birds* 232
Once in a Lifetime, Snow, Les Murray, from *Conversations with Ghosts*★ 242
'One need not be a chamber to be haunted', Emily Dickinson, from *Conversations with Ghosts* 244
Pied Beauty, Gerard Manley Hopkins, unreleased 251
Quarantine, Eavan Boland★ 260

'Ring out, wild bells', Alfred, Lord Tennyson, from *Conversations with Ghosts* 265
Sailing to Byzantium, W. B. Yeats, from *Conversations with Ghosts** 272
'Shall I compare thee to a summer's day', Sonnet 18, William Shakespeare, from *Seven Sonnets and a Song* 277
Sonnets 44 and 45, William Shakespeare, from *Seven Sonnets and a Song* 295
Surely God Was a Lover, John Shaw Neilson, adapted to 'Surely God Is a Lover', bonus track on *Foggy Highway* 307
'That time of year thou may'st in me behold', Sonnet 73, William Shakespeare, from *Seven Sonnets and a Song** 309
Thornbills, Judith Wright, from *Thirteen Ways to Look at Birds* 316
'Though I speak with the tongues of men and of angels', The Thirteenth Chapter of St Paul's First Letter to the Corinthians, adapted to 'Love Is the Law', from *Nothing But a Dream* 318
The Trees, Philip Larkin, from *Nature** 334
'When my love swears that she is made of truth', Sonnet 138, William Shakespeare, from *Seven Sonnets and a Song** 355
The Windhover, Gerard Manley Hopkins, from *Thirteen Ways to Look at Birds* 363
Woman to Man, Judith Wright, from *Conversations with Ghosts* 370

*Solo version sung by Paul Kelly on the audiobook of *Love Is Strong As Death*

Acknowledgements

First and foremost I'd like to thank my publisher, Nikki Christer, who planted the seed for this book. 'Perhaps you could put together a selection of a few of your favourite poems,' she said to me last year. She may have got more than she bargained for.

Selecting the first fifty or so poems was easy. Many had been companions for a long time. But I soon realised there was a whole world of poetry I'd barely explored. So I went hunting. All through last summer I didn't do much else beside lie on the couch reading poetry between bike rides to the beach. Nice work if you can get it.

I put out feelers to friends asking for recommendations. My friends came through, sending me down many and varied paths. And, as mentioned in the introduction, there are those fellow hunters who've been sending me poems over many years.

In particular I'd like to thank (in alphabetical order, of course!) Ezra Bix, James Button, Maxine Beneba Clarke, Siân Darling, Martin Flanagan, Richard Flanagan, Anna Goldsworthy, Robert Gray, Anne Kelly, Lynn Kelly, Martin Kelly, John Kingsmill, John Kinsella, Demos Krouskos, Genevieve Lacey, Bill McDonald, Alex McGregor, Fiona McGregor, Grant McLennan and Hallie Shellam.

Nikki Christer also suggested many poems and authors, as did Melissa Lane, in the middle of doing the massive job of seeking hosts of permissions from authors and publishers around the world. Melissa and Catherine Hill have brought the book home with close copy-editing, research and encouragement. They've been painstakingly backed up by our typesetter, Julian Mole – layout is crucial to poetry – and our eagle-eyed prooøf reader and indexer, Catherine Dunk. Together we've striven to represent each poet's intentions for the layout and final text of their poems as accurately as possible.

Finally, thank you to Alex Ross for his beautiful cover design. I'm very glad to be part of this happy, hard-working team that's made this book for you.

PK, October 2019

Permissions

The publishers gratefully acknowledge the copyright owners for granting permission to reprint the copyright material in this book:

'An Absolutely Ordinary Rainbow', Les Murray, from *Collected Poems*, Black Inc., 2018, reproduced by permission of Margaret Connolly; 'Act of Union', Seamus Heaney, from *North*, Faber & Faber, 2010, reproduced by permission of Faber & Faber Ltd; 'Advice for Good Love', Yehuda Amichai, translated by the author and Ted Hughes, from *Yehuda Amichai Selected Poems*, edited by Ted Hughes and Daniel Weissbort, Faber & Faber, 2018, reproduced by kind permission of Hana Amichai via the Deborah Harris Agency; 'After Love', Maxine Kumin, from *Selected Poems, 1960–1990*, W.W. Norton, 1998, © 1970 Maxine Kumin, reproduced by permission of W.W. Norton & Company, Inc.; 'And so their spirits soared', Homer, from 'The Tide of Battle Turns', Book 8 of *The Iliad*, translated by Robert Fagles, translation © 1990 Robert Fagles, used by permission of Viking Books, an imprint of Penguin Publishing Group, a division of Penguin Random House LLC, all rights reserved, and by permission of Georges Borchardt, Inc., for the Estate of Robert Fagles; 'Asking the Way', Ko Un, translated by Suji Kwock Kim and Sunja Kim Kwock, *Poetry* magazine, November 2014, reproduced by kind permission of Ko Un, Suji Kwock Kim and Sunja Kim Kwock; 'At Grass', Philip Larkin, from *The Less Deceived*, Faber & Faber, 2011, reproduced by permission of Faber & Faber Ltd; 'Aubade with Burning City', Ocean Vuong, from *Night Sky with Exit Wounds*, published by Jonathan Cape, reproduced by permission of the Random House Group Ltd, © 2017; 'Aunt Julia', Norman MacCaig, from *The Many Days: Selected Poems of Norman MacCaig*, Polygon, 2011, reproduced by permission of Polygon, an imprint of Birlinn Ltd, through PLSclear; 'Auto Mirror', Adam Zagajewski, translated by Czeslaw Milosz and Robert Hass, published in *A Book of Luminous Things: An International Anthology of Poetry*, Houghton Mifflin Harcourt Publishing Company, translation © 1996 Czeslaw Milosz; 'Autobiography of Eve', Ansel Elkins, from *Blue Yodel*, Yale University Press, 2015, reproduced by permission through PLSclear;

'Backwards', Warsan Shire, © 2014, reproduced by kind permission of the author; 'The Ball Poem', John Berryman, from *John Berryman: Collected Poems 1937–1971*, Farrar, Straus and Giroux, 2014, © 1989 by Kate Donahue Berryman, reproduced by permission of Faber & Faber Ltd and Farrar, Straus and Giroux, LLC; 'The Ballad of the Lonely Masturbator', Anne Sexton, from *Selected Poems of Anne Sexton*, Houghton Mifflin Harcourt, 2000, reproduced by permission of SLL/Sterling Lord Literistic, Inc., © Linda Gray Sexton and Loring Conant, Jr. 1981; 'Barn Owl', Gwen Harwood, from *Gwen Harwood: Selected Poems*, Penguin, 2001, reproduced by permission of the Harwood Estate (John Harwood); 'A Barred Owl', Richard Wilbur, from *Mayflies: New Poems and Translations*, © 2000 Richard Wilbur, reproduced by permission of Houghton Mifflin Harcourt Publishing Company, all rights reserved; 'Basking Shark', Norman MacCaig, from *The Many Days: Selected Poems of Norman MacCaig*, Polygon, 2011, reproduced by permission of Polygon, an imprint of Birlinn Ltd, through PLSclear; 'beneviolence', Alison Whittaker, from *Blakwork*, Magabala Books, 2018, reproduced by permission of Magabala Books; 'Black Cockatoos', Judith Wright, from *Collected Poems*, HarperCollins Publishers Australia, 2016, © the Estate of Judith Wright 1994, reproduced by permission of HarperCollins Publishers Australia; 'Bride and Groom Lie Hidden for Three Days', Ted Hughes, from *Crow*, Faber & Faber, 2001, reproduced by permission of Faber & Faber Ltd; 'Broadcast', Philip Larkin, from *The Whitsun Weddings*, Faber & Faber, 2001, reproduced by permission of Faber & Faber Ltd; 'Brown', Maxine Beneba Clarke, reproduced with permission from *Carrying the World*, Maxine Beneba Clarke, Hachette Australia, 2017; 'Canoe', Ali Cobby Eckermann, from *Inside My Mother*, Giramondo Publishing, 2015, reproduced by kind permission of the author; 'Celibate's Ode to Balls', Sharon Olds, from *Odes*, published by Jonathan Cape, reproduced by permission of the Random House Group Ltd, © 2016; 'Child Burial', Paula Meehan, from *Mysteries of the Home*, Dedalus Press, 2013, reproduced by permission of Dedalus Press; 'Coming to It', Sam Hunt, from *Coming to It: Selected Poems*, Potton and Burton, 2018, reproduced by kind permission of the author; 'The Composer', W. H. Auden, from *Collected Poems*, Vintage International, Vintage Books, 1991; 'Conjecture Number One Thousand', Caroline Finkelstein, published in *Ploughshares*, Vol. 27, No. 2/3, Thirtieth Anniversary Issue, Fall, 2001; 'Corinna', from *Amores*, Ovid, translated by John Svarlien, published in *Latin Lyric and Elegiac Poetry: An Anthology of New Translations*, edited by Diane J. Rayor and William Wendell Batstone, Taylor & Francis, 1995; 'Country Football', Philip Hodgins, from *Selected Poems*, Angus & Robertson, 1997, © Philip Hodgins 1986, reproduced by permission of HarperCollins Publishers Australia; 'The Cows on Killing Day', Les Murray, from *Collected Poems*, Black Inc., 2018, reproduced by permission of Margaret Connolly; 'Cute', Michel Faber, from *Undying: A Love*

Story, Canongate, 2016; 'Days of 1903', C. P. Cavafy, translated by Edmund Keeley and Philip Sherrard, from *C. P. Cavafy: Collected Poems*, revised edition edited by George Savidis, translation © 1975, 1992 Edmund Keeley and Philip Sherrard, reproduced by permission of Princeton University Press and Professor Keeley; 'The Death of the Bird', A. D. Hope, from *Collected Poems, 1930–1970*, Angus & Robertson, 1972, reproduced by arrangement with the licensor, the A. D. Hope Estate, c/o Curtis Brown (Aust) Pty Ltd; 'Departure', Arthur Rimbaud, translated by John Ashbery, from *Illuminations*, Carcanet Press, 2018, reproduced by permission of Carcanet Press Ltd; 'The Diameter of the Bomb', Yehuda Amichai, translated by Chana Bloch, from *The Selected Poetry of Yehuda Amichai*, translated by Chana Bloch and Stephen Mitchell, University of California Press, 2013, reproduced by kind permission of Hana Amichai via the Deborah Harris Agency; 'Digging', Seamus Heaney, from *Death of a Naturalist*, Faber & Faber, 2006, reproduced by permission of Faber & Faber Ltd; 'Diptych', Robert Gray, from *Coast Road: Selected Poems*, Black Inc., 2014, latest version available at robertgraypoetry.com/poems/diptych/, reproduced by kind permission of the author and Margaret Connolly; 'A Dream of Mountaineering', Po Chü-I, translated by Arthur Waley, from *One Hundred and Seventy Chinese Poems* © 1919 and renewed 1947 by Arthur Waley, reproduced by permission of Constable and Co. Ltd., a division of Little, Brown Book Group; 'Drifters', Bruce Dawe, published in *Australian Poetry Since 1788*, edited by Geoffrey Lehmann and Robert Gray, University of New South Wales Press, 2011, reproduced by kind permission of Liz and Bruce Dawe; 'Driving Alone on a Snowy Evening (After Frost)', Sinéad Morrissey, from *The State of the Prisons*, Carcanet Press, 2005, reproduced by permission of Carcanet Press Ltd; 'Drowning in Wheat', John Kinsella, from *Peripheral Light: Selected and New Poems*, W. W. Norton, 2005, © 2004 John Kinsella, reproduced by permission of W. W. Norton & Company, Inc.; 'Dublinesque', Philip Larkin, from *High Windows*, Faber & Faber, 2015, reproduced by permission of Faber & Faber Ltd; 'Earth Presses Against Us', Mahmoud Darwish, from *Unfortunately, It Was Paradise*, translated by Munir Akash and Carolyn Forché, edited by Sinan Antoon and Amira El-Zein, University of California Press, 2013, © 2013 by the Regents of the University of California, reproduced by permission of University of California Press; 'Elegy from Balmoral Beach', Robert Adamson, from *The Golden Bird: New and Selected Poems*, Black Inc., 2008, reproduced by permission of Black Inc.; 'The Elwood Organic Fruit and Vegetable Shop', Alison Croggon, from *The Common Flesh: New & Selected Poems*, Arc Publications, 2003, reproduced by permission of Jenny Darling & Associates Pty Ltd; 'Eurydice and the Tawny Frogmouth', Robert Adamson, from *The Golden Bird: New and Selected Poems*, Black Inc., 2008, reproduced by permission of Black Inc.; 'Everything Is Plundered', Anna Akhmatova, from

Selected Poems, translated by Stanley Kunitz with Max Hayward, published by Harvill Press, reproduced by permission of the Random House Group Ltd, © 1989; 'The Excrement Poem', Maxine Kumin, from *Selected Poems, 1960–1990*, W. W. Norton, 1998, © 1978 Maxine Kumin, reproduced by permission of W. W. Norton & Company, Inc.; 'Finding a Box of Family Letters', Dana Gioia, from *99 Poems: New and Selected*, © 2012 Dana Gioia, reproduced by permission of The Permissions Company, Inc., on behalf of Graywolf Press, Minneapolis, Minnesota, www.graywolfpress.org, and by permission of Dana Gioia; 'First Sight', Philip Larkin, from *The Whitsun Weddings*, Faber & Faber, 2001, reproduced by permission of Faber & Faber Ltd; 'First Time (I Met My Grandmother)', Ali Cobby Eckermann, from *little bit long time*, Picaro Press, 2017, reproduced by kind permission of the author; 'Five Bells', Kenneth Slessor, from *Kenneth Slessor Selected Poems*, HarperCollins, 2014, © P. Slessor 1944, 1957, 1993, 2014, reproduced by permission of HarperCollins Publishers Australia; 'The fly', Miroslav Holub, translated by George Theiner, from *Poems Before & After: Collected English Translations*, translated by Ian and Jarmila Milner et al., Bloodaxe Books, 2006, reproduced by permission of Bloodaxe Books; 'Folklore', Les Murray, from *Collected Poems*, Black Inc., 2018, reproduced by permission of Margaret Connolly; 'Follower', Seamus Heaney, from *Death of a Naturalist*, Faber & Faber, 2006, reproduced by permission of Faber & Faber Ltd; 'Four A.M.', Wislawa Szymborska, translated by Stanislaw Baranczak and Clare Cavanagh, from *Map: Collected and Last Poems*, © 2015 Houghton Mifflin Harcourt, reproduced by permission of Houghton Mifflin Harcourt Publishing Company, all rights reserved; 'Funeral Blues', W. H. Auden, from *Collected Poems*, Vintage International, Vintage Books, 1991; 'Gift', Czeslaw Milosz, translated by the author, from *New & Collected Poems 1931–2001*, Allen Lane, translated by Czeslaw Milosz and Robert Pinsky © Czeslaw Milosz Royalties, Inc., 1988, 1991, 1995, 2001, reproduced by permission of Penguin Random House UK and The Wylie Agency (UK) Ltd; 'Gifts', Oodgeroo Noonuccal, from *The dawn is at hand: selected poems*, Marion Boyars Publishers, 1992, reproduced by permission of Marion Boyars Publishers; 'The God Abandons Antony', C. P. Cavafy, translated by Edmund Keeley and Philip Sherrard, from *C. P. Cavafy: Collected Poems*, revised edition edited by George Savidis, translation © 1975, 1992 Edmund Keeley and Philip Sherrard, reproduced by permission of Princeton University Press and Professor Keeley; 'The Great Secret', Hafiz, translated by Daniel Ladinsky, from *I Heard God Laughing: Poems of Hope and Joy*, Hafiz, Penguin Books, © 1996 and 2006 Daniel Ladinsky and used with his permission; 'The Hag of Beare', anonymous, translated by John Montague, published in *Contemporary Irish Poetry: An Anthology*, University of California Press, 1980; 'Hardcastle Crags', Sylvia Plath, from *Collected Poems*, Faber & Faber, 2015, published by permission of Faber & Faber Ltd; 'Hatred',

Wislawa Szymborska, translated by Stanislaw Baranczak and Clare Cavanagh, from *Map: Collected and Last Poems*, translation © 2015 Houghton Mifflin Harcourt, reproduced by permission of Houghton Mifflin Harcourt Publishing Company, all rights reserved; 'He is more than a hero', Sappho, translated by Mary Barnard, from *Sappho: A New Translation*, University of California Press, 2012, © 2013 by the Regents of the University of California, reproduced by permission of University of California Press; 'Her Kind', Anne Sexton, from *Selected Poems of Anne Sexton*, Houghton Mifflin Harcourt, 2000, reproduced by permission of SLL/Sterling Lord Literistic, Inc., copyright by Linda Gray Sexton and Loring Conant, Jr. 1981; 'Home', Warsan Shire, © 2014, reproduced by kind permission of the author; 'House', Tusiata Avia, from *Fale Aitu | Spirit House*, Victoria University Press, 2016, reproduced by kind permission of the author; 'The Hungry Grass', Donagh MacDonagh, from *The Hungry Grass*, Faber & Faber, 1947; 'I Ask My Mother to Sing', Li-Young Lee, from *Rose: Poems*, © 1986 Li-Young Lee, reproduced by permission of The Permissions Company, LLC on behalf of BOA Editions, Ltd, www.boaeditions.org; 'I Belong There', Mahmoud Darwish, from *Unfortunately, It Was Paradise*, translated by Munir Akash and Carolyn Forché, edited by Sinan Antoon and Amira El-Zein, University of California Press, 2013, © 2013 by the Regents of the University of California, reproduced by permission of University of California Press; 'i carry your heart with me(i carry it in', E. E. Cummings, © 1952, 1980, 1991 by the Trustees for the E. E. Cummings Trust, from *Complete Poems: 1904–1962*, edited by George J. Firmage, reproduced by permission of Liveright Publishing Corporation; 'I Never Loved You More' and 'I Want to Go with the One I Love', Bertolt Brecht, translated by Johannes Beilharz, from *Die Gedichte*, © Bertolt-Brecht-Erben / Suhrkamp Verlag 2000, used by permission of Suhrkamp Verlag; 'I'm Explaining a Few Things', Pablo Neruda, translated by Nathaniel Tarn, from *Selected Poems of Pablo Neruda*, translated by W. S. Merwin, Anthony Kerrigan, Alastair Reid and Nathaniel Tarn, published by Jonathan Cape © Pablo Neruda and Fundación Pablo Neruda, reproduced by permission of the Random House Group Ltd © 1970; 'I've Been Moved', Kevin Daniel Carmody, © Song Cycles Pty Ltd, administered by Kobalt Music Publishing Australia Pty Ltd, print rights administered in Australia and New Zealand by Hal Leonard Australia Pty Ltd, www.halleonard.com.au, used by permission, all rights reserved, unauthorised reproduction is illegal; 'Immigrant Blues', Li-Young Lee, from *Behind My Eyes*, W. W. Norton, 2009, © 2008 Li-Young Lee, reproduced by permission of W. W. Norton & Company, Inc.; 'In Dream', Anna Akhmatova, translated by D. M. Thomas, from *Selected Poems*, published by Martin Secker & Warburg, © D. M. Thomas 1976, 1979, 1985, reproduced by kind permission of the Random House Group Ltd, © 1985, and Johnson & Alcock Ltd; 'In Paris with You', James

Fenton, from *Yellow Tulips: Poems 1968–2011*, Faber & Faber, 2012, reproduced by permission of United Agents LLP; 'In Praise of Darkness', Jorge Luis Borges, translated by Hoyt Rogers, from *Selected Poems*, edited by Alexander Coleman, Allen Lane, The Penguin Press, 1999, © 1995 Maria Kodama, translation © Hoyt Rogers, 1999, reproduced by permission of Penguin Random House UK and The Wylie Agency (UK) Ltd; 'In Praise of Doubt', Bertolt Brecht, translated by Martin Esslin, from *Die Gedichte*, © Bertolt-Brecht-Erben / Suhrkamp Verlag 2000, used by permission of Suhrkamp Verlag; 'In the Middle of This Century', Yehuda Amichai, translated by Assia Gutmann, from *The Poetry of Yehuda Amichai*, edited by Robert Alter, Farrar Straus and Giroux, 2015, reproduced by permission of Hana Amichai via the Deborah Harris Agency; 'In the Park', Gwen Harwood, from *Gwen Harwood: Selected Poems*, Penguin Books, 2001, reproduced by permission of the Harwood Estate (John Harwood); 'In this world', Izumi Shikibu, from *The Ink Dark Moon: Love Poems by Ono no Komachi and Izumi Shikibu, Women of the Ancient Court of Japan*, translated by Jane Hirshfield with Mariko Aratani, translation © 1986, 1987, 1988, 1989, 1990 by Jane Hirshfield, used by permission of Vintage Books, an imprint of the Knopf Doubleday Publishing Group, a division of Penguin Random House LLC, all rights reserved; 'Incantation', Czeslaw Milosz, translated by Czeslaw Milosz and Robert Pinsky, from *The Collected Poems: 1931–2001,* Allen Lane, © Czeslaw Milosz Royalties, Inc., 1988, 1991, 1995, 2001, used by permission of The Wylie Agency (UK) Ltd and Penguin Random House UK; 'Inevitable', Mahogany L. Browne, published in Poem-a-Day, Academy of American Poets, 7 February 2019, © 2019 by Mahogany L. Browne; 'Ithaka', C. P. Cavafy, translated by Edmund Keeley, from *C. P. Cavafy: Collected Poems*, revised edition translated by Edmund Keeley and Philip Sherrard, edited by George Savidis, translation © 1975, 1992 by Edmund Keeley and Philip Sherrard, reproduced by permission of Princeton University Press and Professor Keeley; 'Japanese Maple', Clive James, from *Collected Poems: 1958–2015*, Picador Australia, 2016, reproduced by permission of United Agents LLP; 'The Journey of the Magi', T. S. Eliot, from *Collected Poems 1909–1962*, Faber & Faber, 2019, reproduced by permission of Faber & Faber Ltd; 'Keats Is Dead So Fuck Me From Behind', from *Hera Lindsay Bird*, Victoria University Press, 2016, reproduced by kind permission of the author and Victoria University Press; 'Last Dawn', Octavio Paz, translated by Eliot Weinberger, from *Collected Poems 1957–1987*, Carcanet Press, 2001, reproduced by permission of Carcanet Press Ltd; 'The Last Hellos', Les Murray, from *Collected Poems*, Black Inc., 2018, reproduced by permission of Margaret Connolly; 'A Letter of Recommendation', Yehuda Amichai, translated by Chana Bloch, from *The Selected Poetry of Yehuda Amichai*, translated by Chana Bloch and Stephen Mitchell, University of California Press, 2013, reproduced by kind permission of Hana Amichai via the

Deborah Harris Agency; 'The Letters of the Dead', Wislawa Szymborska, from *Map: Collected and Last Poems*, translated by Stanislaw Baranczak and Clare Cavanagh, English translation © 2015 Houghton Mifflin Harcourt, reproduced by permission of Houghton Mifflin Harcourt Publishing Company, all rights reserved; 'Life-cycle', Bruce Dawe, from *Sometimes Gladness: Collected Poems, 1954 to 2005*, Pearson Education Australia, 2006, reproduced by kind permission of Liz and Bruce Dawe; 'Life Is Fine', Langston Hughes, from *The Collected Poems of Langston Hughes*, edited by Arnold Rampersad and David Roessel, Knopf, 1994, reproduced by permission of David Higham Associates Ltd; 'Little Bit Long Time', Ali Cobby Eckermann, from *little bit long time*, Picaro Press, 2017, reproduced by kind permission of the author; 'Love', Czeslaw Milosz, translated by the author, from *New & Collected Poems 1931–2001*, Allen Lane, translated by Czeslaw Milosz and Robert Pinsky © Czeslaw Milosz Royalties, Inc., 1988, 1991, 1995, 2001, reproduced by permission of Penguin Random House UK and The Wylie Agency (UK) Ltd; 'Love, never conquered in battle', Sophocles, translated by Robert Fagles, from *The Three Theban Plays*, translation © 1977, 1979, 1982, 1984 by Robert Fagles, used by permission of Viking Books, an imprint of Penguin Publishing Group, a division of Penguin Random House LLC, all rights reserved, and by permission of Georges Borchardt, Inc., for the Estate of Robert Fagles; 'Lucky', Dorothy Porter, from *The Bee Hut* © Dorothy Porter, Black Inc, 2009, reproduced by permission of Jenny Darling & Associates Pty Ltd; 'Lullaby', W. H. Auden, from *Collected Poems*, Vintage International, Vintage Books, 1991; 'Lyric', Alison Croggon, from *This is the Stone*, Penguin Books, 1991, reproduced by permission of Jenny Darling & Associates Pty Ltd; 'The Magpies', Denis Glover, from *Selected Poems: Denis Glover*, Victoria University Press, 2019, reproduced by permission of Denis Glover; 'Man For Whom I Endured', Máire Mhac an tSaoi, translated by Biddy Jenkinson, from *An Paróiste Míorúilteach: Rogha Dánta/The Miraculous Parish: Selected Poems*, edited by Louis de Paor, translated by Peter Sirr, Biddy Jenkinson et al., O'Brien Press, 2011, reproduced by permission of Cló Iar-Chonnacht; 'Man Splitting Wood in the Daybreak', Galway Kinnell, from *The Past*, © 1985 Galway Kinnell, reproduced by permission of Houghton Mifflin Harcourt Publishing Company, all rights reserved; 'A Man's Household', Wislawa Szymborska, translated by Joanna Trzeciak, from *Miracle Fair: Selected Poems of Wislawa Szymborska*, W. W. Norton, 2002, © 2001 Joanna Trzeciak, reproduced by permission of W. W. Norton & Company, Inc.; 'Mary Hogan's Quatrains', Máire Mhac an tSaoi, translated by James Gleasure, from *Margadh na Saoire*, Sáirséal agus Dill, 1971, reproduced by permission of Cló Iar-Chonnacht; 'The Members of the Orchestra', Kevin Hart, from *Wild Track: New and Selected Poems*, University of Notre Dame Press, 2015, reproduced by permission of University of Notre Dame Press; 'Men', Maya

Angelou, from *And Still I Rise*, © 1978 Maya Angelou, used by permission of Penguin Random House Audio Publishing Group, a division of Penguin Random House LLC, all rights reserved, and by permission of Virago, an imprint of Little, Brown Book Group; 'Milk Cream Butter', Philip Hodgins, from *Selected Poems*, Angus & Robertson, 1997, © Philip Hodgins 1993, reproduced by permission of HarperCollins Publishers Australia; 'Mirror', Sylvia Plath, from *Collected Poems*, Faber & Faber, 2015, reproduced by permission of Faber & Faber Ltd; 'The Mistake', James Fenton, from *Yellow Tulips: Poems 1968–2011*, Faber & Faber, 2012, reproduced by permission of United Agents LLP; 'The Mitchells', Les Murray, from *Collected Poems*, Black Inc., 2018, reproduced by permission of Margaret Connolly; 'Morning Birdsong', Ko Un, translated by Clare You and Richard Silberg, from *This Side of Time: Poems*, White Pine Press, 2012, reproduced by permission of White Pine Press; 'Morning Song', Sylvia Plath, from *Ariel*, Faber & Faber, 2015, reproduced by permission of Faber & Faber Ltd; 'Mother', Zbigniew Herbert, translated by John R. Carpenter and Bogdana Carpenter, from *Selected Poems*, Oxford University Press, 1977, reproduced by permission of Oxford University Press through PLSclear; 'Musée des Beaux Arts', W. H. Auden, from *Collected Poems*, Vintage International, Vintage Books, 1991; 'Museum', Wislawa Szymborska, translated by Stanislaw Baranczak and Clare Cavanagh, from *Map: Collected and Last Poems*, translation © 2015 Houghton Mifflin Harcourt, reproduced by permission of Houghton Mifflin Harcourt Publishing Company, all rights reserved; 'Mushrooms', Sylvia Plath, from *Collected Poems*, Faber & Faber, 2015, reproduced by permission of Faber & Faber Ltd; 'My At-Last Lover', Dorothy Porter, from *Crete*, © Dorothy Porter, Macmillan, 2000, reproduced by permission of Jenny Darling & Associates Pty Ltd; 'Night Deepens', Ono No Komachi, translated by Jane Hirshfield with Mariko Aratani, from *The Ink Dark Moon: Love Poems by Ono no Komachi and Izumi Shikibu, Women of the Ancient Court of Japan*, translation © 1986, 1987, 1988, 1989, 1990 Jane Hirshfield, used by permission of Vintage Books, an imprint of the Knopf Doubleday Publishing Group, a division of Penguin Random House LLC, all rights reserved; 'Night Mail', W. H. Auden, from *Collected Poems*, Vintage International, Vintage Books, 1991; 'The Night-Ride', Kenneth Slessor, from *Kenneth Slessor Selected Poems*, HarperCollins, 2014, © P. Slessor 1944, 1957, 1993, 2014, reproduced by permission of HarperCollins Publishers Australia; 'No different, really', Izumi Shikibu, translated by Jane Hirshfield with Mariko Aratani, from *The Ink Dark Moon: Love Poems by Ono no Komachi and Izumi Shikibu, Women of the Ancient Court of Japan*, translation © 1986, 1987, 1988, 1989, 1990 Jane Hirshfield, used by permission of Vintage Books, an imprint of the Knopf Doubleday Publishing Group, a division of Penguin Random House LLC, all rights reserved; 'No End of Fun', Wislawa Szymborska, translated by Stanislaw Baranczak and Clare

Cavanagh, from *Map: Collected and Last Poems*, translation © 2015 Houghton Mifflin Harcourt, reproduced by permission of Houghton Mifflin Harcourt Publishing Company, all rights reserved; 'Now from his breast into the eyes the ache', Homer, translated by Robert Fitzgerald, from *The Odyssey*, Farrar, Straus and Giroux, 1961, reproduced by kind permission of Benedict Fitzgerald, executor for the Fitzgerald Estate; 'Ode to the Clitoris' and 'Ode to the Hymen', Sharon Olds, from *Odes*, published by Jonathan Cape, reproduced by permission of the Random House Group Ltd, © 2016; 'On Seeing the First Flasher', Vicki Raymond, from *Small Arm Practice*, William Heinemann Australia, 1989; 'Once in a Lifetime, Snow', Les Murray, from *Collected Poems*, Black Inc., 2018, reproduced by permission of Margaret Connolly; '1:30 AM', Ko Un, translated by Clare You and Richard Silberg, from *This Side of Time: Poems*, White Pine Press, 2012, reproduced by permission of White Pine Press; 'Ordinance on Arrival', Naomi Lazard, from *A Book of Luminous Things: An International Anthology of Poetry*, translation © 1996 Czeslaw Milosz, reproduced by permission of Houghton Mifflin Harcourt Publishing Company, all rights reserved; 'Ordinary People's Lithograph', Yannis Ritsos, translated by Edmund Keeley, from *Repetitions, Testimonies, Parentheses*, © 1991 by Princeton University Press, reproduced by permission of Princeton University Press and Professor Keeley; 'The Panther', Rainer Maria Rilke, translation © 1982 by Stephen Mitchell, from *The Selected Poetry of Rainer Maria Rilke*, Rainer Maria Rilke, edited and translated by Stephen Mitchell, used by permission of Random House, a division of Penguin Random House LLC, all rights reserved, and by permission of Stephen Mitchell; 'The Past', Kevin Hart, from *Wild Track: New and Selected Poems*, University of Notre Dame Press, 2015, reproduced by permission of University of Notre Dame Press; 'Pillow Talk', Paula Meehan, from *Mysteries of the Home*, Dedalus Press, 2013, reproduced by permission of Dedalus Press; 'A Pity, We Were Such a Good Invention', Yehuda Amichai, translated by Assia Gutmann, from *The Poetry of Yehuda Amichai*, edited by Robert Alter, Farrar, Straus and Giroux, 2015, reproduced by kind permission of Hana Amichai via the Deborah Harris Agency; 'The Planter's Daughter', Austin Clarke, from *Pilgrimage and Other Poems*, Allen & Unwin, 1929; 'Pleasures', Bertolt Brecht, translated by Marcy Jarvis, from *Die Gedichte*, © Bertolt-Brecht-Erben / Suhrkamp Verlag 2000, used by permission of Suhrkamp Verlag; 'A Poem on the Assassination of Robert F. Kennedy', Nikki Giovanni, from *Those Who Ride the Night Winds*, © 1983 Nikki Giovanni, reproduced by permission of HarperCollins Publishers; 'Postscript', Seamus Heaney, from *Opened Ground: Poems 1966–1996*, Faber & Faber, 2002, reproduced by permission of Faber & Faber Ltd; 'Prayer Before Birth', Louis MacNeice, from *Collected Poems*, Faber & Faber, 2016, reproduced by permission of David Higham Associates Ltd; 'Quarantine', Eavan Boland, from *New Collected*

Poems, Carcanet Press, 2012, reproduced by permission of Carcanet Press Ltd; 'The Railroad Station', Wislawa Szymborska, translated by Stanislaw Baranczak and Clare Cavanagh, from *Map: Collected and Last Poems*, translation © 2015 Houghton Mifflin Harcourt, reproduced by permission of Houghton Mifflin Harcourt Publishing Company, all rights reserved; 'Recalling the Past at T'ung Pass', Chang Yang-Hao, translated by C. H. Knock and Gary Gach; 'Resumé', Dorothy Parker, © 1926, 1928 and renewed 1954, 1956 Dorothy Parker, from *The Portable Dorothy Parker*, edited by Marion Meade, used by permission of Viking Books, an imprint of Penguin Publishing Group, a division of Penguin Random House LLC, all rights reserved; 'Riddle 25 from the Anglo-Saxon Riddle Hoard', anonymous, published in *A Feast of Creatures: Anglo-Saxon Riddle-Songs*, edited and translated by Craig Williamson, University of Pennsylvania Press, 2011; 'Rider's Song', Federico García Lorca, translated by Alex McGregor and Paul Kelly; 'Seduction Poem', Alison Croggon, from *The Common Flesh: New & Selected Poems*, Arc Publications, 2003, reproduced by permission of Jenny Darling & Associates Pty Ltd; 'Sex Without Love', Sharon Olds, from *Selected Poems*, published by Jonathan Cape, reproduced by permission of the Random House Group Ltd, © 2005; and from *The Dead and the Living*, copyright © 1975, 1978, 1979, 1980, 1981, 1982, 1983 by Sharon Olds, used by permission of Alfred A. Knopf, an imprint of the Knopf Doubleday Publishing Group, a division of Penguin Random House LLC, all rights reserved; 'Shooting the Dogs', Philip Hodgins, from *New Selected Poems*, Duffy & Snellgrove, 2000; 'Sign of Love', Catullus, from *The Poems*, Gaius Valerius Catullus, translated by A. S. Kline, © 2001, reproduced by permission of Dr Adam Kline; 'A Simple Story', Gwen Harwood, from *Gwen Harwood: Selected Poems*, Penguin Books, 2001, reproduced by permission of the Harwood Estate (John Harwood); 'Sir from Biology', Zbigniew Herbert, translated by Marcel Weyland, from *The Word: Two Hundred Years of Polish Poetry*, Brandl & Schlesinger, 2010, reproduced by kind permission of Marcel Weyland; 'Songs for a Woman', Yehuda Amichai, translated by David Rosenberg, from *Love Poems: A Bilingual Edition*, Schocken Publishing House Ltd, 1986, reproduced by kind permission of Hana Amichai via the Deborah Harris Agency; 'Songs of Grass', Alison Croggon, from *Attempts at Being*, Salt Publishing, 2002, reproduced by permission of Jenny Darling & Associates Pty Ltd; 'Sorcery', Sandra Simonds, from *Steal It Back*, Saturnalia Books, 2015, reproduced by permission of Saturnalia Books; 'Spleen', Charles Baudelaire, translated by William Aggeler, from *The Flowers of Evil*, Academy Library Guild, 1954; 'The Statue of the Virgin at Granard Speaks', Paula Meehan, from *Mysteries of the Home*, Dedalus Press, 2013, reproduced by permission of Dedalus Press; 'Stopping by Woods on a Snowy Evening', Robert Frost, from *The Poetry of Robert Frost*, edited by Edward Connery Lathem, © 1923, 1969 by Henry Holt and Company, © 1951 Robert Frost, used by permission of Henry Holt and Company, all rights reserved; 'The Summer Day', Mary Oliver, from *House of Light*, Beacon Press, 2012, © 1990 by Mary Oliver, reproduced by permission of the Charlotte Sheedy Literacy Agency, Inc.; 'Summer Night', Antonio Machado, translated by Willis Barnstone, from *Border of a Dream: Selected Poems*, © 2004 by the Heirs of Antonio Machado, translation © 2004 Willis Barnstone, reproduced by permission of The Permissions Company, LLC, on behalf of Copper Canyon Press, www.coppercanyonpress.org; 'Sunset', Tu Fu, translated by Kenneth Rexroth, from *One Hundred Poems from the Chinese*, © 1971 Kenneth Rexroth, reproduced by permission of New Directions Publishing Corp; 'Swineherd', Eiléan Ní Chuilleanáin, from *Selected Poems*, 2008, reproduced by kind permission of the author and The Gallery Press, County Meath, Ireland; 'Taklamakan Desert', Ko Un, translated by Suji Kwock Kim and Sunja Kim Kwock, *Poetry* magazine, November 2014, reproduced by kind permission of Ko Un, Suji Kwock Kim and Sunja Kim Kwock; 'Theatre Impressions', Wislawa Szymborska, translated by Stanislaw Baranczak and Clare Cavanagh, from *Map: Collected and Last Poems*, © 2015 Houghton Mifflin Harcourt, reproduced by permission of Houghton Mifflin Harcourt Publishing Company, all rights reserved; 'There's No Place Like Home', Samuel Wagan Watson, from *Love Poems and Death Threats*, University of Queensland Press, 2014, reproduced by kind permission of Samuel Wagan Watson; 'Things I Want Decided', Izumi Shikibu, translated by Jane Hirshfield with Mariko Aratani, from *The Ink Dark Moon: Love Poems by Ono no Komachi and Izumi Shikibu, Women of the Ancient Court of Japan*, translation © 1986, 1987, 1988, 1989, 1990 Jane Hirshfield, used by permission of Vintage Books, an imprint of the Knopf Doubleday Publishing Group, a division of Penguin Random House LLC, all rights reserved; 'A Thirsty Fish', Rumi, translated by Coleman Barks with John Moyne, from *Rumi: Selected Poems*, Penguin Books, 2004, © Coleman Barks, 1995, reproduced by permission of Penguin Random House UK; 'Thornbills', Judith Wright, from *Collected Poems*, HarperCollins Publishers Australia, 2016, © The Estate of Judith Wright 1994, reproduced by permission of HarperCollins Publishers Australia; 'Thought Is Surrounded by a Halo', Gwen Harwood, from *Gwen Harwood: Selected Poems*, Penguin Books, 2001, reproduced by permission of the Harwood Estate (John Harwood); 'The Three Fates', Rosemary Dobson, from *Collected Poems*, Angus & Robertson, 1991, reproduced by arrangement with the licensor, the A. D. Hope Estate, c/o Curtis Brown (Aust) Pty Ltd; 'Tiresias', Alison Croggon, from *This is the Stone*, Penguin Books, 1991, reproduced by permission of Jenny Darling & Associates Pty Ltd; 'to a dark moses', Lucille Clifton, from *The Collected Poems of Lucille Clifton*, © 1987 Lucille Clifton, reproduced by permission of The Permissions Company, LLC on behalf of BOA Editions, Ltd., www.boaeditions.org; 'To Be a Slave of Intensity', Kabir, translated by Robert Bly, from *Kabir: Ecstatic Poems*, © 2004 Robert Bly, reproduced by permission of Beacon Press, Boston; 'To Those Born After', Bertolt Brecht, translated by Des de Moor, from *Water of Europe*, 1999, German version from *Die Gedichte*, © Bertolt-Brecht-Erben / Suhrkamp Verlag 2000, used by permission of Suhrkamp Verlag; 'Today we are in a hospital ward', Tusiata Avia, from *Fale Aitu | Spirit House*, Victoria University Press, 2016, reproduced by kind permission of the author; 'Took the Children Away', Archie Roach, from *Charcoal Lane*, 1990, lyrics reproduced by kind permission of Archie Roach and Mushroom Music Publishing; 'Torture', Ko Un, translated by Clare You and Richard Silberg, from *This Side of Time: Poems*, White Pine Press, 2012, reproduced by permission of White Pine Press; 'The Trees', Philip Larkin, from *High Windows*, Faber & Faber, 2015, reproduced by permission of Faber & Faber Ltd; 'Triads', Vincent Buckley, from *Last Poems*, McPhee Gribble, 1991; 'Try to Remember Some Details', Yehuda Amichai, translated by Chana Bloch, from *The Poetry of Yehuda Amichai*, edited by Robert Alter, Farrar, Straus and Giroux, 2015, reproduced by kind permission of Hana Amichai via the Deborah Harris Agency; 'Uluru Statement from the Heart', 250 Aboriginal and Torres Strait Islander delegates from all around Australia, from the First Nations National Constitutional Convention, 26 May 2017; 'Us', Anne Sexton, from *Selected Poems of Anne Sexton*, Houghton Mifflin Harcourt, 2000, reproduced by permission of SLL/Sterling Lord Literistic, Inc., copyright by Linda Gray Sexton and Loring Conant, Jr. 1981; 'La Vie C'est La Vie', Jessie Redmon Fauset, published in *The Crisis* magazine, July 1922, and *The Book of American Negro Poetry*, edited by James Weldon Johnson, Harcourt, Brace and Company, 1922, reproduced by kind permission of The Crisis Publishing Co., Inc.; 'Waiting for the Barbarians', C. P. Cavafy, translated by Edmund Keeley and Philip Sherrard, from *C. P. Cavafy: Collected Poems*, revised edition edited by George Savidis, translation © 1975, 1992 by Edmund Keeley and Philip Sherrard, reproduced by permission of Princeton University Press and Professor Keeley; 'Watching six seasons of the Nanny while my long-term relationship slowly fell apart', Hera Lindsay Bird, from *Pamper Me to Hell & Back*, Smith|Doorstop, 2018, reproduced by kind permission of the author and The Poetry Business; 'We Did It', Yehuda Amichai, translated by Robert Alter, from *The Poetry of Yehuda Amichai*, edited by Robert Alter, Farrar, Straus and Giroux, 2015, © 2015 by Hana Amichai, reproduced by permission of Farrar, Straus and Giroux, LLC; 'Western Arrernte rain poem', anonymous, recorded and translated by T. G. H. Strehlow, from *Songs of Central Australia*, Angus & Robertson, 1971, reproduced by permission of HarperCollins Publishers Australia and Braydon Kanjira; 'What Kind of a Person', Yehuda Amichai, translated by Barbara and Benjamin Harshav, from *Yehuda Amichai: A Life of Poetry, 1948–1994*, HarperCollins Publishers, 1994, reproduced by kind permission of Hana Amichai via the Deborah Harris Agency; 'When all the others were away at Mass', Seamus Heaney, from 'Clearances', in *New Selected Poems 1966–1987*, Faber & Faber, 1990, reproduced by permission of Faber & Faber Ltd; 'When I Am With You', Rumi, translated by Coleman Barks with John Moyne, from *Rumi: Selected Poems*, Penguin Books, 2004, © Coleman Barks, 1995, reproduced by permission of Penguin Random House UK; 'Where Does Such Tenderness Come From?', Marina Tsvetaeva, translated by Ilya Kaminsky and Jean Valentine, from *Dark Elderberry Branch: Poems of Marina Tsvetaeva: A Reading by Ilya Kaminsky and Jean Valentine*, © 2012 Ilya Kaminsky and Jean Valentine, reproduced by permission of The Permissions Company, LLC on behalf of Alice James Books, www.alicejamesbooks.org; 'White Sunday/Lotu Tamaiti', Tusiata Avia, from *Fale Aitu | Spirit House*, Victoria University Press, 2016, reproduced by kind permission of the author; 'Why I Love Your Body', Dorothy Porter, from *Crete*, © Dorothy Porter, Macmillan, 2000, reproduced by permission of Jenny Darling & Associates Pty Ltd; 'Windy Mick and the Falcon', Neil Murray, from *One Man Tribe*, Charles Darwin University Press, 1999, reproduced by kind permission of the author; 'Wine', Raymond Carver, from *All of Us*, published by Harvill Press, reproduced by permission of the Random House Group Ltd, © 1996, and The Wylie Agency (UK) Ltd; 'Woman to Child' and 'Woman to Man', Judith Wright, from *Collected Poems*, HarperCollins Publishers Australia, 2016, © The Estate of Judith Wright 1994, reproduced by permission of HarperCollins Publishers Australia; 'Women of Corinth', Euripides, translated by Cecelia Eaton Luschnig, from *Diotima: Materials for the Study of Women and Gender in the Ancient World*, diotimawcc.wordpress.com/about/, reproduced by kind permission of Cecelia Eaton Luschnig; 'Your Feet', Pablo Neruda, translated by Donald D. Walsh, from *The Captain's Verses*, © 1952 Pablo Neruda and Fundación Pablo Neruda, © 1972 Donald D. Walsh, reproduced by permission of New Directions Publishing Corp and Agencia Literaria Carmen Balcells; 'Your Kiss', Kevin Hart, from *Wild Track: New and Selected Poems*, University of Notre Dame Press, 2015, reproduced by permission of University of Notre Dame Press; 'Youth', Czeslaw Milosz, translated by the author, from *New & Collected Poems 1931–2001*, Allen Lane, translated by Czeslaw Milosz and Robert Pinsky © Czeslaw Milosz Royalties, Inc., 1988, 1991, 1995, 2001, reproduced by permission of Penguin Random House UK and The Wylie Agency (UK) Ltd.